THE CRISIS OF CONVERSION

Amsterdam Series in Baptist and Mennonite Theologies

The Amsterdam Series in Baptist and Mennonite Theologies (ASBMT) is an academic series rooted in the Believers' Church tradition (Anabaptist-related, Free Church, Peace-Church). Ecumenically engaged and international in orientation, it provides a platform for both younger and established scholars, delivering monographs as well as single-author and edited books. It hosts a wide spectrum of academic fields while at the same time holding to a narrow focus on themes that are of particular importance to and characteristic of the Baptist and Mennonite traditions.

The series is supported by the Dutch Baptist Seminary, the Mennonite Seminary Amsterdam, the Amsterdam Centre for Religion and Peace & Justice Studies, and the International Baptist Theological Study Centre Amsterdam (IBTS). The chairs of the Dutch Baptist Seminary, the Mennonite Seminary, and IBTS (all residing at the VU University Amsterdam) oversee the series.

Scholars who wish to be considered for publication in the series should contact the Managing Editor at ASBMT@ibts.eu.

Series Editors

Henk Bakker (James Wm. McClendon Chair for Baptistic and Evangelical Theologies)
Fernando Enns (Chair of Peace-Theology and Ethics)
David Gushee (Chair of Christian Social Ethics)

Editorial Board

David E. Goatley (*Fuller Seminary*, United States)
Stephen Holmes (*University of St Andrews*, Scotland)
Parush Parushev (*IBTS/St. Trivelius Institute Sofia*, The Netherlands/Bulgaria)
Helen Paynter (*Bristol Baptist College*, England)
Astrid von Schlachta (*Universität Hamburg*, Germany)
Lina Toth (*Scottish Baptist College*, Scotland)

Managing Editor

David McMillan (*IBTS*, Amsterdam)

VOLUME 2

The Crisis of Conversion

Reimagining Religious Experience for a
Postmodern Evangelical Spirituality

J. August Higgins

☙PICKWICK *Publications* • Eugene, Oregon

THE CRISIS OF CONVERSION
Reimagining Religious Experience for a Postmodern Evangelical Spirituality

Amsterdam Series in Baptist and Mennonite Theologies

Copyright © 2024 J. August Higgins. All rights reserved. Except for brief quotations in critical publications or reviews, no part of this book may be reproduced in any manner without prior written permission from the publisher. Write: Permissions, Wipf and Stock Publishers, 199 W. 8th Ave., Suite 3, Eugene, OR 97401.

Pickwick Publications
An Imprint of Wipf and Stock Publishers
199 W. 8th Ave., Suite 3
Eugene, OR 97401

www.wipfandstock.com

PAPERBACK ISBN: 979-8-3852-0461-8
HARDCOVER ISBN: 979-8-3852-0462-5
EBOOK ISBN: 979-8-3852-0463-2

Cataloguing-in-Publication data:

Names: Higgins, J. August. [author].

Title: The crisis of conversion : reimagining religious experience for a postmodern evangelical spirituality / J. August Higgins.

Description: Eugene, OR: Pickwick Publications, 2024 | Series: Amsterdam Series in Baptist and Mennonite Theologies | Includes bibliographical references and index.

Identifiers: ISBN 979-8-3852-0461-8 (paperback) | ISBN 979-8-3852-0462-5 (hardcover) | ISBN 979-8-3852-0463-2 (ebook)

Subjects: LCSH: Evangelicalism. | Spirituality. | Postmodernism—Religious aspects—Christianity. | Christian converts—History and criticism. | Schneiders, Sandra Marie. | Edwards, Jonathan, 1703–1758. | Emerson, Ralph Waldo, 1803–1882.

Classification: BR1640 H54 2024 (paperback) | BR1640 (ebook)

06/21/24

*To my parents,
Allan and Lori*

Contents

Acknowledgments | ix

1 Evangelical Experience and the Crisis of Religious Conversion | 1
2 Sandra Schneiders and the Study of Christian Spirituality: Situating Religious Experience in a North American Context | 44
3 Retrieving the Foundations of North American Evangelical Spirituality: Jonathan Edwards and Ralph Waldo Emerson on the Human Experience of God | 79
4 Conclusion: Toward a Postmodern Evangelical Spirituality | 122

Bibliography | 149
Subject Index | 161

Acknowledgments

I AM GRATEFUL FIRST to Steven Chase, Amy Plantinga Pauw and Amos Yong for their wisdom, feedback, and guidance in shepherding me through my dissertation. I am also grateful for the support and encouragement of the faculty at Oblate School of Theology for taking a chance on a young Baptist student at a Roman Catholic graduate school, and helping me to find, explore, and articulate a generative evangelical spirituality. In particular, I could not have completed this project without the immeasurable support and brilliance of John Markey. To Cliff Knighten, for the countless hours of conversation, seminars, papers, and continued friendship as we navigated the inaugural cohort of the newly created PhD in Christian Spirituality at OST. And to the editorial staff at Wipf & Stock, and David Gushee, David McMillan and the team at the International Baptist Seminary and the Amsterdam Series in Baptist and Mennonite Theology, which I am humbled to present my contribution here in this series. A special thanks to Ryan Martin, my graduate assistant, who helped prepare the index.

To my faith community at Trinity Baptist Church; I am forever grateful to you for providing a safe and exciting place for my own exploration and experimentation in pursuit of a life together.

1

Evangelical Experience and the Crisis of Religious Conversion

Introduction

IN THIS BOOK, I will analyze what I call the crisis of conversion in contemporary North American Anglo-evangelical Christianity and propose a remedy to it. The root of this perceived crisis is an internal contradiction surrounding the evangelical elevation of experiences of religious conversion and the simultaneous epistemological rejection of the validity of human experience more broadly conceived in light of the authority of religious truth. This crisis of conversion, to be explored more deeply in what follows, shines light on an overarching tension within evangelical Christianity concerning the nature and role of human experience and its relationship to divine revelation. Briefly stated, the contemporary crisis of conversion in North American evangelical Christianity points to the self-contradictory status of the nature of human experience as it is expressed phenomenologically in the lived reality of evangelical Christianity. Experiences of conversion are a central marker of evangelical piety, while at the same time intellectual traditions within evangelicalism have negated the validity of human experience at large as a legitimate locus for theological and epistemological reflection. That is, one's conversion experience is simultaneously essential in the phenomenological expression of

The Crisis of Conversion

evangelical spirituality, and at the same time, stripped of its normative power by evangelical epistemological and theological presuppositions. The results of this crisis are both the marginalization of one's own personal experience of faith from the publicly available theological reflection of the community of faith, as well as the establishment of two relatively mutually exclusive communities within evangelicalism; namely, the local church on the one hand, and the academic biblical/theological community on the other.[1] The crisis, as I understand it here, can be traced back to the cultural origins of evangelicalism and its early struggles against both the Enlightenment's rationalism and Romanticism's subjectivism. However, it has become increasingly apparent in the wake of postmodernity's dismantling of the pillars of the modern West's intellectual tradition.[2]

In chapter 1, I will outline the epistemological foundations of evangelicalism based on the recent work of Stanley Grenz and the Neo-evangelical movement of the latter half of the twentieth-century concerning the nature of reality and human access to that reality. From there, I will outline a postmodern critique of Enlightenment epistemology, which poses a significant challenge to the trajectory of evangelical thought in the Twenty-first Century as it relates to the theology of the experience of God in the world.

Chapter 2 will explore the phenomenological underpinnings of human experience more broadly, particularly as articulated through the emerging academic discipline of Christian spirituality. Here, I will suggest that spirituality studies offer evangelicalism a critical methodology that takes seriously the nature of experience through the lived reality of faith in the world that does

---

1. Wells, *No Place for Truth*. Particularly in his third chapter "Things Fall Apart," 95–136, he articulates the growing divide between theological reflection and evangelical ecclesiology. While I am sympathetic with Wells's analysis of the division between church and theology, I am less persuaded by his proposals. See for example Grenz's sympathetic analysis and critique of Well's proposals, Grenz, *Renewing the Center*, 162–66; and Yong, *Hermeneutical Spirit*, 2–4.

2. See for example the following recent evangelical responses to the relationship between evangelicalism, modernity, and postmodernity. Mathews, *Doctrine and*; Sewell, *Crisis of Evangelical Christianity*; Olson, *Essentials of Christian*; Worthen, "Defining Evangelicalism," 83–86; Dochuk, "Revisiting Bebbington's Classic Rendering of Modern Evangelicalism," 63–72; Bebbington, "Evangelical Quadrilateral," 87–96; Rah, *Next Evangelicalism*; Hawkins and Sinitiere, *Christians and the Color Line*; Olson, *Journey of Modern Theology*; Kyle, *Evangelicalism*; Haykin and Stewart, *Advent of Evangelicalism*; Stackhouse, *Evangelical Landscapes*; Wells, *No Place for Truth*.

In particular, the work of Stanley J. Grenz is an important voice in the early development of this issue within evangelical Christianity; Grenz and Olson, *20th-Century Theology*; Grenz, *Revisioning Evangelical Theology*; Grenz, *Theology for the Community of God*; Grenz, *Social God and the Relational*; Grenz, *Named God and the Question of Being*; Grenz and Franke, *Beyond Foundationalism*; Grenz and Smith, *Created for Community*.

Evangelical Experience and the Crisis of Religious Conversion

not reduce experience to purely subjective categories. The key term, "spirituality," will be used here to mean the lived experience of human life in reference towards the transcendent.³

In chapter 3, I will trace and recover the phenomenological foundations of North American evangelical spirituality as articulated by arguably the two most influential figures as it pertains to contemporary North American Anglo Christianity; Jonathan Edwards and Ralph Waldo Emerson. Both Edwards and Emerson were rooted in the aesthetic nature of the human experience of God and the world. And while disagreeing theologically in significant ways, they have, nevertheless, both deeply influenced North American understandings of the spiritual life that continues to inform religious practice and identity today. This critical retrieval of the foundations of North American evangelical spirituality will highlight the turn from a socially rooted conception of religious experience to a firmly individualistic one, as well as the conflation of the Spirit with the aesthetic. In both cases however, the aesthetic and experiential foundations of a North American understanding of the spiritual life remain intact in contemporary North American spiritual identity. Altogether, chapters one through three will underscore the problem that postmodern individualism poses for evangelical spirituality rooted in the practice of religious conversion, and will frame the paradoxical relationship between individualism and spiritual/religious self-identity as expressed in an inculturated North American evangelical context through Edwards and Emerson in the eighteenth and nineteenth centuries.

In chapter 4, I will return to the contemporary postmodern situation, and offer an analysis of Pentecostal/evangelical scholar Amos Yong's novel conception of the *pneumatological imagination*. Yong's pneumatological insight retains the aesthetic and experiential foundations of North American evangelical spirituality as articulated by Edwards and Emerson, while also providing a way out of the epistemological juggernaut of postmodern deconstructionism. Yong's *pneumatological imagination* helps to reconcile the phenomenological, epistemological, and theological conundrum that characterizes the postmodern crisis of conversion in three principal ways. First, Yong confirms the insight from spirituality studies by placing the category of human experience at the center of his investigation. Second, he rehabilitates the epistemological legitimacy of starting with human experience through his utilization of Charles Sanders Peirce's semiotic metaphysics. And third, Yong

---

3. See Sandra Schneider's definition of the discipline of spirituality studies in Schneiders, "Approaches to the Study of Christian Spirituality," 16–33. Specifically see 16–19 for Schneiders's treatment of the material and formal object of the discipline, both of which take up the centrality of human experience.

The Crisis of Conversion

reconciles the evangelical tension between experience and authority theologically through his constructive pneumatology rooted in the Church as an interpretive community critically engaging God, themselves, and the world, in and through the indwelling Spirit.

Evangelicalism and the Experience of Faith

I have chosen the phenomenon of religious conversion as a lens of investigation for two primary reasons. First and foremost, it is largely viewed by both outside observers and those within the movement as a distinguishing characteristic of evangelical spirituality.[4] Second, it is in the very experience of conversion itself, as a special type of the broader category of religious experience for evangelicals, that I find an internal contradiction regarding the relationship between human experience more broadly and the nature of religious authority to be most apparent. This of course is not to suggest that other faith traditions, both within Christianity and beyond, reject conversion experience; nor that these traditions do not also struggle with issues related to human experience and religious authority. Rather, I will argue that human experience in general and the experience of conversion more specifically take on a unique emphasis and pride of place for evangelical Christianity. Often referred to within evangelicalism as being "saved," or "born again," this moment, or series of moments, results in an individual's inward choice or decision to accept the grace of God provided through the death and resurrection of Jesus Christ for his or her personal sins.

These conversion experiences may be a part of a long series of events culminating in a particularly meaningful moment of spiritual clarity centered upon a unique awareness of God, as for example in John Wesley's Aldersgate experience where his heart was "strangely warmed," or C. S. Lewis's famous recounting of his evangelical/Anglican conversion in his spiritual autobiography

---

4. See for example the historical origins of evangelical focus on religious conversion in Hindmarsh, *Evangelical Conversion Narrative*; Hindmarsh, *Spirit of Early Evangelicalism*; and for a more contemporary analysis of the phenomenon of religious conversion within evangelicalism see Balmer, *Mine Eyes Have Seen the Glory*. Theologically, there has also been a great deal of emphasis on conversion for evangelical Christianity; see specifically Olson, *Journey of Modern Theology*, 615–19. As Olson argues, despite the wide variety of specific theological positions held by evangelicals of various stripes, there is a common core of theological positions. "They all claim to be born again, adhere to biblical authority as the supreme norm for faith and practice, believe in the reality of the supernatural including miracles (with varying degrees of interest), are Protestants and stand apart from fundamentalism and theological liberalism and neo-liberalism" (619).

Surprised by Joy.[5] Or, they may be relatively isolated or stand-alone moments where God's presence is felt in a remarkable and memorable way such as the highly emotional "altar calls" of evangelical revival preaching such as George Whitefield of the eighteenth century or Billy Graham of the twentieth century. Similarly, they may be particularly powerful moments of private devotion such as is recounted in Jonathan Edwards's experience of evangelical conversion in his *Personal Narrative*. Edwards's case is instructive for us here regarding the radically transformative power and all-encompassing nature of conversion experiences where he recounts; "[the] appearance of everything was altered: there seemed to be, as it were, a calm, sweet cast, or appearance of divine glory, in almost everything."[6] One's conversion experience or recognition of a series of events culminating in an individual finding his or her religious identity as being converted is central for evangelical Christianity's self-identity.[7] This central mark of evangelicalism is what Stanley J. Grenz (1950–2005), a leading evangelical scholar of the late twentieth century, summed up as "being encountered savingly in Jesus Christ by the God of the Bible."[8] If indeed these type of transformative encounters of the presence of Jesus are typical of contemporary North American evangelical spirituality, then we should, at least provisionally, be able to see evidence of it by taking into account the general reality of conversion as understood by the evangelical tradition broadly conceived.

A Historical Overview of the Origins of Evangelical Christianity

Evangelicalism, while a notoriously difficult movement to precisely define, began to emerge as a distinct expression of the Christian faith around the turn of the eighteenth century.[9] With roots that trace back to the early radical reformations of the late sixteenth century, evangelicalism as a distinctly identifiable

---

5. Lewis, *Surprised by Joy*.

6. Edwards, *Works of Jonathan Edwards* (henceforth *WJE*), 16:793. A host of other examples might be mentioned here as supporting evidence of the power of religious conversion; St. Paul, and St. Augustine, for example point to those conversions that are sudden, dramatic and contained within a singularly powerful moment. Also, Abigail Hutchinson's conversion, as recorded in Edwards, *WJE,* 4. However, along with Wesley and Lewis's conversion accounts, point to the successive and more or less methodical advance of one's conversion towards God in Christ through a series of intellectual, emotional, and spiritual moments that culminate in an eventual awareness of the saving presence of Christ.

7. McClendon, "Toward a Conversionist Spirituality," 249–258.

8. Grenz, *Renewing the Center,* 202. While it is of course true that experiences of conversion are common outside of evangelical Christianity, as we will see, conversion itself takes on a particular significance within evangelicalism as the tradition develops.

9. Hindmarsh, *Spirit of Early Evangelicalism*, 4–5.

style of Christianity does not appear until at least a century later.[10] Part of the difficulty in precisely chronicling the origins of evangelicalism arises in part because of the lack of a singular "evangelical" institution or ecclesial body, and secondly because the moniker "evangelical" has been used to describe groups and individuals that represent not only a variety of traditions, but some even contradictory positions theologically or ecclesially. For example, in the sixteenth and seventeenth centuries, "evangelical" was commonly used to refer to Protestant churches in general, in distinction from Roman Catholicism. The German language bears witness to this as *Evangelischke* means simply Protestant and is the official name of the German Lutheran Church, the *Evangelische Kirche in Deutschland*. This usage, in connection with the etymology of the Greek *evangelion*, highlights a particular flavor of the Reformation principle of *sola Scriptura* by attaching its name and identity with an evangelistic priority of the Gospel message. However, by the eighteenth century, particularly in English-speaking Britain and North America, the term "evangelical" had become increasingly connected to doctrines, practices, and individuals associated with spiritual revival movements within various Protestant churches including Calvinist Reformed churches, Methodists, and the Church of England. Thus, rather than distinguishing between official ecclesial bodies, i.e., between Catholic and Protestant, as had been the common practice following the Reformations of the Sixteenth Century, the label "evangelical" now became a term that distinguished a subset of doctrines and practices within certain Protestant communities.[11]

This more narrow usage rapidly became associated with revivalist figures such as George Whitefield, who has been selected by some scholars as the father of evangelical Christianity, and the Methodist founders Charles and John Wesley beginning in the 1730s. However, revivalism itself does not explain the full picture of the emergence of evangelicalism. Going back to the historical roots of the movement, two traditions are important for the development of evangelicalism in the first half of the eighteenth century, the Pietists and Puritans. Continuing Luther's and Calvin's ecclesial reforms concerning the Word and Sacraments, the Puritans and Pietists went a step further and insisted on individual responsibility as a necessary condition for full inclusion into the Church.[12]

---

10. Grenz, *Renewing the Center*, 33–43.

11. Bebbington, *Evangelicalism in Modern Britain*; Kyle, *Evangelicalism*; Bloesch, *Evangelical Renaissance*.

12. For a more detailed analysis of the influences of early evangelicalism, see chapter 3 of Hindmarsh, *Spirit of Early Evangelicalism*, "The Classical Sources of Evangelical Devotion," 69–101.

Evangelical Experience and the Crisis of Religious Conversion

The Puritans, influenced by early Reformation leaders John Knox (1513–1572) who founded the Scottish Presbyterian Church, and Anglican Bishop John Hooper (1495–1555), advocated that true Christian churches should be "[congregations] of the faithful"[13] and instituted strict church discipline and a moral/ethical requirement for individuals to remain in good standing in the Church. The Pietists, under the leadership of Philipp Jakob Spener (1635–1705), similarly placed the personal dimension of the Christian life at the center of ecclesiology. Pietism stressed the inner transformation of the heart of a person towards love and obedience to God and neighbor as something that was equally as necessary for the Christian life as the objective and largely external understanding of the Reformed doctrine of justification, as well as the formal participation in the sacraments of the Church. This inner transformation was referred to as the new birth, or regeneration, which manifested itself through exhibiting the "fruits" of faith in the individual's new life in Christ.[14] One of the most important results of these influences is, as Grenz comments, that the foundation of evangelical Christianity shifted from the corporate Protestant notion of justification through faith in baptism to the more personal notion of justification through faith in conversion.[15] Thus evangelicalism, especially as it develops in the later half of the eighteenth century, combined a strong since of individual moral/ethical responsibility alongside of an inner-personal appeal to the dynamics of the divine human relationship.

As Whitefield and other British evangelical Christians spread the revivalist spirit across the Atlantic to the North American colonies, the evangelical style of Christianity became firmly rooted in an individual's inner conversion of the heart. Perhaps one of the greatest examples of this type of Christianity is the colonial pastor and theologian Jonathan Edwards (1703–1758) who played a leading role during the North American colonial revivals of the 1730s and 1740s known as the First Great Awakening. Edwards went so far as to suggest that, "God, in his Word, greatly insists upon it, that we be in good earnest, fervent in spirit, and our hearts vigorously engaged in religion," and continued that, "nothing is more manifest in fact, than that the things of religion take hold of men's souls, no further than they affect them."[16] That is for Edwards, true Christianity is viable to the degree that it affects a change of heart, internally from within the life of faith of individual persons.

---

13. Hooper, *Later Writings of Bishop Hooper*, 120–21.
14. Spener, *Pia Desideria*, 64–65, 116; Bloesch, *Evangelical Renaissance*, 109.
15. Grenz, *Renewing the Center*, 43.
16. Edwards, *WJE*, 2:99, 101.

The Crisis of Conversion

Bebbington's Evangelical Quadrilateral

Recently, evangelical scholars in North America and the U.K. have gravitated towards historian David Bebbington's "Quadrilateral" of traits in an attempt to identify a core religious ethos with which to define the distinctive quality of evangelical religious expression across denominational and geographic lines. Bebbington's Quadrilateral defines evangelical Christianity as a religious expression that elevates in a particular way the following: conversionism, activism, biblicism, and crucicentrism.[17] Bebbington's definition accomplishes at least two things related to contemporary evangelicalism.

First, Bebbington's quadrilateral captures what I refer to as evangelicalism's reductionist spirit.[18] This reductionism is not necessarily a watered-down version of Christianity, but rather a tendency to approach the life of faith through the fewest number of means possible. Recently, D. Bruce Hindmarsh provided an interesting commentary on the emergence of early evangelical Christianity through the story of Jesus visiting Martha and Mary as recorded in Luke's Gospel, and Jesus's admonition to Martha that "there is need of only one thing," (Lk. 10:42 *NRSV*) and that Mary, present at the feet of Jesus had found that one thing. Hindmarsh notes that while this passage had long been used as a central text within the contemplative traditions of Catholic Spirituality, by 1765 Whitefield and other evangelical leaders began to utilize this text in an effort to exhort their listeners that "true religion," or religion of the heart, was that "one thing needful."[19]

This evangelical reductionism, or the search for that "one thing needful," is visible at the popular level of evangelicalism in the flat-literalist approach to biblical interpretation, the general rejection of High-Church liturgical forms of worship, a strong skepticism towards philosophy and higher biblical criticisms, as well as a staunch individualism that eschews any necessary mediator, including the local church, between the believer and God.[20] Even if not strictly understood along the scholarly distinctions between the inherency or infallibility of the Bible, evangelical Christians tend to affirm the "plain meaning" of Scripture, which acknowledges that the text itself as plainly read is a reliable source of the revelation of God by the illumination of the Holy Spirit through the individual reader. Walter B. Shurden's study on Baptist distinctives is

---

17. Bebbington, *Evangelicalism in Modern Britain*, 2–17.

18. While true of evangelicalism in general to some degree, it is most evident in the more conservative and fundamentalist branches of evangelicalism.

19. Hindmarsh, *Spirit of Early Evangelicalism*, 1–6.

20. For a similar analysis of the shape of evangelical piety see Bloesch, *Future of Evangelical Christianity*, 111–34.

Evangelical Experience and the Crisis of Religious Conversion

illuminating here through what he calls "Bible Freedom" and "Soul Freedom" as two of the four central freedoms that are central to Baptist life.[21] Bible freedom, according to Shurden, refers to the freedom from external creedal or doctrinal schemas as necessary structures for appropriately reading and interpreting the Bible, and freedom for each and every Christian to be responsible to model their life through obedience to the Bible as the source of revelation of Jesus Christ. Soul freedom asserts the centrality of the individual who alone has the responsibility and therefore freedom to respond to and affirm the life of faith as revealed in the Bible.[22] While not every evangelical tradition would accept Shurden's analysis, he nevertheless provides a good example of evangelicalism's reductionist spirit. In these ways, evangelicalism tends to resort to the lowest common denominator in living out the Christian life; or to state this principle more positively, to focus on the true essence of faith by removing distracting and potentially corrupting extra-biblical practices and ideas from the Christian life, to grasp onto that "one thing needful."[23]

Secondly, in highlighting both the conversionist and biblicist pillars of evangelicalism, Bebbington identifies a central tension within evangelicalism for the locus of religious authority as it relates to the role of experience vis a vis Scripture. Here, I am not suggesting that evangelicals place experience and the Bible on separate but equal grounds, that is certainly the opposite of the case. Rather, evangelicalism, in line with its Protestant heritage, elevates the Bible alone as the witness to the revelation of God in the person of Jesus as the ultimate source of religious authority. Moreover, the veracity of human experience is theologically suspect, and thus generally rejected as a reliable guide to encountering the things of God. At the same time, a genuine *experience* of conversion is a central marker of evangelical piety as well as seen as essential for authentic Christian faith. Thus theologically, evangelicalism questions the nature of human experience as something fundamentally untrustworthy and a leading cause of pluralist subjectivism on the one hand, and at the same time places the experience of Jesus at the very center of what it means to be an evangelical Christian on the other.[24]

---

21. The other two are "Church freedom," and "Religious freedom." Shurden, *Baptist Identity*.

22. Shurden, *Baptist Identity*, 9–32.

23. In a similar vein, Richard Kyle refers to evangelicalism as being "unabashedly populist" which prefers common, simple, and plain approaches to Christianity over complex, sophisticated, and erudite forms. Kyle, *Evangelicalism*, 3. Additionally, this reductionist spirit is seen in the popularity of C. S. Lewis's *Mere Christianity*. While not an Evangelical himself, Lewis's popular theology and apologetic works are some of the most widely read among evangelicals.

24. This would hold true for Arminian/Wesleyan evangelicals the same as it would for

The Crisis of Conversion

Timothy Larsen has provided a complimentary definition of evangelicalism to Bebbington's Quadrilateral in his *Oxford Handbook of Evangelical Theology* that revises and expands Bebbington's definition by providing some historical context to evangelical Christianity:

> 1. An Orthodox Protestant 2. who stands in the tradition of the global Christian network arising from the eighteenth-century revival movements associated with John Wesley and George Whitefield; 3. who has a preeminent place for the Bible in his or her Christian life as the divinely inspired, final authority in matters of faith and practice; 4. who stresses reconciliation with God through the atoning work of Jesus Christ on the cross; 5. and who stresses the work of the Holy Spirit in the life of an individual to bring about conversion and an ongoing life of fellowship with God and service to God and others, including the duty of all believers to participate in the task of proclaiming the gospel to all people.[25]

Both Bebbington and Larsen highlight the individual dimension of religious conversion and the centrality of the Bible as keys for understanding evangelical identity. Thus, the tension introduced above in Bebbington's quadrilateral is also present in a modified form in Larsen's definition as well. Utilizing a more phenomenological approach to understanding evangelical spirituality, Hindmarsh identifies four key paradigms present in the early leaders of evangelicalism; namely "the emergence of revival . . . the formation of voluntary groups for devotion and wider trans-local evangelical networks linked by itinerancy . . . the widespread practice of a a spirited new hymnody . . . and the development of extempore patterns of prayer and preaching."[26] What is interesting here for our present purposes is the absence of doctrinal/theological markers such as the role of scripture or other matters of Christian or Protestant orthodoxy. Hindmarsh does of course recognize the emergence

---

reformed/Calvinist evangelicals. While Arminian/Wesleyan evangelicals talk about the human response to, and/or cooperation with God's agency in salvation through faith, it nevertheless remains true that God's self-revelation in Jesus is a necessary precondition to faith prior to any agency of the human free-will in the process of conversion. See Bloesch, *Crisis of Piety*, 77–94. See also, Grenz, *Renewing the Center* and his assessment of the more recent "neo-evangelical" movement attempting to distinguish itself from the fundamentalists on the right and liberal Protestantism on the right. In Grenz's analysis, this new evangelicalism carries two motifs: "the cognitive-doctrinal and the practical-experiential," (84). These two motifs mirror my perceived tension within evangelicalism, particularly as it relates to the place and role of the Bible.

25. Larsen, "Defining and Locating Evangelicalism," 1.

26. Hindmarsh, *Spirit of Early Evangelicalism*, 10–11.

of a distinctly evangelical theological tradition,[27] but the point here is that evangelical theology followed after, or arose out of, the unique expression of evangelical spirituality—most notably in the experience of personal religious conversion as stimulated through evangelical revival. In light of this brief historical survey of the central defining features of the emergence of evangelical spirituality, I will now proceed to a closer analysis of the nature of Christian conversion in contemporary North American Christianity.

Developing a Theology of Christian Conversion

In his recent book analyzing the state of contemporary North American Christianity, *Moses in Pharaoh's House,* Roman Catholic theologian John Markey (b. 1961) identifies a need for a re-imagined theology of conversion for North American Christianity. Markey argues that most American Christians think of conversion in two basic ways; "the conversion of adherents of other faiths to Christianity, and the conversion from lukewarm church-goer to fervent believer in Jesus Christ as Lord and Savior."[28] According to Markey, this understanding of conversion has become the dominant view, even by American Catholics, due to the influence of evangelical Christianity's ubiquitous "born again" language. The influence of evangelicalism on American Roman Catholicism is not specifically the issue for Markey, but rather that this flat view of conversion falls pitifully short of the dynamic meaning of conversion found in the Gospel message of the New Testament.

Markey finds in the New Testament an understanding of personal conversion to Christ that is "certainly a profound event, but it is life-changing only if it leads to different ways of interacting with one's family, friends, neighbors,

---

27. Hindmarsh, *Spirit of Early Evangelicalism*, 62–65.

28. Markey, *Moses in Pharaoh's House,* 10–11. See also these similar analyses of the phenomenon of religious conversion: Rambo's definition of conversion as a "simple change from absence of a faith system to a faith commitment, from religious affiliation with one faith system to another, or from one orientation to another within a single faith system." Rambo, *Understanding Religious Conversion,* 2. Markey seems to have something like Rambo's phenomenological analysis in mind as he defines the state of the *practice of conversion* as he sees it being lived out in American Christianity. This is of course not to make a normative judgement of whether or not conversion ought to be practiced in this way, simply that as Markey observers it tends to be lived out in this manner. I will turn to this and other issues concerning the nature of religious experience generally, and conversion experience in particular more directly in chapter two below. However, at this initial stage, it is helpful to draw a distinction between normative claims and phenomenological evaluation, though as will be made clear in what follows, that distinction is never absolute as interpretive judgements cannot be absolutely withheld from observations.

The Crisis of Conversion

strangers, and even enemies."[29] Taking a large view of the meaning of the word conversion in general, Markey defines it as "the ability of an individual to adapt to changing circumstances, to develop new habits and skills, and to dramatically change her or his personality because of deeply felt emotional and intuitive experiences."[30] In an earlier work, Markey goes so far as to say "[conversion] can neither be an individualistic, self-centered quest nor a a formalized and objective program without genuinely personal dimensions and diversifications."[31] That is, for Markey, conversion necessarily entails both an intensely personal dimension and a thoroughly social/communal dimension.

Comparing Markey's analysis of conversion with Lewis Rambo's landmark study on the phenomenology of religious conversion, we see a great deal of similarity in terms of the field and scope of conversion. For Rambo, conversion "is a process of religious change that takes place in a dynamic force field of people, events, ideologies, institutions, expectations, and orientations." Rambo identifies three general facets of conversion: (a) conversion is a "process over time"; (b) conversion is a contextual reality influenced "by a matrix of relationships, expectations, and situations"; and (c) conversion when viewed as a whole include factors that are "multiple, interactive, and cumulative."[32] Thus we can reasonably conclude that conversion for both Markey and Rambo ought not to be reduced to the interior, private sphere of an individual's devotional life, but rather results in a kind of change that implicates the entirety of a person's world that includes the individual person but which also extends beyond the purely individualistic frame of reference. Conversion for Marky and Rambo is both a social and individual, private and public reality.

With this understanding of conversion in mind, Markey argues that the stereotypical understanding of conversion by American Christians, especially within conservative Christianity both Protestant and Catholic, is one that is individual, private, and concerned with the internal soul or heart of the person as it relates to her or his relationship with God. This individualistic notion of conversion, Markey suggests, falls short of even a general meaning of the concept of Christian conversion, much less of New Testament conversion to a life of obedience to the will of God as revealed in Jesus Christ and received through the indwelling Spirit. Suspending judgement, momentarily, on the validity of Markey's assessment of the state of the understanding of conversion within North American Christianity, let us first examine Markey's

---

29. Markey, *Moses in Pharaoh's House*, 11.
30. Markey, *Moses in Pharaoh's House*, 82.
31. Markey, *Creating Communion*, 118.
32. Rambo, *Understanding Religious Conversion*, 5.

understanding of conversion more fully as it relates to Christian conversion as expressed in the New Testament.

Donald Gelpi's Theology of Christian Conversion

Markey closely follows the work of Donald Gelpi (1934–2011), who identified five dimensions of personal conversion, which is a slightly revised version of the foundational work of Bernard Lonergan.[33] *affective* conversion, where a person takes "responsibility for his or her emotional healing and development";[34] *intellectual* conversion, concerning the nature of "truth and falsity of one's beliefs";[35] *moral* conversion, whereby a person begins to be "accountable to oneself by choosing values that one wants to embody . . . and by shaping one's moral conduct according to those values";[36] *sociopolitical* conversion, which expands moral conversion and moves a person "out of the personal and into the political sphere";[37] and finally *religious* conversion, which is for Markey that "dimension of the personality that infuses meaning through other dimensions of one's life."[38] These five dimensions are, moreover, interconnected in a process that is both initial and ongoing, and where each dimension is continually interacting with the other four.[39] More importantly, religious conversion *transvalues* all of the other dimensions of conversion by "shifting the fundamental frame of reference in which one experiences affective, speculative, and moral conversion, in a way that casts all experience in a new light."[40] This transvaluing dynamic, unique to religious conversion, highlights the dynamics and counter-dynamics of Gelpi's model of conversion by highlighting how the various dimensions of conversion interact with one another both positively and negatively throughout the whole reality that is Christian conversion.

A central presupposition of Gelpi's notion of conversion is that the seemingly disparate parts of human experience—from affect, memory, and sensory reception, to the various processes of reasoning, decision making and responses—nevertheless "mutually condition one another even though they

33. See primarily Gelpi, *Conversion Experience*. Gelpi, "Conversion," 606–28; Gelpi, *Grace as Transmuted Experience and Social*; Gelpi, *Gracing of Human Experience*; and Gelpi, *Encountering Jesus Christ*.

34. Markey, *Moses in Pharaoh's House*, 86.

35. Markey, *Moses in Pharaoh's House*, 88.

36. Markey, *Moses in Pharaoh's House*, 90.

37. Markey, *Moses in Pharaoh's House*, 92.

38. Markey, *Moses in Pharaoh's House*, 93.

39. Markey, *Moses in Pharaoh's House*, 94.

40. Markey, *Moses in Pharaoh's House*, 97.

engage different kinds of habitual ways of responding to oneself and one's world."[41] That human experience itself tends towards an integrative and therefore holistic reality for a given person or community, naturally leads Gelpi to conclude that a personal conversion in any one dimension of a person's experience implicates and has consequences for the other dimensions of that person as well. That is, an intellectual conversion resulting in a person taking on a sense of personal responsibility and accountability in terms of their new understanding of themselves and/or their world will have an impact on a person's affective, moral, socio-political, and religious frames of reference. And conversely, a person who remains unconverted in their affective life—who eschews or rejects personal responsibility for their emotional or empathic relationship to themselves or their world—will negatively affect or otherwise hold back the other dimensions or frames of reference from their fullest and most generative functioning. Moreover, Gelpi identifies unique effects of each dimension's dynamic and counter-dynamic interaction with the other dimensions of conversion.

On the positive side, affective conversion "animates" the other dimensions by providing a sense of clarity of vision for the future, and heightened creative energy. Intellectual conversion "orders" the other dimensions by solidifying them within more adequate frames of reference and in true beliefs. Personal moral conversion "orients" the other dimensions toward ultimate and absolute values in terms of internal ethical consistency personal integration. Socio-political conversion "deprivatizes" the other dimensions by rooting justice in a public concern for the common good beyond the individual. Religious conversion provides two distinct dynamics to the overall picture of Gelpi's notion of Christian conversion—first, it "mediates" between affective and moral conversion by virtue of it beginning "in the heart" and results in a religious commitment of "faith" that moves a converted person toward obedience through a life of discipleship. And secondly, as we have seen, religious conversion "transvalues" all of the other dimensions of conversion by "suffusing them with religious values and perceptions derived from divine revelation."[42]

On the other hand, Gelpi notes that "each dimension of conversion includes a counter-dynamic force in which the absence of conversion in one realm of experience tends to undermine its presence in other realms of experience."[43] Thus the absence of an intellectual conversion results in a distorted sense of truth and falsity, and leads to fundamentalism and self-delusion. The absence

41. Gelpi, *Encountering Jesus Christ*, 41.
42. Gelpi, *Encountering Jesus Christ*, 44.
43. Gelpi, *Encountering Jesus Christ*, 44.

of personal moral conversion results in narrow individual selfishness and lack of concern or awareness of the personal rights and values of others. Similarly, the absence of socio-political conversion privatizes notions of justice and injustice which reinforce the selfishness of moral counter-dynamics and results in a disregard for the demands of the common good. The absence of religious conversion, in reference to its transvaluative dynamic, results in a less integrated overall process of conversion, and will naturally lack any reference or fidelity to a sense of transcendence, universal identity, or self-purpose.[44]

With the counter-dynamic of affective conversion, Gelpi notes that its absence results in a distorted view of life and human behavior. At this point, the affective counter-dynamic suffers from an overly-psychological analysis where Gelpi describes the effect of the absence of affective conversion in terms of "neurosis" and "psychosis" in a way that obscures the line between a formal psychological diagnosis and Gelpi's theological anthropology.[45] Additionally, by employing psychological terminology, Gelpi misses an opportunity to engage the broader relevance of theological and aesthetic categories such as "harmony/incongruity," "natural/unnatural," and "hope/fear" as a way of showing the animating dynamic potency of affective conversion for a person's emotional, social, and personal frames of reference. While, Gelpi's affective counter-dynamic is helpful to the degree that it highlights the problematic and distorted view of reality from which the other dimensions of conversion respond to, it seems to me that in light of Gelpi's overall theological concern of religious conversion it would have served him better to utilize a different set of vocabulary for this counter-dynamic.

The Lukan "Sermon on the Plain" as a Model for a New Testament Theology of Christian Conversion

Throughout the New Testament, and in line with Markey's and Gelpi's work, conversion toward Christ is never merely a interior private event, nor a singular and momentary experience. Rather, religious conversion as an encounter with the living God in Jesus Christ in the New Testament involves an initial and often radical transvaluation of one's habitual ways of being in the world that is ongoing and decisively alters how a person receives, responds to, and interprets everything else from then on. The evangelist Luke, in his two-volume Luke-Acts, provides a helpful presentation of a New Testament call to a converted life. Particularly Luke-Acts provides a helpful case-study for

---

44. Gelpi, *Encountering Jesus Christ*, 42.
45. Gelpi, *Encountering Jesus Christ*, 42.

The Crisis of Conversion

applying Gelpi's model of conversion to the New Testament witness through his sermon on the plain in chapter 6:17–49.

Luke's version of Jesus's "Sermon on the Plain," a parallel to Matthew's opening pericope of the "Sermon on the Mount" (Matt 5:1–11), provides a vision of the kingdom of God that Jesus inaugurated in his earthly life and ministry. The beatitudes proclaimed in 6:20–23 reveal the qualities of the Kingdom, and when taken together paint a picture of the good, or beatific life. The attributes of the kingdom of God, as given in the beatitudes of Luke 6, align closely with Gelpi's notion of conversion in general; namely taking responsibility for one's place in the world in response to or in the face of an ultimate calling. The more socio-economic focus in Luke's beatitudes in contrast to the spiritual focus in Matthew allows for a nice parallel to Gelpi's concern for a full view of human experience involved in the process of conversion.[46] The juxtaposition of the attitudes of the blessed (6:20b–23) in contrast to the woes (6:24–26) further highlight the dynamics and counter-dynamics displayed in Gelpi's model; the poor/hungry and the rich/full corresponding to Gelpi's sociopolitical conversions, those who weep and those who laugh corresponding to Gelpi's personal moral conversion,[47] and those who are "defamed on account of the Son of Man" and those who are spoken well of corresponding to Gelpi's intellectual conversion. The following section on the love toward enemies both summarizes and expands the implications of the beatitudes and highlight the transvaluative dynamic of Gelpi's notion of religious conversion (6:27–38). Here, Jesus teaches that true conversion into the kingdom of God comes by putting into practice and living out of these beatific qualities of the kingdom of God. Through connecting the kingdom of God of the Beatitudes with Gelpi's model of personal conversion, we find a richness in the call to the converted life that has been largely underdeveloped in the evangelical ethos. To help uncover the roots of this neglect, I will now turn to consider evangelicalism's skepticism concerning the category of human experience more broadly.

---

46. Vinson, *Luke*, 174–85; Buttrick, *Interpreter's Bible*, 118–20; Kraybill, *Upside-Down Kingdom*, 109–12.

47. Luke, recalling the laughter of the 'fool' in the Old Testament Wisdom literature, particularly Prov 17:12; 19:1; and Sir 21:14–15, 20, the contrast between laughter and weeping indicates the true happiness of the righteous life despite or because of apparently unpleasant circumstances contrasted with the superficial laughter of the unrighteous who lead self-centered and morally vacuous lives. Vinson, *Luke*, 181–82.

Schleiermacher and the Evangelical Problem of Experience

While there is some variety as to how various evangelical traditions understand and utilize experiences of conversion, conversion itself is central to an Evangelical identity.[48] One's conversion serves as both the point of entry into the Christian life as well as the source and fount for continuing spiritual growth throughout an evangelical Christian's life. Thus, it is my contention from the outset, that conversion is the *sine qua non* of Evangelical spirituality. At this point it is important to broadly contextualize the notion of "conversion" within the larger issue of religious experience for evangelicals as a way of moving toward an expression of evangelical spirituality in the twenty-first century.

For many outside observers, evangelical Christianity often appears as a purely experiential form of Christianity particularly when viewed ecclesiologically. Evangelical Churches tend to operate congregationally rather than hierarchically, to reject High-Church liturgical forms of worship as restrictive to the freedom of the Spirit of God (John 3:8) and are skeptical of allowing "the Tradition" too great an authority in matters of theological and scriptural interpretation. Reinforcing the reductionist tendency discussed above, ecclesially evangelicalism appears to place a great deal of authority on individual people's experience of God as the foundation for faith and practice in the church.

At the same time, however, there is a way in which evangelical faith and practice is born out of an utter rejection of the validity of human experience. This rejection of the authority of experience stems, at least partially, from the eminent theologian Friedrich Schleiermacher's (1768–1834) influence in the nineteenth century that elevated feeling, or *Gefühl*, as the foundation of Christian piety, thus launching what has become known as liberal Protestantism.[49] Schleiermacher was deeply influenced by German Pietism which elevated the category of human experience of God as a source of revelation and theological reflection. Schleiermacher and the Pietists viewed the reigning Scholastic theology of their day as fundamentally flawed due to its abstract, theoretical, and highly philosophical language that rendered theology, and ultimately Christianity itself, radically disconnected from the experiences of life in the world. In particular, his popular works *On Religion: Speeches to Its Cultured Despisers* (1st edition 1799, 2nd edition 1806) and *Christmas Eve: A Dialogue on the Celebration of Christmas* (1806) drew an early and clear distinction between the inner appropriation of the Christian faith and the external superstructures

---

48. Emerson and Smith, *Divided by Faith,* 2–4; Hinson, "Baptist Approaches to Spirituality," 12–18; Grenz, "Christian Spirituality and the Quest for Identity," 88; Yong, "Word and the Spirit," 235–52.

49. Schleiermacher, *Christian Faith.*

of dogmatic and ecclesial theology. This fundamental distinction would be more fully developed in his magnum opus, *The Christian Faith* (1st edition 1821/22, 2nd edition 1831/32).[50]

Schleiermacher's *Gefühl* as a Source of Christian Revelation

Central to this distinction is the foundational place that he reserves for *Gefühl* in his dogmatics. *Gefühl*, for Schleiermacher refers to a "feeling of absolute dependence" which for the Christian is the foundation and source of our knowledge of God. That is for Schleiermacher, the word "God" is as a referent to an "expression of the feeling of absolute dependence," so that he can conclude by saying that "to feel oneself absolutely dependent and to be conscious of being in relation with God are one and the same thing."[51] Schleiermacher thus placed this feeling of absolute dependence as the singular foundation of faith in God. The Bible, for Schleiermacher, maintained a place of privilege for the Christian because it is itself the record of "an original and authentic"[52] faith in Christ. Implicit in Schleiermacher's understanding of Scripture is that first, there is a clear connection between the prior faith relationship between the biblical authors and God. Second, that the Bible's continued relevance is ultimately related to the faithful and clear expression of this original and authentic faith in Christ. And third, that its contemporary function through the Church's ministry of the word, is found by bringing into contact the witness of the original and prior faith of the apostles with the equally original and prior faith of Christian readers in subsequent ages. That is, the Scriptures serve as the reliable witness and correction to faith in Christ and thus provide shape and structure to the faith as preached by the Church across cultures and time. In all of this Schleiermacher retains the foundational priority of internal "faith" as understood through his use of *Gefühl* over any other external basis of religious authority.[53]

For many Evangelicals in the nineteenth century, however, Schleiermacher took the Pietist emphasis of the believer's inner experience too far when he elevated personal experience as foundational for the Christian faith rather than the Bible.[54] It was perhaps due in part to Schleiermacher's early incor-

---

50. Lamm, "Early Philosophical Roots of Schleiermacher's Notion of Gefühl," 67–105; Clements, "Introduction," 11–15; Simon, "Sentiment Religieux," 69–90; Thandeka, "Schleiermacher's Affekt Theology," 197–216.

51. Schleiermacher, *Christian Faith*. 17.

52. Schleiermacher, *Christian Faith*. 593.

53. Lamm's helpful "Schleiermacher's Spirituality," 32–36.

54. Fortman, *Triune God*, 243–46, 250–56; Olson, *Mosaic of Christian Belief*, 95–96.

poration of the Pietist idea of inner experience as a foundational piece of the Christian life that led him to reject certain core doctrinal positions, particularly the largely forensic and external notion of the substitutionary theory of atonement. This doctrinal dispute would ultimately result in Schleiermacher leaving the *Herrnhuter*, or Moravian Pietists of his family and continue his education within the burgeoning stream of the German Enlightenment.[55] Schleiermacher's work and legacy highlights a tension within evangelicalism between its Pietistic roots that place one's experience of God at the center of the Christian life on the one hand, and its high view of the inspiration of Scripture and core theological positions that were being challenged by the emerging protestant liberalism that Schleiermacher would come to articulate.[56]

If we return to consider the experiential-biblical center of evangelical Christianity in light of Bebbington's and Larsen's definitions we find that Schleiermacher's *Gefühl* places evangelicalism in a precarious situation. For on the one hand, evangelicalism alongside of Schleiermacher's romanticism, sees the personal expression of the individual's faith is of central importance. While on the other, in line with classical Protestantism, both evangelicalism and Schleiermacher see the expansion of modern rational skepticism as a serious threat to the integrity of biblical orthodoxy. The tension that Schleiermacher creates for evangelicals, who were not willing to go as far as Schleiermacher went, then is not necessarily experience verses the Bible as the foundation of Christianity,[57] but rather a much deeper and fundamental question related to the relationship between human experience and the Bible as complimentary modes of divine revelation. In other words, Schleiermacher's proposal posed a fundamental challenge to evangelicalism's Pietist roots that forced it to clarify its own foundations vis a vis both modern biblical criticism on the one hand and anthropocentric experientialism on the other.

In a certain way, Schleiermacher mirrors this tension. Following philosopher Immanuel Kant, Schleiermacher responds to modern rational skepticism by compartmentalizing the foundation of Christianity and protecting it from the perceived threat posed by modern inquiry. That is, Schleiermacher's *Gefühl* achieves something similar to Kant's *Religion within the Boundaries of Mere Reason*. For both thinkers, the external and public trappings of religion, which were becoming more and more susceptible to modern criticism, were themselves deemed unreliable sources of authentic Christianity. The

---

55. Lamm, "Schleiermacher's Spirituality," 5–9.

56. For a more detailed account of Schleiermacher's influence on Protestant theology in the 19th and 20th centuries see Grenz and Olson, *20th-Century Theology*, 39–51.

57. See specifically Grenz and Olson's critique of Schleiermacher, *20th-Century Theology*, 43–46.

The Crisis of Conversion

foundations of true Christianity were thus reconfigured. For Kant, the foundation of religion was re-situated to the realm of morals and ethics; whereas for Schleiermacher, the foundation of religion was removed from the reach of modern rationalism, to the inner life of faith within the individual.

Where evangelicalism would have been receptive to Kant's and Schleiermacher's critique of the modern situation, they were unable to accept either solution. Therefore, the evangelical pillar of an experience of conversion, whereby an individual appropriates his or her faith, stands alongside of the pillar of the objectivity of the Bible as the revelation of the content of his or her faith. In Bebbington's quadrilateral, the activist impulse emerges logically after one's conversion, and similarly, the crucicentristic dimension of evangelicalism is based upon the Biblical witness, interpreted as it is through a particularly individualized understanding of the divine-human relationship. Larsen, who is perhaps attempting to respond to this tension, places a clear stress on the Bible by connecting evangelicalism more explicitly to the original reformers than does Bebbington. Nevertheless, each of his five points are directed toward the individual person, and particularly in points four and five, Larsen continues the evangelical trajectory of a definitive personal experience of God as a defining trait of the Christian life. Thus, for both Bebbington and Larsen, the tension remains between the personal experience of God and the Bible as foundational for authentic Christianity.[58]

In contemporary evangelicalism, the dynamics between human experience and what is considered faithful interpretation of scripture continues to remain a hotly contested issue within evangelical circles as society changes over the decades. Most recently, issues of racism, gender roles, and sexual identity have been the locus of debate among many Evangelical groups.[59] However, these debates are simply the latest manifestations of this central tension concerning which individual or community's experience of God and the world counts as a legitimate starting place for a faithful interpretation of the Bible.[60] These socio-theological debates serve as a witness to the underlying crisis of conversion.

---

58. For a more thorough analysis of Bebbington's quadrilateral see the following: Porterfield, "Bebbington's Approach to Evangelical Christianity," 58–62; Worthen, "Defining Evangelicalism," 83–86; Noll, "Noun or Adjective?," 73–82; Dochuk, "Revisiting Bebbington's Classic Rendering of Modern Evangelicalism," 63–72; Phillips, "Roundtable," 44–45; Kidd, "Bebbington Quadrilateral," 54–57; Elliott, "Bebbington Quadrilateral Travels into the Empire," 46–53; Bebbington, "Evangelical Quadrilateral," 87–96.

59. Emerson and Smith, *Divided by Faith*; Mathews, *Doctrine and Race*; Kyle, *Evangelicalism*; Ziegenhals, "Women in Ministry," 77–87; Knox, "Editorial"; Runn, "Year of Jenn Hatmaker."

60. Cochran, *Evangelical Feminism*.

The Postmodern Crisis of Conversion

Schleiermacher did not create the evangelical tension between experience and the Bible, but rather exacerbated the tension by elevating the experiential pole within the Cartesian/Kantian tradition of conceptual nominalism that dualistically construed subjectivity and objectivity in opposition to one another. Additionally, evangelicalism's reaction to liberal Protestantism has not resolved that tension either. Rather, as a product of the Enlightenment itself,[61] evangelicalism inherited and incorporated a foundationalist theological epistemology within a Cartesian/Kantian conceptual nominalist frame in the pursuit of the Protestant *sola*. Evangelical thought developed in such a way that would ensure that this tension between the supposed objectivity of the biblical witness and the subjectivity of human experience would remain unresolved.[62] Moreover, as postmodern critiques have exposed the deficiencies of foundationalist epistemologies in general by shattering the objective/subjective distinction, it has revealed the universality of the subjective or the particular and contingent. That is, truth is always truth *from* a particular perspective; not, as Modernity would have it, truth in and for itself. Postmodernity's critique of Kantian categories of universal transcendentalism—for example the absurdism of Camus rooted in the irrationality of Kierkegaard's leap of faith—concludes that the Modernist enthronement of reason as a secure foundation for encountering reality was built upon an irrational assertion that subjectivity stands in absolute opposition to objectivity. Kant's categorical imperative has been exposed itself as a leap of faith. In other words, Postmodernity questions the fundamental insight of Modernity that objectivity and its subjective counterpart exist as isolated and self-contained modes of reality that are in need of reconciliation. The history of modern Continental philosophy itself through the German idealism of Hegel, the British empiricism of Hume and Locke, and the German/French Hermeneutical traditions of Gadamer, Heidegger, and Ricœur, may be viewed as a variety of proposals out of the Kantian quagmire of subjectivism culminating in the radical deconstructionism of Jacques Derrida and others in the postmodern turn.[63]

---

61. Grenz, "Concerns of a Pietist with a PhD," 63.

62. Grenz, *Renewing the Center*, 189–90.

63. For surveys of the roots and transitions of modernity and postmodernity see: Kearney, *Wake of Imagination*; Tarnas, *Passion of the Western Mind*; Taylor, *Sources of the Self*; Gillespie, *Theological Origins of Modernity*; and Dupré, *Passage to Modernity*.

For original postmodern critiques of modernity see in particular the French project of deconstruction, especially Derrida, *Of Grammatology*; and the Frankfurt school of Critical Theory, particularly Habermas, *Jürgen Habermas on Society* and I suggest these two representative schools of thought primarily due to the degree that they influence

The Crisis of Conversion

However, what is important to note within this larger narrative is that evangelical Christianity was born in the Enlightenment, and flourished in Modernity. Thus, the postmodern turn has and will continue to effect evangelical Christianity more profoundly than other traditions of Christianity with roots in Classical and pre-Modern contexts.[64] In this way, for Christianity in the West in general, postmodernity presents what might be called a crisis of culture, or relevance, requiring a reconfiguration of methods of engagement and interaction in the world; but for evangelicals, the postmodern challenge is nothing other than a crisis of identity.[65] Central to evangelical concerns surrounding the postmodern critique of foundationalism is the work of Canadian Baptist theologian Stanley Grenz.

Stanley J. Grenz's Evangelical Engagement with Postmodernity

To a large extent, Grenz's theological career was concerned with reorienting Baptist evangelical theology in light of the emerging postmodern philosophical and cultural shifts of the late twentieth century. To that end, he found that at the heart of this refashioning was the need to critically reexamine conventional understandings of conversion. According to Grenz scholar Jay T. Smith, Grenz saw that the practice and thought surrounding experiences of conversion in North America had become problematically intertwined with the prevailing cultural attitudes of individualism and consumerism.[66]

By interpreting the practice of religious conversion within a consumerist and individualist hermeneutic, North American evangelicalism had in a certain sense continued the Enlightenment/Modernity attempt to ground epistemological certainty onto a set of unquestionable foundations. The difference between the earlier foundationalism of Descartes, Kant, and Locke

---

significant theological trajectories. From the French school of deconstruction, comes Paul Ricœur's hermeneutical theology, esp. Ricœur, *Time and Narrative*; Ricœur, *Oneself as Another*; and from Critical Theory, the monumental contributions of liberationist and feminist theology, especially Gutierrez, *Theology of Liberation*; Cone, *Black Theology of Liberation*; and Reuther, *Sexism and God-Talk*.

64. Grenz, *Renewing the Center*, 167.
65. Grenz, *Renewing the Center*, 162–66.
66. Smith, "Generous Theology," 12.

for example, and North American evangelicalism of the Twentieth Century, was where and what constituted a legitimate foundation. Rather than positing the ultimate ground of human inquiry on strictly rationalist foundations, evangelicalism rooted itself firmly in an individualist foundation from which God was seemingly immediately approachable via an individual's engagement with the Bible.[67] That is, for evangelicalism, the individual assumes a pride of place over and against the mediating influences of the church community or other theological traditions. This is not to suggest that evangelical America has not been interested in theological inquiry, or the success and flourishing of the Church, but rather, these realities are seen as ontologically derivative, arising from the priority of the radical autonomy of the individual and his or her conscience before God.[68] Martin E. Marty's penetrating analysis of North American Protestantism refers to this evangelical-styled individualism as "individualism with a vertical dimension."[69]

For Grenz, radical individualism represents one pole of a larger crisis facing evangelicalism, the other pole is the postmodern philosophical critique of Enlightenment foundationalism. The postmodern critique of Modernity deconstructs the modern individual in two important ways. First, by challenging the idealist nature of foundationalist epistemology, postmodernity questions the legitimacy of positing the conception of individual autonomy upon a universal ideal of rational inquiry. This suspicion, in turn, dismantles traditional accounts of the validity of objective and indubitable truth as a legitimate starting point (or end result) of human inquiry. Second, and related to this, by challenging strict foundationalism, postmodernity ironically advances the supremacy of the individual, but now in a manner devoid of a supposedly stable foundation from which to engage the world.[70]

Grenz analyzes the postmodern critique following the structural-linguistic tradition from Ferdinand de Saussure and Claude Lévi-Strauss to the postmodern critiques of Friedrich Nietzsche and Michael Foucault. Through this analysis, Grenz traces the demise of the "self" first through the structuralist move that radically contextualizes the self within embedded cultural-linguistic and social structures.[71] From this de-personalized cultural embeddedness, the structuralists furthered the Modernist agenda

---

67. The sociological work of Robert Bellah is particularly helpful at this point. See Bellah et al., *Good Society*; Bellah et al., *Habits of the Heart*; McLoughlin and Bellah, *Religion in America*.

68. Noll, *Scandal of the Evangelical Mind*, 62.

69. Marty, *New Shape of American Religion*, 55.

70. Grenz, *Social God*, 133–36.

71. Grenz, *Social God*, 128–30.

The Crisis of Conversion

of epistemological foundationalism by attempting to ground the subjectivity of individual identities within objectively observable cultural, linguistic, and social realities. From these "objective" realities then, the goal of the human sciences, in the words of Lévi-Strauss is, "not to constitute, but to dissolve man."[72] Secondly, the post-structuralists further dissolved the self by exposing the limited and fundamentally distorting reality of all particular language systems thus calling into question their supposed ability to reveal universal and ultimate reality. By properly contextualizing the "self" within both sociocultural and historical-linguistic particularities, Nietzsche and Foucault challenged the modern priority of human reason as a reliable medium of coming to know universally objective reality.[73]

According to Grenz, the postmodern "death of the self"[74] is not merely a reference to the rejection of the epistemological and metaphysical pillars of Modernity, but also includes a much more radical notion of the postmodern "embrace of [the self's] demise."[75] This more radical dimension of postmodernity reveals for Grenz an unwitting contradiction within postmodernity itself. In one respect postmodernity certainly has destroyed the fallacy of the naked and objective self standing in absolute relationship to reality; on the other hand, the embrace of this demise has in turn rendered postmodernity an intrinsically "self-referential system."[76] The question must then be asked as to what a self-referential system refers to when the very concept of the self has been left behind?

Grenz argues that the postmodern crisis of the self is more properly understood as a crisis of individualism rooted in a strict foundationalist epistemology.[77] This conception of the autonomous individual gives rise to quintessentially modern ideas of liberty and personal rights, as well as a strict causal logic concerning ideals such as justice and morality that are tied intrinsically to the level of individual volition. This modern individualism is especially apparent in the United States, whose founding documents are thoroughly modern in design based on the supposedly "self evident" principles of individual equality and personal liberty.

---

72. Lévi-Strauss, *Savage Mind*, 247. Quoted from Grenz, *Social God*, 130.
73. Grenz, *Social God*, 130–32.
74. Grenz, *Social God*, 132–33.
75. Grenz, *Social God*, 133.
76. Grenz, *Social God*, 134.
77. For a similar analysis of the situation, see Albert Borgmann's concept of "hypermodernity" that posits that the postmodern turn is actually a reification of Modern conceptions of personal freedom exacerbated by advances in technology in the latter part of the Twentieth Century. Borgmann, *Crossing the Postmodern Divide*.

Evangelical Experience and the Crisis of Religious Conversion

As Grenz analyzes the postmodern situation, he finds that the underlying question is not whether one has an identity (the "self" in the most basic sense), but where and how that identity is constituted. In other words, what (if anything) is in fact "self-evident"?[78] The self-referential element of postmodernity suggests, according to Grenz, that ultimately it is only particularity, otherness, plurality, and diversity that are "self-evident." Moreover, postmodernity claims that attempts to universalize or otherwise objectify reality are not only fundamentally misguided but intrinsically violent and thus morally compromised from the start. Grenz rightly posits that the postmodern conception of the "self" is constituted through being-in-relationships and thus is rooted in contextuality, particularity, diversity, and community rather than in some underlying and supposed universal reality such as reason, or the soul.

Therefore, postmodernity embraces what had been the chief problems of modernity and the Enlightenment—difference, alterity, and subjectivity—as irreducible components of reality itself.[79] Nevertheless, Grenz recognizes that postmodernity's radical telos of utter nihilism is not only indefensible, but that its nihilistic sympathy is in fact an external recapitulation of modern foundationalism. The shift between postmodern nihilism and modern foundationalism is one of location and not of utter rejection. That is, rather than resting on modernist *a priori* positive universal categories, the postmodern self is constituted through the negative rejection of intrinsic universality while at the same time externalizing the ground of the self to the Other but in a similarly absolute fashion. In this way, Grenz sees postmodernity itself as a post-foundationalist system rooted in the negation of the autonomous self, rather than an anti-foundationalist or non-foundationalist system as some commentators have argued.[80]

Grenz cautions against interpreting this postmodern identity crisis as necessarily catastrophic, even though he by and large seems to agree with the scope of change incumbent with the postmodern situation.[81] The primary challenge (or opportunity?) that postmodernity creates for evangelicalism according to Grenz is the radical breakdown of the Modern notion of "selfhood," or perhaps one step further, the issue of individualism itself.[82] Methodologically, Grenz saw that postmodernity's rejection of the "self" was ultimately the result of a significant epistemological and metaphysical shift that fundamentally

---

78. Grenz, *Social God*, 133.

79. Grenz, *Social God*, 136.

80. Grenz, *Renewing the Center*, 168–75; Grenz, *Social God*, 130, 136.

81. Grenz, *Revisioning Evangelical Theology*, 16–17; Grenz and Franke, *Beyond Foundationalism*, 49–51.

82. Grenz, *Social God*, 50–57, 279–82.

questioned the validity of the autonomous individual as a legitimate foundation.[83] To return briefly to the preceding discussion concerning the issue of experience for evangelicalism, Grenz's analysis of modern foundationalism helps to shed light on not only the evangelical skepticism of Schleiermacher's elevation of the category of experience, but also on the foundationalist approach to biblical hermeneutics that characterizes the liberal/fundamentalist theological divide to this day. Moreover, the nature of evangelical approaches to religious experience and religious authority highlights the severity of the challenge that postmodernity poses for evangelicalism as both the classical conservative and classical liberal narratives are being called into question.[84]

While I agree with Grenz's analysis of the postmodern demise of the "self," as well as the paradoxical reification of the "other" inherent in postmodern expressions of individualism; by situating the postmodern challenge to Christian orthodoxy within the context of "hypermodernity," Grenz fails to account for a deeper reality implicit in the postmodern project of deconstruction. Hypermodernity is a type of critique of modernity that views the emerging cultural situation not as a "post-modern" rejection and replacement of the claims of Modernity with something recognizable as postmodern, but rather as a deepening and accelerated form of modernity, or "hyper" modernity. Like the postmodern critique, hypermodernity sees the flaws of Modernity in its individualist and materialist impulses. However, unlike the postmodern critique, hypermodernity fails to take into account the deeper layer of critiques inherent in postmodern deconstruction.[85]

Postmodernity does not, in general, view this present age of transition as simply a last gasp of modernity, but rather sees the current situation as an elongated and increasingly violent upheaval of the very foundations of Modernity itself. Thus while the hypermodern critique seeks to relate the critical and deconstructive philosophical and cultural revolutions of the latter part of the Twentieth Century to the Modern era, as a type of raw or aggressive

---

83. Grenz and Franke, *Beyond Foundationalism*, 38–42.

84. Grenz and Franke, *Beyond Foundationalism*, 4–9.

85. See Borgmann's appraisal of the nuances between hypermodernity and postmodernity in his *Crossing the Postmodern Divide*. Central to Borgmann's analysis is that hypermodern society acknowledges certain overarching postmodern critiques and then responds by elevating and strengthening other elements of modernism, namely the belief in perpetual social progress through technological advancement, and a reification of scientific objectivism as the foundation of social epistemology. In both cases, these elements have the adverse effect of intensifying the fragmentation of society through a radicalized individualism. Moreover, by embracing and absolutizing modern ideas in the face of postmodern critiques of modernity, hypermodern society turns its back on the project of deconstruction, which for postmodern thought, provides a possible trajectory out of the inevitable contradictions of the social presuppositions of modernity.

expression of a nevertheless intrinsically modern paradigm; the postmodern critique seeks to move past, beyond, or otherwise outside of Modern structures of society, commerce, culture, and thought.[86] A contemporary snapshot of the situation of the Western world might reveal little difference between the hypermodern and postmodern narratives, as we are currently witnessing a particularly violent and aggressive cultural individualism alongside an increasingly aggressive and rapid materialism spurred on through the proliferation of technological commodities.[87]

However, the difference between the two accounts of the situation lies not by looking back toward Modernity, but rather looking ahead to what is yet to come. In looking ahead, hypermodernity sees a refashioned and streamlined modernity; a sort of second naiveté reaffirming classical liberalism's narrative of social progress. Postmodernity's nihilistic vision of the future is at once more bleak and less clear. Grenz's analysis, when viewed in the context of the postmodern/hypermodern conversation, seems to reside more comfortably with hypermodernity, precisely because the future of Evangelical theology is for Grenz ultimately a recapitulated return to Modern sources, albeit with a greater awareness of some of the now obvious dangers of naively modern pursuits of truth.[88]

This is most obvious in Grenz's theological solution to the postmodern death of the self.[89] Here, Grenz attempts to shift from strict foundationalist conceptions of individualized selfhood in favor of a more communal/social model of selfhood in dialogue with Jean-François Lyotard, Michel Foucault, and Friedrich Nietzsche on the one hand, and George Herbert Mead, Wolfhart Pannenberg, and C. S. Lewis on the other. This communal approach bears certain affinities with postmodern sensibilities, and is itself, I think, a move in a positive direction. Grenz, attempts to construct a Christian theological anthropology that takes into account the postmodern critique of modernity by recasting the autonomous self as the "ecclesial self" rooted in the relational identity of God's triunity and the revelation of this relational ontology through the word of God.[90] Of central importance for Grenz's ecclesial self is the early concept of the *imago Dei*, of human persons being created in the image of

---

86. Borgmann, *Crossing the Postmodern Divide*, 48–52.

87. Borgmann, *Crossing the Postmodern Divide*, 110–12.

88. Grenz, *Revisioning Evangelical Theology*, 15–17; Grenz, *Social God*, 123–25; Grenz, *Renewing the Center*, 68–169.

89. See Grenz, *Social God*, 130–37; for his analysis of the postmodern 'death' of the self, and his proposal, 312–22.

90. Grenz, *Social God*, 312.

The Crisis of Conversion

God.[91] Grenz uses the *imago Dei* as a lens through which he refashions the nature of human identity from one constructed on universal principles of unity or monistic origins, to one that is fashioned through personal/relational categories.[92] Here Grenz, like the hypermodern critique, seems content to address the problem of individualism, and its related problem of materialist consumerism, by attempting to pull the human person out of a solipsistic understanding of identity, to one that emerges out of a larger web of relations in community.[93] For Grenz, the *imago Dei*, achieves its fullest expression in the life of Jesus Christ and his community of disciples that becomes the Church.[94] Grenz's theological anthropology is thus intrinsically trinitarian in construction, thoroughly communal in design, as well as being biblically focused in orientation.[95]

It is from within this internal critique of postmodernity that Grenz's constructive postmodernesque anthropology emerges through a reimagining of the concept of the *imago Dei* found in one of his more important works, *The Social God and the Relational Self*. Grenz's functional anthropology echoes the respective cultural-linguistic worldviews of the Old and New Testament original audiences where the language of Christian anthropology emerges. Scholars point to linguistic connections between royal imagery and the language of Genesis 1:26 *selem* (image), and *demut* (likeness), where kings and rulers would erect statues or empower individuals to be their "image" and "likeness" and to re-present the king. By emphasizing the linguistic element of the Old Testament, Grenz highlights the importance of interpretation in the function of humanity re-presenting God. This anthropological hermeneutic relies, among other things, on the faithful interpretation of the function of the people who are created in the image and likeness of God, what would ultimately become the "if-then" language of the Covenant between YHWH and Israel.[96]

In the New Testament, Grenz takes the Old Testament foundations of the functional nature of the image of God as covenant and casts it in a christological light. This christological move allows Grenz to recast the *imago*

91. Grenz, Social God, 331–32.
92. Grenz, Social God, 141–43.
93. Grenz, Social God, 305–12.
94. Grenz, Social God, 251–64.
95. In Grenz's own language, he refers to this three-part program as: The Trinity as the "structural motif of Evangelical theology," The Church as Community as the "integrative motif of Evangelical theology," and the Bible as the Word of God as the "Orienting motif of Evangelical theology." See Grenz, Renewing the Center, 211–17.
96. Grenz, Social God, 202; see also Walter Brueggemann's helpful treatment of the issue of the interpretation of covenant for the Hebrew people in his, *Old Testament*, 207–10.

Dei eschatologically, which brings his earlier insight of the functional and relational qualities of the *imago Dei* to full completion through the work of Christ.[97] Grenz then sees the biblical narrative showing a continual unfolding of the *imago Dei* from the creation of man and woman in the garden of Eden culminating in the historical event of Jesus Christ and then presently lived through eschatological hope in our sharing in the resurrection.

While this move is on the one hand, simply following the unfolding of the revelation of God in Christ, anthropologically, this creates a couple of complications in Grenz's argument as a whole. Ultimately, it is not simply the covenant that is fulfilled in Christ, but the *imago Dei* as well. Thus, Grenz interprets Paul in Romans five as reorganizing humanity's relationship to God by shifting the *imago* from Adam "who is a type of the one who is to come" (Rom. 5:14) to Jesus. According to Grenz, Paul fuses the anthropological language of the *imago Dei* with the soteriological language of Christ's atonement. While the functional dimension of the image of God remains through the ongoing participation in the paschal mystery soteriologically and therefore eschatologically, the location or "embeddedness" of the image of God in the world has shifted from humanity in general to Christ exclusively. It seems then to suggest that Grenz's *imago Dei* is more properly a soteriological, rather than an anthropological category here in that it is through our participation in Christ, the new Adam, that human persons share in or participate in the image of God.[98]

Moreover, in his proposal, Grenz fails to account for a major vein of postmodern critique. Specifically, Grenz fails to address the ambiguous nature of the relationship between word and reality that has been recognized by hermeneutical phenomenology and philosophical deconstructionism. For all of Grenz's helpful analysis of the transition from epistemological foundationalism to the various branches of postfoundationalist theories,[99] Grenz falls back on a foundationalist solution, where the Bible, as the objective Word of God, becomes the sole source of the revelation of God to humanity. While certainly, for Christians, Scripture should occupy a unique and irreducible position as it relates to Christian formation and practice; by so uncritically focusing on the Word of God as that which is written in the Old and New Testaments; Grenz, and the larger evangelical community, equate the revelation of God, and by

---

97. Grenz, *Social God*, 223–28.

98. See Grenz, *Social God*, "From Humankind to the True Human: The Imago Dei and Biblical Christo-Anthropology," 185–222.

99. He highlights in particular the eschatological coherentism of Wolfhart Pannenberg as his preferred theological and epistemological model moving forward. Grenz and Franke, *Beyond Foundationalism*, 43–45; Grenz, *Social God*, 311.

The Crisis of Conversion

extension the presence of God on this earth, with the Bible in such a manner that obscures God's wider presence throughout the world. This in turn leads to a dismissal of the human person as a locus for perceiving and experiencing the presence of God. Therefore, I find within Grenz's conception of the *imago Dei*, a tendency within evangelical Christianity more broadly to reduce the locus of Christian revelation to the Bible, thereby designating everything else that isn't literally scripture as, strictly speaking, devoid of revelatory potential. While on the surface this may appear to be an attractive theological option, particularly for those who are frightened by the various social and cultural challenges that "traditional" Christianity faces in the West, it is precisely in this radical division between scripture and the rest of the world, that the evangelical crisis of conversion is exposed.

As we have seen from both the ambiguous relationship of experience in light of Schleiermacher's *Gefühl* on the one hand, and its spiritual/theological biblical reductionism as seen in Bebbington's methodological work on the other, evangelicalism has found itself in a precarious position in light of the mounting cultural and intellectual shifts of the nineteenth and Twentieth Centuries as evidenced by Grenz's creative though ultimately unsuccessful attempt to integrate postmodern concerns within a broadly evangelical theological and hermeneutical framework. This precarious situation has finally begun to expose the problematic position of the category of human experience as a constitutive element of evangelical thought and practice, namely the crisis of conversion as I have outline it here. Moreover, given that the general contours of both the liberal Protestant and secular postmodern critiques of the previous two centuries, and the evangelical responses to these traditions have revolved around semiotic and hermeneutical issues related to history, text, power, and truth, I will argue that any viable solutions to this present crisis of conversion will have to come to terms with the relationship between text and reader and the possibility of normative claims more generally in such a way as to avoid the dualistic foundationalism of modernity, and its postmodern nihilistic counterpart. To that end, a closer look into the postmodern critique is needed, both in order to have a better sense of the magnitude of the present crisis, and more importantly to search for a viable alternative for the future of evangelical Christianity.

Postmodernity's Critique of Enlightenment Foundationalism: Edmund Husserl and Jacques Derrida

For Christianity at large, and evangelicalism in particular, the postmodern challenge ushered in by deconstruction highlights the potentially idolatrous stance of the written word in relation to the reality of the presence of God as it is commonly understood and practiced in evangelical Christianity. This potentially idolatrous stance is perhaps most clearly seen in Edmund Husserl's (1859–1938) phenomenological critique of modern epistemological foundationalism, and the semiotic deconstruction of Jacques Derrida (1930–2004). Through engaging the work of Husserl and Derrida here, a potential solution will emerge by recovering a constructive space for the category of human experience in the process of normative meaning making that will guide the remainder of this book.

Husserl's phenomenology attempts to do two primary things. First, it offers a thorough critique of post-Enlightenment and Modernist assumptions concerning the radical objectification of a given reality as existing in essential independence from human knowledge and experience of it. That is, for post-Enlightenment thinkers, the subjectivity of human epistemology and experience was thought to be absolutely derivative of and extrinsic to the nature of reality in and of itself. Husserl, on the other hand, recognized that not only did these assertions contradict the empirical and plain experience of human beings in the world and their relationship to reality, that indeed they were essentially flawed presuppositions. In response, Husserl outlined a new method for engaging the Enlightenment problem of "subjectivity," through an investigation of what he called phenomenology, or the realm of pure consciousness.[100]

Secondly, and through his new method, Husserl reconstructed the metaphysical foundationalism of post-Enlightenment thought in a way that recognized the irreducible role of human experience (*Erlebnis*) as both contingent upon the nature of reality and at the same time constructively active in reality. That is, for Husserl, lived-experience is ultimately and simultaneously interpretive (confirming a basic insight of post-Enlightenment metaphysics) and generative, or meaning-making (shattering the objectification of post-Enlightenment metaphysics). This phenomenological ontology, what we might call here his phenomenological foundations, identified experience as the constitutive connection between the embeddedness of concrete existence (*Dasein*) and intuitional essence (*Eidos*); or that which mediates the essentially interdependent nature of the objective and subjective.[101]

---

100. Husserl, *Ideas*, 1–4.
101. Husserl, *Ideas*, 12–17.

The Crisis of Conversion

Central to his project are two interrelated concepts; intentionality and the method of phenomenological reductions (*Epoche*). The phenomenological reductions establish Husserl's method of phenomenological investigation by "bracketing," or "reducing" a reality as given to its essential or eidetic existence. This reduction is functionally similar to the scientific method of empirical investigation, as well as a sort of reversal of the epistemological methodology of post-enlightenment deductive metaphysics. Whereas the scientific method attempts to bracket out a single material, psychological, or logical element of reality and isolate it from its "natural stance" in order to investigate its essential nature, and where post-Enlightenment epistemology attempted to bracket out human subjectivity from investigation of Truth in its "natural stance" in order to investigate the foundations of reality in and of itself; Husserl on the other hand, brackets out this "natural stance" in order to investigate the exact opposite, namely the realm of pure consciousness, or the essence of experience itself. Once he makes the move from the natural standpoint to the phenomenological standpoint he finds that scientific empiricism as well as post-Enlightenment epistemologies were themselves conceived and established through a virtually similar (though unconscious) process of phenomenological reductions. That is, that the assumptions of both scientific empiricism and post-Enlightenment epistemology assume the form of "hypotheses" or in Husserl's terminology "possibility," but not the actual fact of *Dasein*.[102]

Relatedly, Husserl's concept of intentionality forms in many ways the results, as it were, of the phenomenological reductions. The realm of pure phenomenology takes the shape of general but nevertheless real possibility. It is general in that it is possibility as such, and real in that the nature of possibility, as possibility, necessarily exists. For Husserl then, the move from possibility to particular actuality is one of intention. The shape of experience, of consciousness, and of human rationality is thus characterized by the volitional category of intentionality.[103]

Furthermore, this suggests that the actualization of mere epistemological possibility to real phenomenological insight is necessarily and essentially an "intentionality of" or an "experience of" something. That is, consciousness itself is always and already directed towards something-ness and thus provides the context for the nature of human experience as essentially embedded, or that irreducible connection between *Dasein* and *Eidos*. Experience is not the "object" or "end" of Husserl's phenomenology, but rather the very means by which reality, truth, and meaning, actually exist at all. Thus, in the final analysis, the phenomenological *Epoche* is not directed at experience as object

---

102. Husserl, *Ideas*, 87–88, 97.
103. Husserl, *Ideas*, 34, 43–44.

but rather lays open the nature of experience as lived through his development of the phenomenological method and its central component of intentionality. And similarly, the phenomenon of experience is for Husserl, not properly a thing either but rather, is similar to the Heideggerian notion of the particularity of a person's "being in the world."[104]

By recasting the relationship between objectivity and subjectivity in terms of human interpretation of reality, Husserl fundamentally challenged the driving impulse of post-enlightenment epistemologies which saw subjectivity as a fundamental problem to be overcome through processes of purely rational investigation as a means of removing the distortions of personal bias. Instead, Husserl established subjectivity itself as an irreducible element of reality, and moreover, an element that had generative as well as distorting potential. And while it would be anachronistic to include Husserl as a postmodern thinker, who would celebrate the demise of objective foundationalism and embrace some form of metaphysical pluralism, he nevertheless set the table for later voices, such as Derrida and his postmodern deconstruction.

The work of Jacques Derrida, a leading figure of postmodern thought, advances and critiques Husserl in important ways. Derrida advances the notion of alterity, or otherness, that naturally results from Husserl's bracketing on the one hand, as well as the isolation of "self" from other intrinsic to his usage of *Erlebnis* or lived-experience. On the other hand, Derrida also critiques Husserl in a similar fashion by deconstructing the presumed immediacy of Husserl's *Erlebnis* as a result of the radical temporality of the phenomenological reduction. It is the interplay of this critique and advancement that Derrida's deconstruction becomes informative for the future of evangelical spirituality.

Derrida's *Of Grammatology*, published in 1967, is an early yet foundational text that introduce many of the central elements of deconstruction that he would develop throughout the rest of his career. Chief among them is the provocative neologism *différance*, which plays off of the dual meaning of deferral, or to put off, and difference, or otherness itself. If Husserl sought to establish the possibility of actual knowledge of objective reality through the irreducibility and immediacy of the experiencing subject; Derrida subverts this project by exposing the dubious origins of such a quest by virtue of the essential distanciation inherent in temporality, marked by the presence of the "trace." That is, the supposed immediacy posited in Husserl's "experiences of" as intentional intuitions, is betrayed by the very embeddedness of concrete existence. As Derrida argues: "the order of the signified [or a given reality] is never contemporary, is at best the inverse or the subtly discrepant

---

104. Husserl, *Ideas*, 98.

parallel—discrepant by the time of a breath—of the order of the signifier."[105] Here we see Derrida deconstructing Husserl's own phenomenological critique of enlightenment foundationalism by revealing a similar foundationalist objectification of the immediacy of Husserl's understanding of pure consciousness.

As an example of the movements of deconstruction, Derrida's critique of Husserl highlights two significant advances related to the possibility of normative claims. First, it advances Husserl's phenomenological critique by more satisfactorily shattering the illusion that normativity itself is derived from the external imposition of the objectivity of reality onto the internal subjectivity of the perceiving subject; and yet also refusing the opposite, that normativity can be reduced to mere subjective volition. Rather, Derrida argues that while the "difference between signified and signifier is *nothing*,"[106] confirming to some degree Husserl's articulation of the irreducibility of subjectivity in the process of knowing; that neither is "being," the Husserlian *Dasein*, "a primary and irreducible signified ... " But rather the signified is itself "rooted in a system of languages and an historically determined ... *significance*." That is, even the knowing subject itself should not be objectively posited as the ontological ground of meaning making. Instead, the signifier along with the signified are structured triadically alongside of the emerging significance. In this way, the signifier, that which is signified, and the significance that emerges are for Derrida irreducible elements not only of the hermeneutical task of interpretation, but of the nature of reality construed semiotically.

Second, deconstruction confirms Husserl's bracketing of the phenomenological stance as a way of inhabiting the structures of our world precisely because as phenomena, reality is necessarily always and already inhabited. While the elusive presence of the trace inherent in difference continually defers our efforts to definitively posit the original sign through which all significance depends, the presence of the trace also negates the assertion that the significance of that which is signified exists independent from the sign. Because something remains in the movements of deconstructing, deconstruction itself is deferred. To totalitize deconstruction as the end result or radical *telos* of reality would be to ultimately collapse deconstruction into construction, and thus return to the beginning of the problem: namely the problem of difference.

Perhaps it is fair to suggest that for Husserl, and especially Derrida, the fundamental critique of Enlightenment rationality was not that we are confused or wrong about the nature of reality, and its recognition of the fundamental "problem" of subjectivity; but rather an inability or unwillingness to

---

105. Derrida, *Of Grammatology*, 19.
106. Derrida, *Of Grammatology*, 24.

come face to face with our own essential complicity in the reality that we create, or the dubious assertion of "objectivity" itself. The external, or universal, or objective, projection of normative claims in the theo-philosophical sense of "ought" and "is," results in an idolatrous deception reducing the reality of the signified to that of the signifier through a flawed processes of signification. This is Derrida's insight concerning the concealing of the dubious origins of both science and philosophy through the illegitimate "*closure* of the *epistémè*,"[107] or the secured source and foundation of knowledge. Through the movement of deconstruction, we come to something informative and constructive for the re-situation of human experience for evangelical understanding of divine revelation through the self-implicating nature of human experience in general through in the intentionality of our inhabitation; continually deferring the temptation of epistemic closure through the self-disclosive unfolding of the revelatory encounter of God.

Furthermore, Derrida represents a sort of fruit of an earlier debate between the structuralists and poststructuralists of the Twentieth Century. The project of deconstruction that he inaugurated is instructive for us here in that he called into question the Western intellectual tradition's elevation of the written word over and against the spoken word as supreme in terms of both correspondence to the word's referent in reality as well as its supposed objectivity in terms of communicating meaning and truth, which I have identified as the source of the present crisis of conversion. What was at stake in these debates between the structuralists and poststructuralist was the question of the relationship between meaning and truth, or interpretation and reality, and its implications for the nature of normative claims.

The structuralist Ferdinand Saussure (1857–1913), sought to investigate a universal semiotic system in which various language systems might be able to be understood under a single rubric of interpretation. However, Saussure's perennialist approach failed to adequately take into consideration the reality-encompassing nature of any given language system, thus ruling out any attempt to find a neutral "common ground" outside of a particular language system with which to reconcile or integrate distinct systems. In religious studies, Mircea Eliade's work on the sacred/secular distinction,[108] George Lindbeck's socio-linguistic "ad-hoc apologetics," and much of the nineteenth-century worldwide ecumenical movements stand out as examples of a Saussurean structuralist approach to the study and practice of religion. While paying attention to the supposed universality of language itself,

---

107. Derrida, *Of Grammatology*, 101.
108. Eliade, *Sacred and the Profane*; Eliade, *Quest*; Eliade, *History of Religious Ideas*.

The Crisis of Conversion

Saussure misses the radical difference of particular linguistic systems in terms of their discrete and immanent reality-forming function.

Ludwig Wittgenstein's post-structuralist linguistic approach takes a step closer with the concept of language games, but lacks any awareness of the real relationship of differing sign systems, that is a conflation of icons and indices in traditional semiotic language. Derrida's deconstructionism takes things even one step further, challenging not only the linguistic turn of the Wittgenstein's poststructuralism, but questioning the very nature of the word/*logos* at the heart of Western thought itself. Here, Derrida deconstructs language theory by exposing the underlying conceptual nominalist premises of the structuralist and post-structuralist schemes altogether. Wittgenstein, like Saussure before him, becomes trapped in a false nominalistic dialectic between the two poles of speech and reality; that language "shows" reality, but cannot of itself "say" anything.

Expanding on insights from a host of philosophical specialties including hermeneutics, critical theory, linguistics, and semiotics, Derrida argues that the Word as written obscures and distorts reality to a far greater degree than the Word as spoken. Derrida contends that in light of an overarching postmodern awareness of the radically contingent, particular, and contextual nature of reality in general (i.e. Wittgensteinian language games), that the relatively greater permanence and mobile nature of the Word as written, vis a vis the word as spoken, is far more easily ripped from its contingent origins and therefore more easily removed and manipulated from the realities to which it attempts to speak, taking a monumental insight from Schleiermacher's foundational work in hermeneutics that "a person thinks by means of speaking."[109] The Word as spoken, precisely due to its more fragile and bounded existence as a concrete event in a particular time and place, is able to retain a greater affinity to its proclaimed reality. That is, according to Derrida, the Word as spoken contains within itself, by virtue of its essence as spoken, the presence of its referent to a greater degree than the Word as written. Derrida calls this reversal of the written over and against the spoken the "self-enslavement to the perceived permanence of the written."[110] Derrida's hermeneutics is therefore rooted in the question of the nature and meaning of reality, rather than a linguistic concern with the nature and meaning of language.

---

109. Schleiermacher, *Hermeneutics*, quoted in Clements, *Friedrich Schleiermacher*, 158.

110. Derrida *Of Grammatology*, 41. The irony of this argument based on the written words of Derrida is not lost, nor does the difficulty in overcoming the challenge of the written necessarily result in the utter rejection of the written. Rather, Derrida here seeks to present to our consciousness the idolatrous relationship between the written, the human mind, and the real. A relationship that Grenz fails to take into account.

By placing his semiotic critique at the more fundamental question of ontology, Derrida calls into question Modernity's quest for objective certainty that has fueled the various Kantian/Cartesian foundationalist epistemologies of the past few hundred years, including evangelicalism's objectification of Scripture that we saw with Grenz. Derrida's deconstructionist critique exposes a fundamental flaw in the epistemological presuppositions of evangelical thinking, one that Grenz was apparently unaware. However, the contemporary Malaysian-American evangelical-pentecostal scholar, Amos Yong, provides a helpful corrective to Grenz through his seminal postmodern hermeneutical method, which he calls the *pneumatological imagination*. I will consider Yong in greater detail in the concluding chapter, but initially it will be helpful to trace the basic contour of the pneumatological imagination as it provides a creative solution to both the nihilistic spiraling of deconstructionism on the one hand, and evangelical fideistic foundationalism on the other.

Towards a Constructive Postmodern Evangelical Experience: Amos Yong's "Pneumatological Imagination"

Like with Grenz, Yong is aware of the serious nature of the challenges wrought by the postmodern turn, particularly those of globalism and the religio-ethical importance of the "other." Moreover, like Grenz, Yong sees the general postmodern situation as something that offers Christianity in particular, but also religious thought and practice in general, very real advantages in terms of religion's place in the public theater. This is not to say that Grenz or Yong uncritically or totally acquiesces to postmodernity, but that both thinkers in some sense do their theology from within a postmodern framework. On the other hand, while Grenz interacts more explicitly and directly than does Yong with the primary literature of postmodern literature, Yong's work, as I read him, appears to inhabit postmodern questions and habits of thought more intuitively. Yong then might be thought of as continuing where Grenz left off; that is, Yong takes the postmodern situation as articulated through Grenz and others as the launch pad for his own theological reflection. Moreover, Yong has embraced or embodied a key feature of postmodernity in a more integrative way than Grenz was able to. In particular, Yong's theological anthropology as self constituted through being-in-community which leads to what Gelpi, a significant dialogue partner with Yong, calls, an "inculturated" theology.[111]

---

111. Gelpi, *Inculturating North American Theology*; Gelpi, *Gracing of Human Experience*; Yong, "In Search of Foundations," 3.

The Crisis of Conversion

An inculturated theology, for Gelpi, means one that not only assumes a culturally pluralist world, but views the fact of pluralism as a legitimate reality. From this place of pluralism, inculturation recognizes that "distinctive historical and cultural heritages lay legitimate claims to equally distinctive hopes and aspirations correlative to their situations and traditions."[112] This definition then embodies key features of postmodernity as outlined above by Grenz; in particular, the relational and social constructionism that is internally self-referential. The self-referential element in Gelpi's and Yong's understanding of inculturation though is not self-*centered* but rather oriented towards the "Other." For Yong, the postmodern world(s) is one characterized by global villages where the categories of "insider-outsider with regard to communities or participation are no longer water-tight."[113] Thus, Christianity can no longer rest on the universal assumptions of Modernity that saw objective truth as something that can be recognized universally; but moreover, Christianity itself, as it develops within discrete cultural "villages" is not something which can be neatly separated from the cultural bed in which it emerges. Therefore, Yong attempts to develop an inculturated methodology that takes cultural embeddedness as the starting point. This methodology is what he ultimately calls the "pneumatological imagination."[114]

Yong's "pneumatological imagination" points to the pneumatological rationality that undergirds Christianity, and that this pneumatological rationality, alongside of and illuminating the incarnation of Christ, establishes the hermeneutical frame from within which Christian communities live and have their being.[115] This hermeneutic is trinitarian, or what Yong calls "trialectical," in shape rather than dialectical (read dualistic) and is expressed by Yong as Spirit-Word-Community.[116] Ultimately, the value of Yong's work is the articulation of the irreducible, constructive, and meaning-forming dimension of Community as a corrective to the Individualism that has been at the basis of Evangelical Christianity since its beginnings in the late 16th Century. Moreover, as a continuation of the conversation begun above with Grenz's analysis of the postmodern situation, Yong's pneumatological imagination provides a helpful way forward for Evangelical spirituality moving into the twenty-first century.

---

112. Gelpi, *Inculturating North American Theology*, 1.
113. Yong, *Spirit-Word-Community*, 303.
114. Yong, *Spirit-Word-Community*, 22, 76.
115. Yong, *Spirit-Word-Community*, 101–05.
116. Yong, *Spirit-Word-Community*, 14. Throughout this book, I will use capitalized Spirit, Word, and Community, as technical terms related to Yong's hermeneutical framework. Spirit, also will refer to the Holy Spirit, and will be made clear in the context.

The pneumatological imagination, furthermore, helps to flesh out the social component of Grenz's theological notion of the "ecclesial self" precisely through Yong's more thorough articulation of the constitutive and therefore constructive role of community itself as a normative dimension of human existence and of the experience of God in this world. That is, as Spirit-Word-Community, Yong's trinitarian hermeneutics not only establishes the body of Christ as the locus of the Christian life, but shows that the church as Community is instrumental in bringing the Word and the Spirit into the world. By construing hermeneutics trialectically rather than dialectically, Yong recognizes that interpretation as meaning-full engagement with the other is essentially perichoretic in nature.[117] Therefore, Yong argues that each of the three moments of this hermeneutic are constitutive for the others, so that the "relationship between Spirit and Word is played out in the context of Community," the "relationship between Word and Community is mediated by Spirit," and the "relationship between Spirit and Community is anchored in Word."[118]

While the structure of Yong's pneumatological imagination provides some conceptual improvements on how to think about the nature of the relationship between God and World, the dynamics of the pneumatological imagination in terms of its function and content are far more important. As suggested above, the context of the pneumatological imagination is Community, the embeddedness and therefore the inter-relationality of one to another. Implicit in this context is the recognition that one does not "possess" community, but rather that one is always and already with-in communities. Furthermore, as each community and in dynamic and collaborative tension with other communities, "lay legitimate claims to . . . distinctive hopes and aspirations"[119] the task of interpretation, of making meaning out of the difference, lays claim to the whole person. That is, the question of reality, meaning, and identity are not separable, even as they are not the same, precisely because the social foundations of the Self-in-Community are embedded throughout the whole of the task of life.

Theologically, the claim of the pneumatological imagination on Christian communities is expressed as conversion. Conversion for Yong, as we saw above with Gelpi, is a dynamic and complex process that operates in no less than five modes: affective, intellectual, moral, sociopolitical, and religious.[120] This dynamic view of conversion, is in itself a major advancement over the

---

117. Yong, *Spirit-Word-Community*, 21.

118. Yong, *Spirit-Word-Community*, 20.

119. Gelpi, *Inculturating North American Theology*, 1.

120. Yong, *Spirit-Word-Community*, 222; Gelpi, *Gracing of Human Experience*, 292–99; Gelpi, *Inculturating North American Theology*, 37–42.

The Crisis of Conversion

merely religious conversionism inherent in evangelical thought and practice, as evidenced by Grenz collapsing the *imago Dei* into a category of religious conversion with little to no implications for the rest of the person. For Yong, conversion is not something that happens distinct from the hermeneutics of the pneumatological imagination but is in fact co-terminus with it; and mirroring the perichoretic nature of the trialectic, these modes of conversion are what he and Gelpi call transvaluative, meaning that each type of conversion effects and implicates the other types.[121] That is, the hermeneutical process of the pneumatological imagination is both "world-affirming (re-productive) [and also] world-making (creative)."[122] As world-affirming, the hermeneutical trialectic provides the tools to make sense of the experienced world from within the community; and as world-making, the hermeneutical trialectic provides the power to engage the world beyond the community. Conversion, in like manner, refers to the processes of taking responsibility for one's life from within the confines of the community,[123] and also the transformation that comes through the affective, intellectual, moral, sociopolitical, and religious engagement of the world.[124]

By linking the pneumatological imagination with Gelpi's dynamic conversion, Yong is able to bring spirituality to the center of his methodological proposal. While Yong is not primarily concerned with the language of spirituality as such, particularly as it is used in the academic study of spirituality, nevertheless, the pneumatological imagination has significant implications for spirituality. Here I use Sandra Schneiders's definition of spirituality: "The experience of conscious involvement in the project of life-integration through self-transcendence toward the horizon of ultimate value one perceives."[125] I find that Yong's pneumatological imagination as it functions through the dynamics of conversion and engagement with the other closely parallels the dynamics of involvement, life-integration, and self-transcendence in Schneiders's definition.

Yong's pneumatological imagination is not a mere conceptual category from which to engage in intellectual speculation, but rather because of its world-making and world-affirming modalities, it is primarily a tool for engaging with and living in the world. Similarly, spirituality is for Schneiders ultimately that "conscious involvement" with what is of ultimate value, not

---

121. Gelpi, *Gracing of Human Experience*, 329–31; Yong, *Spirit-Word-Community*, 145.

122. Yong, *Spirit-Word-Community*, 222.

123. Yong, *Spirit-Word-Community*, 198–202; Yong, *Hospitality and the Other*, 63.

124. Yong, *Spirit-Word-Community*, 304.

125. Schneiders, "Approaches," 16.

merely consciousness of. The issue of Schneiders's ultimate value is mirrored by the total claim that the pneumatological imagination makes on a person-in-community through the holistic dynamics of conversion as outlined above. And, ultimately, the trialectical shape of Yong's hermeneutics reveal the "horizon of ultimate value" for the community and thus make a normative claim on the lives of those persons for whom that hermeneutic is operative.

Additionally, Yong's pneumatological imagination provides an alternative model for resolving the thorny issue of experience and the interpretation of Scripture for evangelical spirituality. The key is the hermeneutical shape of the postmodern self-in-community. As the Community is both the context of one's encounter with Word through the Spirit, via one's continuing holistic conversion, as well as the medium of interpretation of the Word, there need not be a radical distinction between experience and scripture as two mutually exclusive realities. This of course, does not mean that any interpretation is valid, the same as it does not mean that any experience whatsoever is authentically one of conversion. Rather, through the dynamics of conversion, which take on a more holistic and therefore transformative function, one's experience and reading of scripture are continually in the process of transformation through the dynamic encounter of Spirit-Word-Community.[126]

The pneumatological animation places both experience and the interpretation of God's self-revelation in the world within the trialectic of Spirit-Word-Community so that through the dynamics of the hermeneutics of the community the experience of the text and the experience of the people relate perichoretically in Christ and through the Spirit. This also calls into question the legitimacy of the literalist/fundamentalist approach to Scripture as something which is a priori, self-evident, and complete in and of itself.[127] Not only does that approach to Scripture severely limit the power of Scripture to speak in new situations and to new contexts, but it fundamentally destroys the nature of Scripture as the witness to the revelation of God to the world.[128] Scripture itself embodies Yong's Spirit-Word-Community hermeneutic. As the God-Self-World relationship exists as dynamic encounter, so too does the relationship of Experience-Scripture-Community.

---

126. Here Yong and Schneiders are picking up on a fundamental insight from Hans Georg-Gadamer's seminal notion of the "fusion of horizons" in Gadamer, *Truth and Method*. See my analysis of the fusion of horizons as it relates to the question of experience and spirituality, Higgins, "Spirit and Truth," 469–90.

127. Yong, *Spirit-Word-Community*, 232–33.

128. On this important point, see Schneiders's seminal work, *Revelatory Text*.

Conclusion

In conclusion, I argue that Yong's pneumatological imagination serves as a more helpful way forward for postmodern Evangelicalism than Grenz trinitarian *imago Dei*. As Grenz's *imago Dei* shifts from humanity to Christ and the New Humanity in Christ cast eschatologically as a primarily future reality, he loses the imperative and holistic claim that Yong's conversion dynamic provides.[129] While Grenz does indeed attempt to highlight the responsibility that comes with being converted into the New Humanity in Christ, that transformation is cast in rather dualistic terms as the imposition of Christ's humanity on to the person first, and then the application of that change as a secondary response.[130] On the other hand, Yong's pneumatological imagination elevates the person-in-community under a holistically normative position in relationship to God, to the Community, and ultimately to the World, that I think captures the heart of the Gospel call more effectively.

Moreover, as suggested above, Grenz's transfer of the *imago Dei* from humanity to Jesus fails to address the social-self of the postmodern situation. Rather, Grenz's anthropology re-affirms the Modern fissure between self and world as distinct objects and serves to further reinforce the us/them dichotomy, resulting in a further fragmented vision of humanity. From Grenz's analysis of the situation, the ecclesial self, that is those participating in the only true community in Christ stand apart from and over against the rest of humanity in an eschatologically absolute way.[131]

In stark contrast, the pneumatological imagination is constituted by and sustained in the encounter of the other, thus Yong's community in Christ through the Spirit is oriented toward the other and for the other in an eschatologically absolute way. This allows Yong to say that "salvation refers to . . . the transformation of communities, societies, and even nations into realms of justice, peace, and righteousness; to the mending and redemption of the world, the cosmos, as a whole; to eschatological union with God."[132] Christian communities for Yong then, through the pneumatological imagination participate as "guests and hosts in the divine hospitality revealed in Christ by the power of the Holy Spirit" through the continual and dynamic engagement of the other.[133]

---

129. Grenz, *Social God*, 238–40.
130. Grenz, *Social God*, 252–58.
131. Grenz, *Social God*, 312–17.
132. Yong, *Hospitality and the Other*, 63.
133. Yong, *Hospitality and the Other*, 127.

Evangelical Experience and the Crisis of Religious Conversion

Yong's pneumatological imagination therefore, provides a new way of approaching the classical Evangelical problem of religious experience and fidelity to the Bible, by recasting the relationship from a mutually exclusive one that pitted human experience against revelation, to a trialectic relationship of Community-Experience-Scripture whereby the individual and the community are mutually engaged in the process of interpretation that is itself mediated experientially through the ongoing movement of the Spirit in the world. Furthermore, by expanding the role of experience in general, the pneumatological imagination is helpful in recovering and exploring the notion of Evangelical spirituality through the dynamic structure of a more holistic understanding of conversion.

2

Sandra Schneiders and the Study of Christian Spirituality

Situating Religious Experience in a North American Context

THE UNCOMFORTABLE RELATIONSHIP BETWEEN religious experience and Scriptural authority that characterized theological and biblical studies for evangelical scholars throughout the twentieth century has exacerbated the contemporary crisis of conversion, as outlined in the previous chapter. This suggests that it is time for evangelicals to take a step back and reevaluate the underlying assumptions that presume human experience on the one hand and the faithful handling of Scripture on the other exist in dialectical opposition to one another, and as such have a mutually exclusive effect on understanding and interpreting divine revelation. To that end, this chapter will analyze the nature and role of religious experience as utilized in the emerging disciple of spirituality studies in an effort to achieve a more adequate understanding of religious experience in its phenomenological or lived expression. Additionally, a better understanding of religious experience, as it is developed in the North American Pragmatist philosophical tradition, will allow us to more accurately situate ontological and epistemological issues related to divine revelation and individual or communal religious experience together in a way that avoids the problematic dualisms of evangelical foundationalist presuppositions critiqued in the previous chapter.

The Study of Christian Spirituality: A Methodological Overview

The term "spirituality," while a relatively recent concept in the sense in which it is variously used today, is of course a modern locution for an ancient reality that has been around arguably since the beginning of human life itself. As Philip Sheldrake and others have noted, the term is derived from the Latin root *spiritualitas*, a translation of the Greek word *pneuma*, "spirit," and its adjective *pneumatikos*, "spiritual," as found in the New Testament, and particular the Pauline epistles.[1] Today, spirituality refers to at least a few broad categories in contemporary usage. First, the term is often used as a mark of distinction from the merely religious, such as the phrase "I am spiritual, but not religious." Second, the term refers to norms and practices of discreet religious traditions, such as Franciscan spirituality, or Islamic spirituality. And thirdly, spirituality is used, in a similar way to that of the term religious, referring to that part of reality that is directed towards or in response to transcendent reality, in whatever form that may come, so that to say that a person is spiritual in this sense is the same as saying that person is religious. Thus, there is a good deal of confusion related to the wide semantic range of the term—often times even at odds with one another—as is the case that spirituality may be used as something that is synonymous or at least compatible with religion, and also used to mean something that is in direct opposition to religion.

Sheldrake in particular, has done extensive work in retrieving the historical uses of spirituality, and is helpful for contextualizing how spirituality has shifted in meaning and usage from age to age. For example, "spirituality" shifted in usage from the more ancient/biblical term referring to the quality and direction of a person's life vis a vis his or her relationship to God (the *sarx/pneuma* distinctions found in Paul) to the Medieval use of spirituality as referring to both an episcopal gathering or ecclesiastical possessions. Moreover, it shifted again to the later Scholastic distinction between the soul as contrasted to the body, and denoting individual concerns of devotional piety and spiritual theology of the early Modern period. Finally, it shifted a third time to the existential concerns of a holistic and integrated view of spirituality in the contemporary period.[2]

Spirituality, as a subject distinct from the academic study of doctrinal theology, begins to emerge in the twelfth century with the rise of European

---

1. Howard, *Brazos Introduction to Christian Spirituality*; Perrin, *Studying Christian Spirituality*; Sheldrake, *Spirituality and History*; Sheldrake, *Spirituality*.

2. McGinn, "Letter and the Spirit," 26-29; McGinn, "Mystical Consciousness"; Sheldrake, *Brief History*, 2-3; Sheldrake, *Spiritualty and History*, 40-61.

Cathedral schools, precursors to modern Universities, which moved theological education outside of the monastic communities of the classical period. In this move, Sheldrake suggests that theological concerns were no longer integrated into the daily life of monastic religious communities. Rather, theological pursuits became "secularized" and were now able to be explored outside of personal commitments to a monastic way of life. Thus, theology began to be seen as a distinct intellectual pursuit that could exist in isolation from the pastoral concerns of the spiritual life. Secondly, spirituality was subsumed under theology as a sub-discipline where the practical concerns of prayer and discipline could be organized according to the increasingly abstract categories of the emerging Scholastic systemization of theology.[3]

Sheldrake's historical analysis of the relationship between theology and spirituality indicates that the shifts begun in the twelfth century represent a new moment for spirituality from what it had meant previously. For early Christians, Sheldrake suggests that there was not a clear distinction between theology and spirituality. That is, for the early church to think theologically was synonymous to living spiritually, drawing on the New Testament origins of *pneuma* highlighted above. This not only confirms Sheldrake's tracing of the distinctions between theology and spirituality that emerge from the twelfth century onward, but also provides evidence that the modern phenomenological distinction between spirituality as a lived phenomenon and spirituality as critical reflection had not been so clearly distinct for the early church. This insight is supported by Bernard McGinn's work in the history of Christian mysticism, who notes a parallel move in the language and nature of mysticism, from an early integration of mystical and theological language to a gradual distinction and eventual subordination of mysticism under theology through the Medieval period, and a recent renewal of interest in the twentieth century.[4]

Towards a Definition of the Phenomena of Spirituality

To complicate matters further, a general distinction has been raised between first and second orders of spirituality in the contemporary conversation by utilizing insights from phenomenology and hermeneutics. Spirituality may refer to the first-order phenomena itself as that which is lived, experienced, or practiced by individuals and traditions throughout history, and to the second-order refection on those lived spiritualities in pastoral application, devotional

---

3. Sheldrake, *Explorations in Spirituality*, 54–59.

4. McGinn, *Foundations of Mysticism*; McGinn, *Essential Writings of Christian Mysticism*; McGinn, "Mystical Consciousness," 44–63; McGinn, *Varieties of Vernacular Mysticism*.

guides and teachings, or academic study and research. In a similar vein, Walter Principe has noted three layers of abstraction when it comes to speaking about spirituality: "(1) as the real or existential level of lived experience (2) as the spiritual doctrines and practices of significant groups or different spiritual traditions, and (3) as a discipline or study."[5] Principe's categories help to organize some of the chaotic nature of the use of spirituality, but it appears to be of little use in helping to define precisely what particular thing "spirituality" refers to across these three levels and how it might be distinguished from similar categorizations of theology, history, or any number of other topics dealing with human persons and the transcendent. Nor does he help clear up matters from the historical complexities of these terms in their classical origins, through the Medieval period, and into the Enlightenment and modern contexts. Evan B. Howard, has on the other hand, helpfully formulated Principe's three-tiered structure by speaking of spirituality as "a relationship with God . . . " (1) "as lived in practice," (2) "as dynamics are formulated," and (3) "as explored through formal study."[6] While Evan's re-formulation of Principe's structure here is helpful in terms of giving some clarity to the various levels in which spirituality may be discussed, and he offers some clarity in the inclusion of spirituality as a relationship with God, we are nevertheless still left unsure of what precisely spirituality as a phenomenon is at any of these layers as something that is distinct enough from other religio-theological categories as to warrant its own terminology, much less its own distinct field of study.

In response to the wide historical and lexical range of spirituality, numerous definitions have been put forward to help bring clarity and focus to what "spirituality" refers to. Arthur Holder, in his introduction to the *Blackwell Companion Christian Spirituality*, defines spirituality simply as "the lived experience of Christian faith and discipleship."[7] This broad definition has its uses, particularly in delineating Christian spiritualities from other traditions: Buddhist, Jewish, etc, it however is limited in terms of articulating or identifying the relationship between spirituality and the two other terms in his definition, faith and discipleship. A host of scholars have offered their own definitions which can be organized into three broad categories; ranging from the more narrow and explicitly theological/religious in nature to the universally existential, with the hybrid hermeneutical definitions in between the two, incorporating important elements from both the theological/religious and universal/existential types.

---

5. Principe, "Toward Defining Spirituality," 127–41; Principe, "Theological Trends," 54–61.

6. Howard, *Brazos Introduction*, 15.

7. Holder, "Introduction," 5.

The Crisis of Conversion

Theological/religious definitions tend to highlight the doctrinal character of spirituality, and in the case of Christian spirituality generally emphasizes the Triune nature of God the Father, Son, and Holy Spirit, as an expression our embodiment of faith, such as Sheldrake's definition of spirituality as "a conscious relationship with God, in Jesus Christ, through the indwelling Spirit and in the context of the community of believers";[8] or Gaspar Martinez's "Spirituality is a global and communitarian itinerary in search of God that stems from an encounter with the Lord and consists in following Christ by living according to the Spirit";[9] or Peter Phan's "Christian spirituality is not a way of life based on normative ethics or universalizable principles but one that is sustained by the Spirit, modeled on Jesus, and oriented towards the Father."[10] These theological definitions, highlight the close relationship of faith and practice that illuminates and understand spirituality as embodied and theologically authentic experiences and practices of faith.

On the other end of the spectrum are existential definitions that attempt to define spirituality as a universal human phenomenon across theological boundaries of discreet religious traditions, often to include even secular, non-theistic, and atheistic experience within an understanding of spirituality as an essential element of human existence itself. Prominent examples of these types of definitions include William Cenkner's understanding of spirituality as "personal existential integration that allows one simultaneously to deal with and to rise above dichotomies offers recognizable success for achieving moments and even extended periods of intelligibility."[11] Or the famous early twentieth century Hindu guru Sri Aurobindo Ghose's notion of an "awakening to the inner self and entering into the greater reality of the universe."[12] And Owen C. Thomas's definition as "the sum of all the uniquely human capacities and functions: self-awareness, self-transcendence, memory, anticipation, rationality (in the broadest sense), creativity, plus the moral, intellectual, social, political, aesthetic, and religious capacities, all understood as embodied."[13] Rather than define spirituality according to theological formulations, as we saw above, these definitions begin from the human situation itself and are more interested in the expression of self-transcendence as such regardless of one's personal theological commitments. This is not to suggest that those who use these definitions are not personally committed to certain theological or

---

8. Sheldrake, *Spirituality and History*, 60.
9. Martinez, *Confronting the Mystery of God*, 140.
10. Phan, "Systematic Issues in Trinitarian Theology," 25.
11. Cenkner, "Theme and Counter-Theme," 87–95.
12. Ghose, *Life Divine*.
13. Owen, "Some Problems in Contemporary Christian Spirituality."

religious traditions, but that for them spirituality cannot be simply reduced to theological presuppositions. Spirituality here is ultimately a supremely human reality with tangential reference to God or any other theological category.

In between the theological/religious definitions on the one hand the universal/existential definitions on the other, are what I call the hermeneutical definitions. These definitions, while generally employing the language of the universal/existential category, incorporate important elements of theological/religious understandings of spirituality as well. Examples here include Roger Haight's definition of spirituality as "the way persons and groups live their lives with reference to something that they acknowledge as transcendent."[14] And similarly Daniel Helminiak's "[spirituality] deals with people's visions of meaning, purpose, and values insofar as in some way these foster self-transcendence."[15] For both Haight and Helminiak, spirituality is concerned with the pluralist nature of experience as self-transcendence as we see with the universal/existential definitions and that is absent in the theological/religious types. And at the same time, these hermeneutical definitions include a normative dimension like those of the theological/religious definitions that are absent in the universal/existential category. For Helminiak, this normative dimension is articulated as "meaning, purpose and values" and in Haight it is articulated as "with reference to something . . . transcendent." The theological/religious scaffolding of spirituality is thus preserved though left incomplete and unarticulated.

These hermeneutical definitions of spirituality reveal a methodological tension within contemporary understandings of spirituality between plurality and normativity, or between experience and authority. All three categories of definitions in one way or another can be read as attempts to address this tension. The theological/religious definitions situate authentic spiritual experience within the accepted boundaries of theological norms, whereas the universal/existential definitions prioritize the diversity of human experience itself as normative, in terms of what might be properly understood as authentic spirituality. The situation is more nuanced when it comes to the hermeneutical definitions, which in some way attempt to maintain the tension without resolving to one option over the other.

---

14. Haight, *Spirituality Seeking Theology*, x.
15. Helminiak, "Role of Spirituality," 197–224.

The Crisis of Conversion

Sandra Schneiders's Hermeneutical Spirituality

One of the most widely used definitions of spirituality is offered by Sandra Schneiders, of the Graduate Theological Union in Berkley, California, home of the first doctoral program in the study of Christian spirituality in the United States.[16] For Schneiders, spirituality is "the experience of conscious involvement in the project of life-integration through self-transcendence toward the horizon of ultimate value one perceives."[17] As the standard definition of the hermeneutical type described above, Schneiders's understanding of spirituality is both comprehensive in terms of its adaptability to the wide variety of potential spiritual experience and expression, as well as its ability to be utilized within the framework of religious and theological commitments. Additionally, Schneiders's more expansive definition over Haight's and Helminiak's provides greater clarity and precision regarding the tension between experience and authority suggested above. Specifically, Schneiders's definition achieves greater clarity in three key concepts central to the vocabulary of spirituality; namely, the role of human experience, the process of transformation inherent to spirituality as experience, and the personal experience of the transcendent.

Spirituality is according to Schneiders first and foremost, "an experience of conscious involvement." While incorporating consciousness as a constitutive element in experience, Schneiders elevates experience as the methodological key for spirituality.[18] Following Paul Ricœur's work, Schneiders argues that

16. Schneiders, "Discipline of Christian Spirituality and Catholic Theology," 196–212.

17. Schneiders, "Approaches," 16; Schneiders, "Study of Christian Spirituality," 5–6.

18. There has been a vigorous debate within the field of spirituality studies as to whether "experience" or "consciousness" is the most adequate term for the field, and both of these terms come with their own benefits and ambiguities. Proponents on both sides view the other term as insufficiently vague or unwieldy to be helpful in articulating the spiritual life.

For proponents of consciousness, they claim that terminology and methods of inquiry borrowed from psychology provide a clearer path forward by interrogating the inner dimensions of the human psyche as that locus of the human person that spirituality's most interested in. As we have already seen, Philip Sheldrake and Bernard McGinn prefer consciousness as more adequately illuminating the religious (Sheldrake) or mystical (McGinn) dimension of the spiritual life, understood primarily in the interior life of the soul of a person. Steven Chase, similarly opts for consciousness as developed through Jungian psychoanalysis as that with exposes the inherent tensions and contradictions within an individual which provides the motivation for seeking holistic integration cultivated through the spiritual life. (cf. Sheldrake, *Spirituality and History*, 45, 60; and McGinn, "Mystical Consciousness" Chase's position comes out of class notes based on his unpublished lectures for a doctoral seminar on "Spirituality and Theology."

On the other hand, Schneiders, as seen in her definition here, and David Perrin (cf. Perrin, *Studying Christian Spirituality*, 20–21), have opted for the language of experience as a more comprehensive term than that of consciousness to talk about the spiritual life

experience is both a subjective reality and always an "experience of," meaning that on the one hand experience is always an individual's own experience, locked away inside of one's own subjectivity and therefore is essentially incommunicable as such; while on the other hand, as an experience *of* something, an experience's referent can be articulated mediately through verbal, literary, artistic, and behavioral "texts."[19] This back-and-forth dynamic of experience as individual "experiences of," establishes the basic hermeneutical structure of Schneiders's understanding of Christian spirituality that is central to both the lived reality of spirituality, following Holder's notion of lived experience, and also clears out a unique space of inquiry within the several specialized fields of religious studies.

Schneiders along with others in the discipline of spirituality have identified this unique space for spirituality as "experience"; both as the material and formal object of the discipline. That is, spirituality is primarily concerned with faith as it is actually lived, expressed, or experienced by real people throughout history, as the discipline's material object, or what it is that is being studied. And, it is the particularity of experience itself that constitutes the discipline's formal object, or the aspect under which it is studied.[20]

Second, Schneiders's definition clarifies what spirituality, as experience, is through the dynamics of transformation, as that which reveals or gives evidence of "the project of life-integration through self-transcendence." This suggests that while experience as such is the general locus of spirituality, according to the material and formal objects of the discipline, it is more specifically transformative experience that is of primary concern for spirituality as both lived reality and critical reflection.[21] It is at this point that the phenomenon of spirituality begins to take more definite shape, precisely through the actualization of human experience as lived. This clarification has important implications for our emerging understanding of spirituality, as it points to the need to develop hermeneutical categories from which to properly identify and interpret transformational experiences; namely those experiences that tend toward greater life-integration, as well as the need to develop tools and practices with which to cultivate such experiences through the ongoing process of self-transcendence.

---

that illuminates both the interior world of an individual's psyche, but also the public, visible, and active world of embodied existence. I find Schneiders's use of experience in particular to be persuasive for reasons that will be articulated in the analysis that follows.

19. Schneiders, "Approaches," 17–18.

20. Frohlich, "Spiritual Discipline," 65; Schneiders, "Study of Christian Spirituality," 5.

21. Schneiders, *Revelatory Text*, 44–46.

This brings us to the third and final component of Schneiders's definition of spirituality as that which tends "toward the horizon of ultimate value one perceives." On its own, this component could be interpreted as simply allowing anything whatsoever to be inserted here as the perceived horizon of ultimate value; sexual gratification, the accumulation of material wealth or personal dominance over others, the common good, enlightenment, or the kingdom of God, to name but a few. Certainly, each of these have been pursued by individuals throughout history in such a manner as to allow the designation of it being their "spirituality." For spirituality to mean everything, however, is the same as it meaning nothing at all. It is equally unhelpful on the other hand, to dismiss *a priori* all other values or pursuits other than those a particular person or group profess as ultimate, as this would simply collapse spirituality into intellectual dogmatism. The key to finding a way out of the seemingly inevitable quagmire of sheer pluralism on the one hand or absolute individualism on the other, is to return again, perhaps counterintuitively, to the category of experience as it has informed the preceding elements of Schneiders's definition of spirituality.

First, returning to experience in reference to the perceived horizon of ultimate value reminds us what spirituality is not; namely the "horizon of ultimate value that one perceives." Rather spirituality–in both its lived expression, and as a subject of inquiry–is the *experience of...* that which tends towards the horizon of value that one perceives. This is also a crucial point in identifying the boundaries and relationship between spirituality as a discipline and other areas of study. Strictly speaking, the horizon of ultimate value as such would fall under the purview of "normative" disciplines such as philosophy, ethics, physics, and theology. In this regard, spirituality is akin to biblical studies in its relationship to systematic theology, in that it interrogates what is there as given—the scriptural texts in the case of biblical studies, or religious experience in the case of spirituality—leaving aside, where appropriate, normative questions related to the adequacy, veracity, or utility of the material under investigation.[22]

Second, and more importantly, Schneiders's definition suggests that there is an essential interdependence between experiences that tend towards the horizon of ultimate value and the dynamics of transformation that result in life-integration and self-transcendence. It is in this interplay of the dynamics of transformation that I am persuaded to utilize the language of experience over other suggested terms, such as consciousness. While they overlap in terms of scope and flexibility, I find that experience more readily lends itself to illuminate the integrative dynamics of Schneiders's definition, particularly in terms of the actualization of spirituality as lived. Moreover, these dynamics

---

22. Schneiders, "Study of Christian Spirituality," 10–13.

inform Schneiders's two methodological keystones, namely interdisciplinarity and the self-implicating nature of spirituality.

The interdisciplinary aspect of spirituality has received a great deal of attention, and need be not be rehearsed again here.[23] What is important for our present purposes is that interdisciplinarity itself can be seen as a postmodern response to the fracturing of the holistic nature of human inquiry in general as a result of the rigid compartmentalization of traditional academic disciplines that have operated in relative isolation from one another. It is precisely on the instance of the centrality of human experience, as a holistic phenomenon, that has informed the study of spirituality's interdisciplinary posture. Moreover, the integrative principle of the hermeneutical process of interpretation at the heart of Schneiders's understanding of spirituality, naturally lends itself to the synthesizing effects of both human knowledge and experience rooted in Hans Georg Gadamer's seminal concept of the "fusion of horizons."[24]

The self-implicating keystone of Schneiders's methodology finally brings us to reconsider the dialectical relationship between religious experience and religious authority that has precipitated the evangelical crisis of conversion. To assert that human experience in general is self-implicating is on its face tautological, in that the sum of any given person's experience forms the immanent horizon of their existential reality and thereby constitutes that person's individuality vis a vis other persons. In other words, a given person's experience naturally implicates them because it is that person who is involved as experiencing subject. This infinite regression of the subjectivity of experience has played no small role in the general apprehension or utter rejection of experience as a viable hermeneutical standpoint, particularly for those concerned with preserving doctrinal, theological, or ecclesial traditions. However, by asserting that spirituality is self-implicating, Schneiders is making a deeper claim. Spirituality is self-implicating more specifically as intentional involvement in the dynamics of transformation through life-integration and self-transcendence that we saw above. This point is important to consider methodologically, as it indicates how spirituality as experience is

---

23. See the following studies that take up the issue of interdisciplinarity within the field of Christian spirituality. Agnew et al., *With Wisdom Seeking God*; Helminiak, *Spiritual Development*; Lombard, "Biblical Spirituality and Interdisciplinarity," 211–12; Schneiders, "Spirituality in the Academy"; Schneiders, "Study of Christian Spirituality"; Wolfteich, "Animating Questions," 121–43; Schneiders, "Hermeneutical Approach," 49–64; Frohlich, "Spiritual Discipline," 65–78; and the seven essays that comprise "Part V: Interdisciplinary Dialogue Partners for the Study of Christian Spirituality," in Holder, *Blackwell Companion to the Study of Christian Spirituality*.

24. Gadamer, *Truth and Method*; for an analysis of Gadamer's hermeneutics in relationship to Schneiders's methodology see Higgins, "Spirit and Truth."

self-implicating, and also sets the terms for the critical reflection and scholarly analysis of spirituality as transformative experience.[25]

The three constitutive elements in Schneiders's definition analyzed above, help to situate the question of self-implication within the overarching intentionality of human experience more generally through the dynamics of transformation. And it is through properly identifying the phenomenon of spirituality as experience through the hermeneutical lenses of the life-integrating and self-transcendent dynamics of transformational encounter, that ultimately allows Schneiders to identify the particularity of religious experience from human experience at large, and also to bring to bear the critical hermeneutic of transformational dynamics towards a perceived horizon of ultimate value. At this point it is necessary to contextualize this ultimate horizon, which is for Schneiders always supplied by the particularity of the experience in question.[26] For Schneiders, this frame is the Christian religious tradition, and more specifically the primary texts of the Christian Scriptures. By taking this position, Schneiders argues from the standpoint of Christian spirituality, again always as experience, that the primary objective in engaging the Christian scriptures as a reader is ultimately transformation rather than simply gathering new information.[27]

The transformative dimension of Schneiders's biblical spirituality reinforces her hermeneutical understanding of experience both through the dynamics of integration and transcendence, and in the actual encounter between text and reader. In both instances, the self-implicating nature of Schneiders's methodology comes into play. According to the dynamics of transformation, the Christian Scriptures are self-implicating to the degree that they orient the reader towards the horizon of ultimate value. It is in this experience of transformative encounter that the Scriptures are properly interpreted as divine revelation according to the theologically rich phrase, "the word of God."[28]

In claiming that the Bible is the word of God, Schneiders is not referring to either the literal act of God's speech being written down, nor to some supernatural quality of the propositional claims contained within it; rather, for her, the Bible is the word of God because it implicates the reader according to the dynamics of life-integration and self-transcendence as it reveals the horizon of ultimate value, namely God's self. According to the actual encounter between

---

25. Schneiders, "Approaches," 29–31.

26. Schneiders, "Study of Christian Spirituality," 17–19.

27. Schneiders, *Revelatory Text*, 13–14; Schneiders, *Written That You May Believe*, 18–22.

28. Schneiders, *Written That You May Believe*, 16–20; Schneiders, *Revelatory Text*, 40–44.

reader and text, the Christian Scriptures are self-implicating according to the text being revelatory of God's self-disclosure. When seen in this light, the Scriptures, as the word of God, provide not merely propositional data about God and the qualities of Christian discipleship, though it does indeed provide that; but more importantly, it provides the locus of an inter-personal encounter with God. This response of the reader to the self-disclosure of God as revealed in the text implicates the reader in that it requires her or him to deal with the mode in which it is delivered, namely as an experience. The "objective" data contained within the text, becomes then secondary to the primary purpose of the Scriptures as a witness to an experience of life-integration and self-transcendence towards the horizon of infinite value found in Jesus Christ. This existential, or spiritual, stance—functionally synonymous terms for Schneiders here—[29] vis a vis the reader before the text, presents new opportunities to gain new insights from the text as revelatory, that is, as the locus of an experience of the self-disclosure of God. In this way, Schneiders argues that there is no fundamental difference between the revelatory nature of authentic religious experiences of the horizon of ultimate value in general that reveal God, and the revelatory experience of God through the Scriptures in particular. That is to say that in both instances they may be properly understood as spiritual, or moments of genuine revelation.

Schneiders's spiritual stance draws a fundamental methodological distinction within the field of Christian religious studies between the methods of biblical spirituality and those historical critical methodologies that have been dominant for the past several hundred years. At the same time, by engaging the spiritual or revelatory dimension of Scripture as experience of divine self-disclosure, Schneiders orients the reader to consider the truth claims of the text existentially. Central to Schneiders's argument is the question of whether the texts of sacred Scripture provide a meaningful account of the self-disclosure of God to the world? Internally, Schneiders argues that indeed these texts do attempt to tell us something true about God's agency in the world, which is most clearly revealed in the life, ministry, death, and resurrection of Jesus of Nazareth.[30] Therefore, in addition to the proper excavation of the historical world behind the text, and the literary world of the text—which are the primary contributions of the historical-critical, and textual analyses of modern biblical exegesis—a full account of the Christian Scriptures, must in some way be able to account for the claims that the text brings to the reader in the world before the text.[31]

29. Schneiders, *Revelatory Text*, 14.
30. Schneiders, *Written That You May Believe*, 69–74.
31. Schneiders draws heavily on the notion of "appropriation" in the act of

The Crisis of Conversion

These claims challenge the reader to consider for themselves the ultimate horizon presented in the text. Here the biblical data and Christian history provide the "positive data of Christian religious experience"[32] as constitutive disciplines of spirituality's interdisciplinarity mentioned above. Alongside these constitutive disciplines, is theology which provides second-order reflection on the primary data of history and biblical studies on the one hand, and also a framework for interpreting and articulating one's own experience on the other. An apparent contradiction emerges here in Schneiders's thought, as on the one hand her articulation of spirituality as a discipline of study brackets normative claims that would *a priori* attempt to adjudicate the authenticity

---

interpretation that is rooted in a Gadamerian notion of the "fusion of horizons" or the interaction between the various worlds at play in any act of interpreting a "text." However, this appropriation, is not to be understood as a fideistic a priori assertion of a given text's veracity; but rather a reorientation of the relationship between text and reader so that these questions assume their proper existential position. In this way, Schneiders's improves on Gadamer's hermeneutics by taking into account both Ricœur's seminal "Second Naïveté" in dialogue with Jürgen Habermas's critical theory. In so doing, Schneiders articulates a robust and nuanced argument for the necessity of the categories of human experience as integral to the process of Biblical interpretation.

Ricœur, "Hermeneutics and the Critique of Ideology," 63–100; Ricœur, "Appropriation," 182–93; also Ricœur's "hermeneutical wager" that is arguably the functional equivalent to Schneiders's spiritual stance of the reader to the text, as outlined in *The Symbolism of Evil*, 353–57. Like Schneiders, Ricœur here suggests that the way of the subjective/objective dualism that plagues the philosophical debates of the structuralists and post-structuralists; and similarly the irreducible historical distantiation of the text from the reader from perspective of the historical-critical methodologies of modernist approaches to biblical studies; and even the dislocation of the truth claims within the text from Gadamer's method of the fusion of horizons, is to bring to bear the existential weight of the symbolic meaning contained within the text on the act of interpretation itself. That is to experience the text as a locus of self-disclosure that necessarily requires the reader to take up the truth-claims of the text existentially in the process of interpretation as self-implicative appropriation.

Moreover, Schneiders in following Habermas, notes the oppressive and violent consequences of appropriation as a means of controlling interpretation inherent in Gadamer's conception of tradition within his hermeneutical process. For Schneiders, this informs her feminist consciousness, whereby she challenges the authoritative patriarchal "tradition" that has marginalized and de-legitimated feminine experience as a suitable existential frame of reference from which to interpret and engage with the meaning of a given text. In this way, Schneiders's focus on experience serves a critical function that both exposes the violence undergirding authoritative interpretations of Scripture, and also creates the possibility for new and liberative interpretations of the text to speak meaningfully to and from experiences that have been systematically silenced throughout the tradition of biblical interpretation. See Schneiders, *Revelatory Text*, 183–86; Schneiders, *Written That You May Believe*, 146–48, For a summary of Habermas's critical theory see his essays, "Dogmatism, Reason, and Decision," "The Tasks of Critical Theory in Society," and "The Concept of the Lifeworld," in Habermas, *Jürgen Habermas on Society and Politics*.

32. Schneiders, "Study of Christian Spirituality," 7.

of a given experience in terms of its conformity to the external authority of some system, theological or otherwise; while on the other hand, as we have just seen, the self-implicating linchpin at the center of her methodology would appear to immediately require spirituality as experience to be subject to questions and interpretations concerning the appropriateness of a given "experience of" a specific horizon of ultimate value.

Schneiders is no doubt aware of this tension as her work on the revelatory quality of the Christian scriptures indicates. For Schneiders, all of human experience is, like the Bible, potentially revelatory, meaning that it becomes revelatory through the act of interpretation.[33] And while Schneiders references the intentionality of the phenomenon of experience itself as always being experiences of particularities, she does not integrate this insight with her distinction between the self-implicating nature of spirituality as *experience of* vis a vis the normative nature of theology as proper or legitimate *interpretation of*. While Schneiders has made a convincing argument that the focus on experience as such is the unique and valuable contribution of spirituality to religious studies, an articulation of how the phenomena of religious experience relates to the interpretive and prescriptive dimensions of religious studies is left under-developed.

This underdevelopment is due in part to the nature of Schneiders's research in biblical studies. As a biblical scholar, she is therefore not primarily interested in articulating a nuanced and more developed philosophical analysis of human religious experience more broadly, but rather with the hermeneutical nature of the study of the Christian scriptures. Moreover, as one of the founders of the contemporary discipline of the study of spirituality in North America, the bulk of Schneiders's work in defining the field and articulating its methodological principles has been done in the context of presenting the distinguishing features of spirituality in relationship to other disciplines within the humanities more broadly, and advocating for spirituality's place within the sub fields and specializations of religious studies more particularly. In this endeavor she has been manifestly successful.[34] Now more than thirty years later, the discipline of spirituality studies no longer has to defend its rightful place within the academy and as a result we are able to critically explore the foundations of the now well-established discipline. To that end, I propose that a critical reassessment of the semiotics of human experience, particularly as it has

---

33. Schneiders, *Revelatory Text*, 39.

34. See for example an early exposition of spirituality's place within the umbrella field of religious studies and in particular its relationship to theology. Schneiders, "Theology and Spirituality," 253–74.

The Crisis of Conversion

developed in the North American Pragmatist philosophical tradition, will help provide a more developed articulation of spirituality as religious experience.

Towards a North American Semiotics of Religious Experience

I have chosen to place Schneiders's methodology in conversation with the North American philosophical tradition regarding human experience for two main reasons. First, it allows us to contextualize the North American evangelical crisis of conversion outlined in the previous chapter with Schneiders's development of the discipline of spirituality. In this respect, I will continue the project of a North American inculturated theology by Donald Gelpi by applying key insights from his analysis of the American Pragmatist tradition to the concerns of Schneiders's spirituality and from there, draw out some initial conclusions regarding the unique position of the category of human experience as it relates to the development of the crisis of conversion within the broad evangelical tradition in the US. And more importantly, the North American philosophical tradition has had a particular fascination with human experience, which, as we will see, has on the one hand helped inform the underlying presuppositions of personal autonomy and individualism at the heart of the crisis of conversion, and also provides a semiotics of religious experience that may indeed provide a viable way forward on the other. This contextualization will itself be a sort of interdisciplinary conversation as Schneiders's work is squarely situated in the German and French Continental traditions of phenomenology and hermeneutics rather than with North American figures. However, this contextualization, or re-contextualization as it were, of Continental ideas in the new context of North America has a long history, and is at least in part a distinguishing characteristic of the American intellectual tradition more broadly.[35]

Contextualizing Religious Experience in North America

The history of the North American intellectual tradition, from the perspective of the European West at least, is in itself rooted in a type of religious experience. European imperialism, ecclesiastical missionary impulses, and theo-political sectarianism coalesced during the sixteenth and seventeenth

---

35. See William James's opening apology to his 1901–1902 Gifford Lectures, *The Varieties of Religious Experience*, where he a bit humorously notes the heavily one-sided flow of ideas from Europe to North America, as he a North American delivers these prestigious lectures to an European audience. William James, *Varieties*, 11–12.

centuries into a brutally successful form of colonialism in the Americas. Whether it was the earlier Spanish, Italian, Portuguese, and French Catholics, or later the English, Dutch, and Scottish Protestants, the colonization of the New World and its indigenous peoples, and the African slave trade have left an indelible mark on the religious landscape of what is now North and South America. The complicated history of European exploration is not of central concern here, other than to connect the emerging globalization of European culture and its influence throughout the New World on the one hand, and the theological and spiritual foundations of the colonization of North America on the other. From as early as the Puritan John Winthrop's famous 1630 sermon "A Model of Christian Charity," we find that the early colonists understood themselves in Christian missiological terms from the very beginning, as seen here in Winthrop's conception of the colonies as a city upon a hill:

> We shall find that the God of Israel is among us, when ten of us shall be able to resist a thousand of our enemies; when He shall make us a praise and glory that men shall say of succeeding plantations, "may the Lord make it like that of New England." *For we must consider that we shall be as a city upon a hill. The eyes of all people are upon us. So that if we shall deal falsely with our God in this work we have undertaken, and so cause Him to withdraw His present help from us, we shall be made a story and a by-word through the world.*[36]

Moreover, as Perry Miller and others have shown, the nascent New England colonies quickly combined ecclesial, spiritual, political, and economic interests into a fairly hegemonic society that would dominate colonial life for more than a century.[37] While much of the literature on Puritan society, stemming from Miller's classical presentation of the "New England Mind," has tended to focus on the intellectual world of this synthesis, more recently scholars have begun to recognize the foundational role that Puritan spirituality, or piety, had in formulating and buttressing the ecclesial-political institutions of the early colonies.[38] Thus we may reasonably conclude that the migration and colonization of the English to North America was as a response to and development of a particular kind of religious experience. An experience that

---

36. Winthrop, "Model of Christian Charity."

37. Miller, *Seventeenth Century*; Miller, *From Colony to Province*; Hambrick-Stowe, *Practice of Piety*; Porterfield, *Female Piety in Puritan New England*; Nuttall, *Holy Spirit in Puritan Faith and Experience*; Cohen, *God's Caress*; Bremer, *Puritan*.

38. Hindmarsh, *Spirit of Early Evangelicalism*; Hindmarsh, *Evangelical Conversion Narrative*; Schwanda, *Emergence of Evangelical*; Schwanda, "'Hearts Sweetly Refreshed,'" 21–41.

separated the Puritans from the larger religious culture of sixteenth-century England, and provided them with a sense of purpose that propelled them to seek out a new place from which to live out this sense of divine calling.

Here we find early resonance with Robert Bellah and his team's recent cultural sociological study of middle-class America, following the nineteenth-century French diplomat Alexis de Tocqueville's prediction of the looming crisis of American individualism.[39] The Puritans combined a proto-individualist spirit in the form of radical protestant separatism in New England with a strong sense of personal agency and responsibility for their own sense of salvation being worked out in a theocratic civic society. As colonial sensibilities matured into a nationalist spirit through the latter half of the sixteenth century, this synthesis had solidified by the seventeenth century into what Mark A. Noll described as "Christian Republicanism" in his landmark study, *America's God*.[40] What is of particular interest for our present purposes, is that from Winthrop, Bellah, and Noll, we find a consistent theme that prioritizes the select chosen few (the Puritans) and eventually the individual person exclusively as the locus of authority, whether that authority be socio-political, economic, or theological. In the following chapter, I will examine in more detail how Jonathan Edwards, the last great leader of the Puritan era, and Ralph Waldo Emerson, a central figure in the nineteenth century romanticist movement known as Transcendentalism, utilized human experience at the individual level and its relationship to theological and intellectual authority. But for now, I will turn to consider the philosophical development of a semiotics of religious experience as it was worked out by the North American intellectual tradition at the turn of the twentieth century.

Towards a North American Semiotics of Religious Experience: William James

William James (1842–1910) is one of the most well-known of the classical pragmatists, alongside his contemporaries Charles Sanders Peirce, John Dewey, and Josiah Royce. His 1901–02 Gifford Lectures, published as *The Varieties of Religious Experience*, helped to shape the course of religious studies in the United States in the twentieth century, and has been particularly important for the study of spirituality.[41] In the *Varieties*, James sets out to provide an em-

---

39. Bellah, *Good Society*; Bellah, *Habits of the Heart*; Tocqueville, *Democracy in America*.

40. Noll, *America's God*, 73.

41. While James enjoys a certain celebrity within contemporary religious studies, it was C. S. Peirce who was the most original thinker of the classical pragmatist group and

pirical, or scientific, account of religious experience which he locates within the subjective world of the individual person: "Religion ... shall mean for us *the feelings, acts, and experiences of individual men in their solitude, so far as they apprehend themselves to stand in relation to whatever they consider the divine*" (Italics are original to James).[42] Thus religion, as James was interested in exploring it in his lectures, was preeminently an individual affair that remains locked within "the inner dispositions of man himself which form the centre of interest," a particular relation that "goes direct from heart to heart, from soul to soul, between man and his maker."[43] Here we find James situating the category of "religion" within the category of experience, which is for him at once a more broad and more immediate category, and the proper location for understanding religion itself. James's reasoning for understanding religion in such a way is both methodological and constructive.

At the methodological level, James finds the "intellectualism" of philosophical/systematic foundations of religion to be largely inconsequential to the concerns of individual believers. In his closing lecture "Philosophy," James critiques these intellectual arguments, particularly the development of God's supposed metaphysical attributes as it has developed in the Catholic and Protestant intellectual traditions. He asks rhetorically; "what seriousness can possibly remain in debating philosophic propositions that will never make an appreciable difference to us in action?."[44] And more pointedly, "what specific act can I perform in order to adapt myself to God's simplicity?."[45] These critiques need not be interpreted as a call for an anti-intellectual account of religion or religious experience, but rather a challenge to the presumed adequacy of a purely philosophical foundation for deducing the veracity of religious claims. Instead, James, like we saw with Schleiermacher previously, wants to ground our understanding of religion in general in the raw data of subjective immediacy through the experience of the divine and the practical implications thereof, precisely because that is where for him, we will ultimately find the essence of religious belief. That is, for James, the reason

---

whose ideas served as the foundation for James and Dewey's later success. Josiah Royce on the other hand, maintained a commitment to idealism alongside of pragmatist concerns; he was nevertheless a central voice in the conversation at the turn of the twentieth century and made significant contributions to the philosophy of religion, particularly in Roman Catholic circles towards the latter half of the twentieth century as we will see below. James more so than any of these other figures has featured prominently in the discipline of spirituality over the past several decades.

42. James, *Varieties*, 32.
43. James, *Varieties*, 31.
44. James, *Varieties*, 338.
45. James, *Varieties*, 339.

why religious belief in general has the power of veracity at the individual and societal levels has more to do with the nature of experience and very little to do with abstract formulations of metaphysical attributes, logical arguments, or doctrinal statements.[46]

At the constructive level, the prioritization of experience allows him to work out his understanding of religion based upon the observable results of religious experiences. Here James's understanding of the veracity of religious claims, rooted as they are in the observable practical implications of concrete religious experiences rather than in abstracted doctrines, situates both religious belief and religious experience pragmatically, or through the process of verification via the testing of hypotheses. Commenting on Peirce at this point, James argues that (a) the goal or telos of human inquiry is "the attainment of belief"; (b) that beliefs are "rules for action"; and (c) that "the whole function of thinking is but one step in the production of habits."[47] These three markers correspond to Peirce's important and original metaphysical categories of Firstness, which is the quality of presentness or genuine possibility; Secondness, the quality of struggle or genuine particularity; and Thirdness, the quality of laws or genuine generality. Thus, for Peirce, the particular process of actualization from possibility to actuality, that collectively tends towards generalized hypotheses of reality is what constitutes our experience of reality. Following this, James argues that any final test for the truthfulness (or usefulness) of a given phenomenon must come from the results or the merit of the phenomena so considered as it is used in thought or practice; what he calls "philosophical reasonableness, and moral helpfulness."[48] This is the case for James's understanding of human inquiry in general, as well as for particular religious experiences.

This leads James to suggest that there must be real and discernible elements to those experiences that are given a religious valuation that distinguish them from the total range of human experience, where "we can meet nowhere else."[49] At the general level, the designation of an experience being religious carries with it an existential weight for the individual, and it involves an "absolute addition to the Subject's range of life";[50] this absolute addition in turn is expressed along a psychological/emotional spectrum from melancholy, to

---

46. See an extended analysis of James's strategy here in Lash, *Easter in Ordinary*.

47. James, *Varieties*, 338. See Peirce, "The Fixation of Belief," and "How to Make our Ideas Clear," "The Universal Categories," and "The Categories Continued," in Peirce, *Collected Papers*, 5:223–33, 248–65, 29–46, 47–63.

48. James, *Varieties*, 23.

49. James, *Varieties*, 42.

50. James, *Varieties*, 44.

happiness, and finally insight.[51] At the level of particular religious experiences, and following his empiricist methodology, James seeks to identify and isolate these religious elements in their purest and most exaggerated form within the full spectrum of human experience so that it may be most clearly seen both within itself and in relation to the whole. This dynamic range of absolute addition is worked out in the substantive analyses of the *Varieties* that characterize the three modes of religious experiences James considers: the melancholy inherent in experiences of conversion (Lectures IX-X), the happiness in the experiences and progression of saintliness (XI-XV), and the insight gained in mystical experience (XVI-XVII).

In terms of James's articulation of a semiotics of religious experience, his analysis of mystical experience, the "root and center" of personal religious experience, is instructive for our purposes in working out the relationship between experience and authority.[52] James identifies four distinguishing marks of mystical experience; ineffability, noetic insight, transiency, and passivity.[53] While the latter two markers are generally present in James's accounting of mystical experience, it is the first two, namely the ineffability and noetic insight that are essential to mystical experience. That is for James, the phenomenon of mysticism must be something that is on the one hand directly experienced, and on the other lead to a depth of truth and revelatory significance that in itself remains inarticulable. This dynamic interaction between the immediacy of experience, and the mediated nature of noetic insight is an important development for our purposes in articulating a semiotics of religious experience. James's categories offer an improvement concerning the nature of experience to what we saw in Schneiders related to the dynamics of self-implication and the question of normativity above. The tension that Schneiders left implicit and unresolved between experience and authority is shown in the work of James to be hermeneutically related in the nature of human experience itself, understood pragmatically. The immediacy of James's understanding of religion as individual experience of the divine, ineffable as it remains in mystical experience, yields itself to the unfolding of noetic insight as the individual is drawn into themselves through an encounter with the divine other. The noetic quality of James's understanding of religious experience on the one hand proceeds hermeneutically, as the individual is challenged by the transcendence of the mystical experience and subsequently attempts to articulate the process of transformation that they have begun in light of the experience. Despite the inarticulability of mystical experience, the *Varieties* are full of primary source

---

51. James, *Varieties*, 27.
52. James, *Varieties*, 290.
53. James, *Varieties*, 290–91.

material of autobiographical and eye-witness accounts of mystical insight, ranging from Teresa of Avila, Swami Vivekananda, Walt Whitman, Hegel, Dionysius, Sufism, and Saint Paul. Thus, despite the apparent paradox of the noetic and inarticulate markers of mystical experience, something indeed is communicable as evidenced by the writings of the great mystics. This tension between subjective experience and communicable noetic insight is never completely resolved for James as he attempts to work out the authoritative nature of the noetic content of religious experience. He claims that religious experience is authoritative only for the person who had the experience. For all others, the authoritative appeal has merely potentially persuasive power.[54]

From the analysis thus far, there is a significant degree of compatibility between James's understanding of religious experience and Schneiders's notion of spirituality. They both are interested in religion from the point of view of personal experience, and it is through experience that religious claims come to bear on the responses of the individual person. Moreover, there is a dialectic at play between the particularity of experience and larger claims of coherence of a given experience with a transcendent reality, whether that is explicitly the Christian God or some other form of transcendence. And, more importantly, they both make a clear distinction between first order experience and second order reflection. Where Schneiders devotes the majority of her argument staking out the phenomenological nature of a unique field of inquiry vis a vis philosophical and theological doctrines, James is concerned with staking out the phenomenological nature of religious experience itself vis a vis human experience more broadly.

Nevertheless, there is a compatibility in terms of how both thinkers situate the question of the veracity of religious experience within the phenomenon of experience as such. Their results are similar: there is an implicit authoritative claim that is made on the individual in the experience itself that is strictly speaking unavailable for critique at the level of its origin for those whom are outside of that experience. For James, the noetic insight of religious experience is present potentially in the experience and thus can only be presented as a hypothesis for others. And for Schneiders, a given experience becomes revelatory for an individual through the dynamics of transformation in response to a horizon of ultimate value. Moreover, the designation of the religious or spiritual element of the experience is for both authors something that is supplied by the subject. That is, for both Schneiders and James, the uniquely spiritual or religious element of an experience lies in the responses, or "fruit" that result from the experience and not from something universally accessible in the object of the experience. Interestingly, both James and Schneiders critique

---

54. James, *Varieties*, 289–92, 322–27.

the supposed objectivity of theological and philosophical idealism stemming from Cartesian and Kantian subject/object dualisms on this point, precisely because these epistemologies cannot account for the inherent subjectivity of human experience as it is actually lived.

Without diminishing the significant compatibility between the two, there is one point where Schneiders's notion of spirituality improves upon James's notion of religious experience as it is developed in the *Varieties*. The issue is the "arbitrary" notion of religion that James sets up in the *Varieties*.[55] By defining religious experience as a purely personal phenomena, and setting aside institutional concerns, James ignores a crucial element in the phenomenon of religious experience itself; which problematically, distorts his pragmatic project. This problematic emerges towards the conclusion of his lectures where he attempts to "extract from the privacies of [particular] religious experience some general facts which can be defined in formulas upon which everybody may agree."[56] These general reflections represent "interpretive and inductive operations, operations after the fact, consequent upon religious feeling, not coordinate with it, not independent of what it ascertains."[57] James's conclusions are worth quoting at length:

> Summing up in the broadest possible way the characteristics of the religious life, as we have found them, it includes the following *beliefs*:—
> 1. That the visible world is part of a more spiritual universe from which it draws its chief significance;
> 2. That union or harmonious relation with that higher universe is our true end;
> 3. That prayer or inner communion with the spirit thereof—be that spirit 'God' or 'law'—is a process wherein work is really done, and spiritual energy flows in and produces effects, psychological or material, within the phenomenal world.
>
> Religion includes also the following psychological characteristics:—
> 4. A new zest which adds itself like a gift to life, and takes the form either of lyrical enchantment or of appeal to earnestness and heroism.
> 5. An assurance of safety and a temper of peace, and, in relation to others, a preponderance of loving affections.[58]

---

55. James, *Varieties*, 30.
56. James, *Varieties*, 330.
57. James, *Varieties*, 30.
58. James, *Varieties*, 368.

The Crisis of Conversion

And concerning the question, "ought we to consider the testimony [of the wide variety of religious experience] true?" James concludes:

> The warring gods and formulas of the various religions do indeed cancel each other out, but there is a certain uniform deliverance in which religions all appear to meet. It consists in two parts:—
> 1. [An] uneasiness, reduced to its simplest terms, is a sense that there is *something wrong about us* as we naturally stand.
> 2. [A] solution . . . that *we are saved from the wrongness* by making proper connection with the higher powers . . .
>
> *He becomes conscious that this higher part is coterminous and continuous with a MORE of the same quality, which is operative in the universe outside of him, and which he can keep in working touch with, and in a fashion get on board of and save himself when all his lower being has gone to pieces in the wreck.*[59]

These conclusions are fine so far as they go to deduce a phenomenological description of religion, and even helpful in terms of articulating a starting place for engaging in ecumenical and interfaith dialogue. However, these conclusions are internally problematic and fail to satisfy the standard of truth when considered from James's own pragmatic conception of experience. James, as we saw previously with Schneiders, wants to argue to for the uniqueness of experience as such in his understanding of religion. And according to his utilization of Peirce's pragmatic principle, the fruits of such experience provide the final test in the truthfulness of conceptions related to the experience resulting in "production of active habits."[60] And while these habits, for pragmatists, tend towards generalized patterns of thought and action, they are nevertheless necessarily conditioned by the actualization of particular phenomena. It is unclear how James's conclusions (a), result in the production of active habits, and (b) are conditioned by the actualization of religious experience as James has analyzed. It seems rather, that James's conclusions correspond to an *a priori* metaphysical theory of the coterminous nature of the transcendent with the world. This pantheistic model is central to his conception of "over-beliefs" which provide a general character for James's understanding of religious belief,[61] while at the same time, James is rightly critical of the tendency of the philosophic tradition to reduce religious insight into a pantheistic/monistic

---

59. James, *Varieties*, 384–85.

60. James, *Varieties*, 338.

61. James, *Varieties*, 388. See also Matthew Bradley's commentary on Over-Belief in James's thought in his introduction to the *Varieties*. Bradley, "Introduction," xxv–xxviii.

dualism.[62] At the root of this problematic is the hard distinction he draws between primary experience and secondary reflection.

James consistently distinguishes between the raw experience and subsequent reflections and this forms the basis for his critiques against philosophical or theological doctrines as external judgements on the validity of religious experience, particularly as saw in his analysis of mystical insight. Coupled with his individualistic construal of the nature of religion, James is not able to account for the role that the habit-forming role of religious traditions play in the very nature of religious experience, or the necessarily mediated nature of experience central to Thirdness in Peirce's pragmaticism.[63] Early on in the *Varieties* James clarifies this distinction in relation to religious experience, where he finds that purely naturalistic explanations, whether they be psychological or scientific, fail to correspond to the nature of religious experience as it happens in the lives of individual persons. So that, in order to get closer to an adequate understanding of the general phenomenon we must base the value of religious experience only through "judgements based on our own immediate feeling primarily; and secondarily on what we can ascertain of their experiential relations to our moral needs and to the rest of what we hold as true."[64]

Yet it is precisely in the act of judgements rooted in the particularity of "immediate feeling" that such generalities which James concludes as the markers of religious experience fail to adequately grasp religion as it is experienced. This is so precisely because religious experiences do not occur generally and separate from the interpretive habits conditioned through the mediation of historical religious traditions. Wayne Proudfoot has critiqued the experiential turn in modern religious liberalism stemming from Schleiermacher and James at this point by noting that the search for an "autonomous moment of human experience" upon which to ground religious belief cannot be found apart from "reference to concepts, beliefs, grammatical rules, and practices."[65] Moreover, it is in the realm of the social world of language and tradition, that "institutional" branch of religion cast aside in the *Varieties,* where we find these beliefs being initially formed.

Fellow Pragmatist John Dewey (1859–1952), offers a similar critique to that of Proudfoot on the fundamental relationship between the raw phenomena of the objects of human experience and the abstracted systems of

---

62. James, *Varieties,* 108, 324.

63. "Pragmaticism" is a neologism of Peirce, who wanted to maintain sufficient distinctions between his own work in philosophy, and similar projects that refer to themselves as pragmatists, such as James himself. Peirce, *Collected Papers,* 276–77.

64. Peirce, *Collected Papers,* 23.

65. Proudfoot, *Religious Experience,* 228.

The Crisis of Conversion

interpretation and belief about the nature of reality. In *Experience and Nature*, and his 1930 Gifford Lectures, *The Quest for Certainty*, Dewey argues that human experience is essentially comprised of three interrelated functional stages, or moments; initial raw experience which is viewed as the basic, sensory, and more or less immediate interaction between the objective thing (which could be another subject) and the experiencing subject which I will call for our present purposes "experience 1";[66] second, we find "experience 2," a second stage in which there has been "continued and regulated reflective inquiry" on the materials of the primary experience;[67] and third, we find a return to the original experience 1 with the reflective products of our extended inquiry of experience 2 which creates for itself a new kind experience, "experience 3."[68] The labels experience 1, 2, and 3, are of course not be understood as three independent experiences with hard boundaries, but rather should be understood as the irreducible elements and natural dynamics of what Dewey means by experience itself.[69] That is, the relationship between what we have called experience 1 and experience 2 is best understood as the experiencing subject's reflexive incorporation of the immediacy of some initial experience, thus there is a necessary continuity between them. The same should be said about experience 3, with one important difference. For Dewey, the link between experience 1 and experience 2 is quite a natural and basic reality of experience in general in terms of the cognitive process of the awareness of the experiencing subject and the ability to organize, categorize, and interpret the material of primary experience temporally.[70] Experience 3 however requires a degree of intentionality that was absent in the previous two components of lived experience. One of Dewey's main critiques of the project of modern philosophy, particularly in the wake of Kant's dualistic project, is that critical reflection, experience 2, has become abstracted from experience 1 precisely because of the absence of this third dimension.[71] In this way, experience 3 serves as a sort of telos or end for Dewey. By putting up the results of critical reflection back onto the material of the primary experience in a new way it serves to both elongate that initial experience in more highly reflective and therefore critical way, and it more importantly serves to ground our critical reflection on the real world lived-experiences of human persons thereby

---

66. Dewey, *Experience and Nature*; Dewey, *Quest for Certainty*.
67. Dewey, *Experience and Nature*, 6–7.
68. Dewey, *Experience and Nature*, 19.
69. Kaminsky, "Dewey's Concept of an Experience," 318.
70. Dewey, *Experience and Nature*, 7–8.
71. Dewey, *Quest for Certainty*, 59, 273–76; Dewey, *Experience and Nature*, 8–9.

protecting philosophical reflection from become so abstracted as to become functionally irrelevant.[72]

Of central concern for Dewey here is that critical reflection about the nature of reality, especially about religious and philosophical realities, must be grounded in and informed by the actual experience of those realities. Where for much of Modern thought, following Kant's segregation of "pure" and "practical" reason, Dewey argues that all truth is practical, in that our conceptions about reality that are "true" as such to the degree that they correspond to our experience of these realities, or that these conceptions provide some usefulness in our acting upon lived experiences in the world.[73] In line with James's stated conclusions, Dewey's notion of truth rooted in the reality of lived-experience provides a properly contextualized method for critical inquiry that is tested against the data of experience. However, where James's theory of religious experience becomes mired in a dualistic distinction between individual private experience and shared traditions of interpretation, Dewey's notion of experience includes the process of interpretation as a constitutive element of experience itself. Similarly, Schneiders's understanding of religious experience also necessarily includes interpretive moments that provide clarity and shape to those experiences oriented towards horizons of ultimate value. Moreover, James's and Schneiders's more direct engagement on Christian religious experience brings greater clarity to the spiritual dimension of human experience than Dewey allows. Where Dewey is interested in articulating a philosophy of human experience in pursuit of the truthfulness of religious and philosophical conceptions, he does not develop or expand this fundamental insight into a more specifically theological or religious context.

In effect then, by dismissing the presence of external factors, such as interpretive frameworks and the process of traditioning, James has undercut a constitutive element to the nature of religious experience itself. Where James helps provide us with the helpful dynamic categories of immediacy and mediation within the phenomenon of experience itself, by exclusively focusing on private individual religious experience, he lacks a properly social category from which experience is mediated. Schneiders, by contrast, while defining spirituality according to a general understanding of experience of ultimate value similar to James, she pays close attention to the intentionality and particularity of religious experience, and thereby incorporates the processes of social traditions and language within her hermeneutically structured definition

---

72. For more detailed treatments of Dewey's notion of experience see Schlitt, *Experience and Spirit*, 101–7; Kaminsky, "Dewey's Concept of an Experience," 316–30; Rosenthal, "John Dewey"; and Tibbetts, "John Dewey."

73. Dewey, *Quest for Certainty*, 57–60.

of spirituality that help to break James's notion of religious experience out from its extreme individualism. Moreover, Schneiders's use of tradition and a wider social lens is an important part of her feminist critique against the role that religious traditions have played in misogyny and violence against women throughout history. James's theory of religion lacks this critical edge in part due to his individualist reduction of religion; a symptom that is mirrored in the evangelical crisis of conversion.

Towards a North American Semiotics of Religious Experience: Josiah Royce

James's contemporary and fellow Pragmatist, Josiah Royce (1855–1916) offers a helpful corrective here concerning the role of tradition and traditioning in the notion of religious experience. Much of Royce's work and legacy can be attributed to his interactions with his life-long friend and colleague James.[74] As we saw above, in the *Varieties*, James argues for a radically individualistic notion of religious experience that, "goes directly from heart to heart, from soul to soul, between man and his maker."[75] While both James and Royce would fall under the category of pragmatism, they differ quite radically in their interpretation of the nature of the human person and also of religious experience. Royce rejected James's individualistic notion of the human person in favor of a more socially constructed anthropology rooted in community rather than in individualized existential subjectivity, that was heavily influenced by the philosophy and semiotics of Peirce who Royce first heard in a series of lectures in 1898, and that would inform Royce's mature thought beginning with his own Gifford Lectures given in 1899–1900 and published as *The World and the Individual* (1899), and continuing with *The Philosophy of Loyalty* (1908), *The Sources of Religious Insight* (1912), and *The Problem of Christianity* (1913).[76]

Religious experience for Royce is a much more complicated issue than we saw with James. For Royce, James's reductionism of religious experience to the level of the individual was untenable, and therefore he sought to ground religious experience in something other than the individual. Beginning with *Sources*, Royce lays out what he finds as the central elements of religious experience which include the individual, but also is expanded to include social and communal structures as sources as well.[77] For Royce, James's elevation of the

---

74. Royce, *Basic Writings*, 1:205–8; Buckham, "Contribution of Professor Royce," 227.
75. James, *Varieties*, 31.
76. Miller, "Josiah Royce and George H. Mead," 68.
77. Royce, *Sources of Religious Insight*, 34.

human individual alone with God, is ultimately doomed since it is the human individual who, according to his own Protestant heritage, stands in need of salvation and therefore is not in a position to be the arbiter of his or her own salvation. Social structures such as the family, church and state, and society help to overcome, or mediate this deficiency but they in the end suffer the same fate as the individual.[78] Thus Royce also includes reason, the power of the will, and loyalty as central pieces in his metaphysic of religious experience as they all assist in breaking out of the seemingly inescapable subjectivism inherent in human finitude.[79] While the groundwork is begun in his *Sources*, his solutions are worked out in *The Problem of Christianity*.

The "problem" of Christianity for Royce is related to the difficulties arising out of the historical reality of modern human persons and their relative temporal distance to the Master (Jesus). This is not simply an academic problem of the "historical Jesus," though it does include such inquiry. Rather, the problem is one of religious experience itself. Given that historical Christianity almost immediately distinguished between the life events of Jesus on this earth, and the principles of faith handed down to us through the "creed,"[80] how does the contemporary person understand his or her relationship to the life of Christian faith that is rooted in contemporary understandings of God and the world and has been handed down in various modified forms through history on the one hand, and to the person of Jesus himself on the other? The problem then is one of interpretation. The Christian creed is most obviously a historical process of interpretation summarizing and teaching the faith of the Church from one generation to the next generation of believers. Jesus, however, occupied a unique moment in history and we must now experience his life and teaching through the same process of historical interpretation. Simply stated, the problem for Royce is that Christianity has never been simply "a religion taught by the Master. It has always been an interpretation of the Master," and this interpretation "even in its simplest expressions, has always gone beyond what the Master himself is traditionally reported to have taught while he lived."[81]

Thus, whatever religious experience is within the Christian tradition, it can never be simply a matter of individual experience, because the very origins of Christianity itself were never simply a matter of a single individual. It seems then that Royce does not disagree with James's individual interpretation

---

78. Royce, *Sources*, 19.

79. Royce, *Sources*, 12, 34, 48, 62, 76.

80. "Creed" here is used by Royce to designate not only the creedal formulations of the first several centuries, but of the overall reality of "the faith" handed down through the historical processes of the tradition.

81. Royce, *Problem of Christianity*, 66.

The Crisis of Conversion

of religious experience because it is fundamentally incorrect, but rather that individual religious experience is never merely one single individual's experience.[82] Relying heavily on Peirce's semiotics, Royce attempts to ground all human understanding, as interpretation, to a fundamentally social reality realized in community. For Christianity this community of interpretation is the Church who through the mediation of tradition continually interprets the life, ministry, and message of salvation through Jesus Christ. Moreover, this Christian community of interpretation is experienced through the presence of the life of the Holy Spirit.[83] Therefore, while not destroying the individual, Royce places the individual person within a community of interpretation through which the individual experiences and understands the world about him or her. The Church, by carrying out the mission of salvation taught by the Master and guided by the Spirit throughout history, becomes for Royce the symbol of the universal community, which ideally would include every single person. Royce's vision of the Church as the Universal Community inextricably binds together the individual and the Church as community of interpretation to such a degree that salvation, or religious experience more broadly, can only be found in the union, or some other interaction, between the individual and the Church.[84] It is within the matrix of this universal community of interpretation that Royce expounds upon the nature of religious experience.

Royce's doctrine of signs brings some clarity and focus on his "problem" of Christianity.[85] For Royce, all reality is known through the interpretation of

---

82. Royce, *Sources*, 14–15.

83. Markey, "Clarifying the Relationship between the Universal and the Particular Churches," 310.

84. Royce, *Problem*, 95. While this may appear to be similar to *Extra Ecclesiam nulla salus*, originating with the 3rd Century bishop Cyprian during the Novatian controversy, Royce seems to be using the Universal Community in a more Hegelian and therefore metaphysical way rather than some doctrinal statement concerning the requirement of church membership or baptism for personal salvation.

85. A detailed analysis of Peirce's concept of *thirdness* is beyond the scope of this chapter. However, it is a central element in Royce's thought, so a brief word is in order. In Peirce's categories of Being, he introduces his notion signs or symbols by identifying three categories of Being; Quality, Relation, and Representation. Quality is that which refers to the ground or pure abstraction of a thing, i.e., "blackness." Relation is that which identifies the Quality of the ground by contrasting it with other qualities, i.e., we know this stove to be black by it being related to the quality of blackness. And finally representation or "thirdness" is the interpretant which unites the particular Relation to the abstract Quality, a particular substance. Peirce's simple example of "This stove is black" shows the three elements of the Quality "blackness," the Relation of the particular stove to the quality of blackness, and the Interpretant naming that stove as black. Thus, all of reality is mediated through the process of signs through human language. Our words function as interpretants mediating the ground or universal Quality of reality with particular instances of

signs. Accordingly, we can know or experience a given particular reality as such *only* because we can interpret that particular reality vis a vis other particular realities; that is we say that a ball is round because we know what roundness is, and that roundness is not squareness, etc. The quality of roundness exists outside of that particular ball's round shape, and moreover we judge the quality of the particular ball based on our awareness and understanding of the quality of roundness, and not the other way around. In true Idealist form then, Royce grounds human experience in general, and including religious experience, not within an individual's experience itself, but rather within a larger of community of interpretation from which we learn to interpret a given reality as it is experienced. It is the community of interpretation then that shapes the way in which we understand and experience this world. Therefore, it becomes readily apparent that, for Royce, all of reality is in fact socially construed and dynamic, rather than individualistic and static.[86] We will now move on to address Royce's thought in relation to the problem of subjectivity within religious experience as outlined above with Schneiders and James.

As we saw, there is a tension inherent in the category of religious experience between the apparent plurality of possible and actual experiences on the one hand, and the sense that the ultimate referent of religious experiences is, at least in theory, something universal. For Schneiders, this tension is expressed in her "horizon of ultimate value"[87] whereas for James it is the "absolute addition to the Subject's range of life"[88] For Royce, there is a similar tension in his understanding of the nature of God as the transcendent and the interpretive nature of religious experience. This tension is laid out most clearly in the following passage:

> And, if in ideal, we aim to conceive the divine nature, how better can we conceive it than in the form of the Community of Interpretation, and above all in the form of the Interpreter, who interprets all to all, and each individual to the world, and the world of spirits to each individual . . . In him the Community, the Individual, and the Absolute would be completely expressed, reconciled, and distinguished.[89]

As human persons cannot exist outside of or apart from our socially-constructed reality, neither can God exist outside of or distinct from the

---

things. See Peirce, "On a New List of Categories," 287–98.
  86. Royce, *Problem*, 324–25, 346–47.
  87. Schneiders, "Approaches," 16.
  88. James, *Varieties*, 44.
  89. Royce, *Problem*, 318–19.

The Crisis of Conversion

Community of Interpretation. While there are strong overtones to a Hegelian metaphysic of Absolute Spirit, Royce himself seems wants to distance his own idealism from that of Hegel's system, so we must not draw too close a connection between the two systems of thought.[90] However, it does seem to follow that Royce is vulnerable to the charge of pantheism, where the reality of God is not, in essence, distinct from the subjective nature of the world as historical interpretive process. While Royce does not explicitly equate humanity in its ideal community with God, there is a significant blurring of the lines between the Community of Interpretation that is the Church, and the Universal Community that is the sum total of all reality, inclusive of the divine nature itself. In the ideal, there is little distinction between the Universe and God.

While the above analysis may seem to suggest that Royce, like we saw with James, might capitulate back to the individual's experience as the final interpreter of religious experience; it is helpful to recall that Royce argues for a radically social understanding of human experience in general. If individuals are the sole arbiters of religious experience, religious experience becomes nothing more than absolute relativism where each person creates their own version of the divine, as James clearly illustrated in his *Varieties,* and perhaps to a lesser degree, Schneiders's horizon of infinite value might initially suggest. For Royce, individuals are by nature "wayward and capricious"[91] thus the community serves as the means to transcend individual fragmentation and thus is more capable of arriving nearer to truth. However, in rejecting individualistic relativism, Royce does not revert to a form of objective foundationalism, dogmatically shouting that he is right and everyone else's opinions are wrong. Rather the concept of the community of interpretation which exists as a collection of individuals and yet transcends every single individual serves the process of mediating truth claims, and because it is a *process*, truth is never separated from the act or the will to interpret. Individuals may interpret incorrectly, and even the community of interpretation may in particular instances misuse or misinterpret things, such as the misogynistic and racist attitudes and policies still operative within Christian communities today as Schneiders notes. However, communities of interpretation, both as really existing and in the ideal, can move toward truth in a way that is simply impossible for individuals and particular religious experiences. For, as communities of interpretation provide the ground for individual interpretations of reality, the individual interpretations become integrated into the community of interpretation. Thus, as people and societies transition over time, so do the communities of interpretation. In this way, both the relativism of James's

---

90. Royce, *Problem*, 38–39.
91. Royce, *Problem*, 84.

individualism and the dogmatism of objective foundationalism are avoided in Royce's conception of communities of interpretation and human experience as the interpretation of signs.[92]

Royce's concept of Loyalty becomes central for the social nature of human experience, including religious experience. Loyalty is simply defined as "the willing and thoroughgoing devotion of a self to a cause, when the cause is something which unites many selves in one, and which is therefore the interest of a community."[93] For Christianity, loyalty is expressed most perfectly through love of God and love of neighbor, thus reinforcing the social reality of the community and giving the Christian community its universal mission. Loyalty also serves as a correction to individual sinfulness, thereby holding the community itself to the universal ideal—binding the universal community to the divine nature. The problem then for Royce, as noted by David Miller, is to be able to "account for the freedom and creativity of the individual."[94] Referring back to the beginning of our discussion of Royce, Christianity has since its very foundation been concerned with both the life and teachings of Jesus as well as the continued interpretation and expansion of those teachings by the Church and its doctrinal expressions. This Christian Tradition becomes the received community of interpretation of which individuals are a part of and thus function as a source of individual interpretations of religious experience. Simply stated, religious experience is defined according to the interpretation of religion as received from a community of interpretation to an individual. This is not quite the same thing as saying that the religious experience is merely the interpretation of the community, but rather the community of interpretation serves as the lens from which individuals interpret their experiences.[95] Contrary to James's notion that the external and ecclesial forms of religion are something that can be separated from "personal religion pure and simple,"[96] Royce sees the church itself as the method of experiencing and understanding God. So like experience itself, the definition of religious is a product of the community of interpretation mediated to the individual. We are left with a similar problem here as before, what role does the individual have, in if any at all, in religious experience?

Interestingly enough, Royce confronts this problem by yet another appeal to the virtue of community. The universal community exists as an ideal, or the quality of community, that all specific relative communities represent

92. Royce, *Problem*, 319.
93. Royce, *Problem*, 83.
94. Miller, "Josiah Royce and George H. Mead," 83.
95. Royce, *Problem*, 361.
96. James, *Varieties*, 31.

The Crisis of Conversion

to one degree or another. As all individual persons are less than perfect, so too all human communities are less than the ideal. The community's role in mediating reality to individuals is also responsible for setting the boundaries for that reality. Individuals who step out of those boundaries have in a sense rejected the community and are no longer a part of it, thus protecting and continuing the community's interpreting function. This means that at some basic level, a community is dependent on the freewill choices of individuals to remain loyal to the community. For the Christian community, this loyalty is expressed through love and forgiveness. The power of forgiveness, for reconciliation, and ultimately atonement is a supreme power of the Christian community, and it is also the greatest mechanism for accomplishing its universal mission, the expansion of the kingdom of God on earth. The community in this sense operates as a collection of individuals and would not, even could not, otherwise exist in light of the various other polarizations and differences between them. However, the function of the Christian community here transcends the individual members in its ability to reconcile estranged persons. So, while again the focus is on the community, the act of loyalty on the part of individual persons to the person of Jesus ensures that the mission of the community will continue and so a symbiotic relationship is formed between the community and its many individual members held together in light of the call and presence of God.[97]

For Royce, then, human experience in general and religious experience in particular are similarly constituted. Experience is for Royce, as we saw above, the interpretation of signs. And, any particular individual person, experiences the world through the aid of pre-existing, larger realities called communities of interpretation. Thus, there is always three fundamental elements at play in the reality that is lived human experience: the interpreter, i.e., the experiencing person; that which is interpreted, i.e., the experienced phenomenon; and the interpretation, i.e., the particular meaning or significance of the experienced phenomenon to the interpreter out of all potential meanings or possible interpretations available to the interpreter, namely the realm of interpretation that is the community of interpretation. Experience for Royce, as we saw with Dewey is dynamic process rather than static object; and like with James, experience mediates the nature of the world around us as individual persons. Moreover, it is teleologically oriented as we saw with both Dewey and James towards the pragmatic implications of the experience in terms of the formation of our beliefs, habits, and abilities for future experiences. Royce, however, does make significant improvements to James's understanding of religious experience more particularly. Royce's three-fold nature of experience helps

97. Royce, *Problem*, 176–79.

to properly situate the individual within a larger and external social frame, so that where in James's *Varieties*, religious experience is reduced to internal immediate perceptions between an individual and the divine, for Royce there is always present communities of interpretation mediating meaning and value to a given particular experiences of the divine. This mediating reality helps to inform a particular given religious experience while also providing new insights and potential meaning for future experiences. In this way, Royce pays attention to the relative continuity and cumulative power that traditions have on the process of interpretation in any given experience in a manner that I find to have great compatibility with Schneiders's hermeneutical spirituality.

Conclusion: Schneiders's Hermeneutical Spirituality as Christian Religious Experience

In chapter one, I argued that one of the main culprits in the evangelical crisis of conversion was a foundationalist epistemology that reduced the revelatory presence of God to an objectification of the Bible. This objectification isolates Scripture from the rest of human experience in a way that obscures one's ability to recognize the presence of God in the world; this reduction is mirrored in James's isolation of the interior of the individual from the external traditions of faith for his understanding of religion. Sandra Schneiders's foundational work helping to establish the contemporary discipline of the study of Christian spirituality has given renewed attention to the dimension of the human experience of God as a critical source for understanding not only the lived experience of Christian women and men through the ages, but also a deeper awareness of the presence of God in the world at large. Of particular importance here is Schneiders's notion of the self-disclosive nature of the revelatory experience of God, that mitigates the temptation to objectify God through a literalist interpretation of the Bible. At the same time, this focus on experience immediately raises questions concerning the proper interpretation of religious experience, particularly in reference to the traditional authorities of Christianity's doctrinal traditions and the Biblical witness. Specifically for Schneiders, these questions coalesce around the tension between the self-implicating nature of spirituality as religious experience, and the methodological bracketing off of normative claims from the phenomenon of experience itself. This mirrors the central problematic of the evangelical crisis of conversion as outlined in the previous chapter, namely the tension between the central role of individual religious experiences of conversion and the theological/philosophical dismissal of human experience as a viable category for Christian revelation.

The Crisis of Conversion

As a step toward resolving this tension, at least partially, I have situated Schneiders's work alongside of the work of the North American Pragmatist tradition's articulation of a semiotics of religious experience. Here, in the work of James and Royce, we find one way to situate the category of human experience in general within a wider social context in such a manner as to give room for the unfolding of authentic religious insight through an individual's particular experience. James's helpful analysis of the phenomenology of religious experience, including the ineffability and noetic nature of mystical experience highlighted both the immediacy of human experience, corresponding in a certain sense to the self-implicating dimension of religious experience from Schneiders, and the process of unfolding interpretation inherent in human experience, corresponding to the self-transcendent dimension of Schneiders's analysis. However, the individualist slant to James's understanding of religious experience resulted in a distorted view of religious experience vis a vis human experience in general by cutting out the fundamental role of tradition for interpreting the noetic content of a given religious experience. Royce offers a helpful corrective at this point through his concept of communities of interpretation that both help articulate particular experiences and also give shape to the "results" of particular and collective interpretations of experiences through loyal and prolonged engagement of individuals within particular communities of interpretation. These communities of interpretation correspond and help clarify the horizon of ultimate value that is the telos of Schneiders's understand of spirituality as spiritual experience.

In summation, these collective methodological insights help to recast the evangelical crisis of conversion in terms of a more faithful understanding of the nature of reality, including the reality of God, through a more expansive understanding of the nature of human experience that is one, more faithful to the phenomenon of experience itself, and two, widens the frame of reference for evangelical understandings of conversion in a manner that is more faithful to the New Testament call toward the kingdom of God. A conversion that is at once personal and continually expansive, modeled after the work of Don Gelpi and John Markey in chapter one above. In the following chapter, I will shift gears and provide some historical context to the evangelical crisis of conversion by examining the works of Jonathan Edwards and Ralph Waldo Emerson as representative North American figures concerning the experiential foundations of the North American religious-spiritual ethos.

3

Retrieving the Foundations of North American Evangelical Spirituality

Jonathan Edwards and Ralph Waldo Emerson On the Human Experience of God

IN 1911, TEN MONTHS after the death of William James, Josiah Royce gave an address to Harvard University's Phi Beta Kappa society in honor of his friend's life and legacy. In that address, Royce placed James alongside of two others as the most influential and representative American thinkers to date; Jonathan Edwards and Ralph Waldo Emerson.[1] Certainly within the histories of philosophy, religion, and literature in North America, these three men continue to exert tremendous influence. A witness to this fact is the relatively continuous stream throughout the twentieth century and into the twenty-first, of publications, dissertations, and monographs that treat some combination of these three figures.[2] Of particular interest here is the recent dissertation

---

1. Royce, "William James and the Philosophy of Life," 205–7.

2. Below is a sampling of works of the past several decades related to some combination of Edwards, Emerson, and James. Miller, *Jonathan Edwards to Emerson*; Lips, "Spirit's Holy Errand"; Scott, "Faith and Chaos"; Martin, "Beholding and Jubilant Soul"; Morris, "Jonathan Edwards and Pragmatism"; Ramsey, "Ineluctable Impulse," 303–22; Shaw, "Speaking for the Spirit"; Proudfoot, "From Theology to a Science of Religions," 149–68; Brantley, *Coordinates of Anglo-American Romanticism*; Gilpin, "Theology of Solitude," 31–42; Harrison, "Toward a Theology of Experience"; Koopman, "Pragmatism as a Philosophy of Hope," 106–16; Milder, "From Emerson to Edwards," 244–61; Knutson, *American Spaces of Conversion*; Robinson, "Road Not Taken," 45–61; Higgins, "Aesthetic Foundations," 152–66.

The Crisis of Conversion

by Andrea Knutson, published in 2011 by Oxford University Press, *American Spaces of Conversion: The Conductive Imaginaries of Edwards, Emerson, and James*, wherein Knutson traces the intellectual legacy of seventeenth-century conceptions of conversion and the Calvinist/Puritan doctrine of preparation, understood as the "pursuit of belief," from the eighteenth through the early twentieth-century in the writings of Edwards, Emerson, and James.[3]

This pursuit of belief manifests itself first through the Puritan *ordo salutis*, particularly as reconstructed through the conversion narratives recorded by the great Puritan divine Thomas Shepard (1605-1649) of his congregants in the First Church of Newtown (now Cambridge, Massachusetts). For Shepherd, and his congregants, one's conversion was interpreted through a careful process of internal discernment of the successive work of the Spirit present in the soul of the person, understood as means of grace integrating the heart, mind, and will towards sanctification. However, as Knutson articulates, what emerges out of the early Puritan's interpretation of their experiences of conversion, is not testimonies rejoicing in the assurance of salvation, but rather, an ambiguous and "open-ended" reality where assurance of one's regeneration was "continually deferred" as means of grace were often interpreted as unpredictable, and where a single "moment of grace did not necessarily provide assurance of salvation."[4] The state of uncertainty inherent in the interpretation of the experience of conversion itself, occasions, for Knutson, what she calls the "conductive imaginary: a conscious space organized, or that self-organizes, around the dynamics and tensions between emergent stored up truth, uncertainty and certainty, and perception and objects perceived."[5] That is, the transcendent dimension of the covenant of election established by God in the Calvinistic theology of Puritanism represents the truth, certainty, and object of religious conversion; and the immanent frame of the individual's always uncertain perception of one's attainment of conversion through the experiences of the Spirit as means of grace result in a shift in the early American conceptions of the reality of regeneration as merely "possible within a broadly defined spectrum of spiritual experience that emerges from two primary and opposing descriptions of conversion presented in the Bible: man's voluntary return to God and God's turning of man to [Godself]."[6]

Secondly, this early Puritan pursuit of belief would be recast in the writings of Edwards through the concept of the "sense of the heart" that allowed for an individual to move beyond notional understandings of God's grace, love,

3. Knutson, *American Spaces*, 4.
4. Knutson, *American Spaces*, 20-22, 27-32.
5. Knutson, *American Spaces*, 4.
6. Knutson, *American Spaces*, 5.

and election, towards an experience of these realities. Here, Knutson summarizes the performative thrust of Edwards's notion of the sense of the heart as that which "[collapsed] the gap between mind and thing . . . [and was the] goal of religious experience, though neither he nor Shepherd, because of their belief in original sin, could trust that experience."[7] Through the sense of the heart, as Amy Plantinga Pauw, Michael J. McClymond, Gerald R. McDermott, and others have noted, Edwards revised certain elements and emphases of his Calvinist/Reformed tradition concerning election as that found in Shepherd, from one where the individual wrestled with their own election and tended to dismiss assured experiences of one's conversion or direct knowledge of God, towards placing the aesthetic/affective experience of conversion as a sort of participation in the Trinitarian divine life itself as central mark of genuine Christian piety.[8] Thus for Knutson, Edwards's notion of conversion rooted in the perception of gracious affections meant that individuals "know they have undergone conversion . . . and more importantly, saints themselves are the most effective judges of whether the transformation is real because *they feel the difference.*"[9] The conductive imaginary of Edwards shifted the interpretation of the process of religious conversion from one that was concerned primarily with conforming one's own perception of religious experience to the institutionalized and external progression of the Puritan *ordo salutis,* to one that was concerned with the perception of the inner conformity of a person's affect, intellect, and will within an individual's experience of God.

By the time we get to Emerson in the Nineteenth Century, New England Puritanism rooted in Calvinist theology had given way to Arminian thought in the form of Unitarianism as the dominant religious outlook at Harvard where Emerson would attend from 1817–1821. This shift placed human freedom at the center of one's religious identity in a way that would depart not only from the specific theological content contained in the earlier *ordo salutis* of classical Puritanism, but also from even Edwards's recasting of religious conversion in terms of the internal consistency of the human experience of a divinely ordered and determined reality as well.[10] While Emerson retained a basic conviction of a transcendentally determined reality, he recasts it aesthetically in terms of an individual's "escape from slavery to society and carnal

---

7. Knutson, *American Spaces,* 60.

8. McClymond and McDermott, *Theology of Jonathan Edwards,* 669; Pauw, "'Supreme Harmony of All,'" 11–12; Delattre, *Beauty and Sensibility,* 121.

9. Knutson, *American Spaces,* 67.

10. Kuklick, *History of Philosophy in America,* 50–51, 70; Miller, *Errand into the Wilderness,* 200; Goen, "Editor's Introduction," 84.

The Crisis of Conversion

passion by assent through inner illumination to the divine source of life."[11] In this way, Knutson identifies Emerson's conductive imaginary as a "universal impulse to believe," a method which habituates individuals to a way of thinking "that moves them into experiencing the feeling of transcending the world of fact and the forces of doctrine, language, and history"; inviting his readers to "become natural philosophers of the soul, continually groping our definitions of the world and self as we engage in the project of incessant regeneration."[12]

Andrea Knutson's articulation of the development of the conductive imaginaries, particularly of Edwards and Emerson, provide a helpful framework that organizes the "advancing spirit" of American philosophy and literature around the nature and interpretation of experiences of religious conversion. This framework will help inform the following analysis of the phenomenology of religious experience more broadly in the work of Edwards and Emerson, which will help to contextualize the historical foundations of the contemporary crisis of conversion as outlined in the first chapter. Moreover, Edwards's and Emerson's status as representative American figures will help us flesh out the methodological implications of Sandra Schneiders's work in the field of Christian spirituality and the Pragmatist tradition's semiotics of religious experience from chapter two, that will be informative for my subsequent integration of religious experience and the future of evangelical spirituality via Amos Yong's pneumatological imagination in the concluding chapter.

In the remainder of the chapter, I will contextualize a major vein of the North American theological and spiritual tradition concerning the intersection of theological aesthetics, and the human experience of God. This relationship serves as one of the cornerstones of contemporary Christian spirituality studies. Contextualizing the work of Edwards and Emerson within the field of spirituality is beneficial for my purposes for at least a couple of reasons; first, as we saw in the previous chapter with the work of Sandra Schneiders, spirituality studies takes the category of lived human experience of the divine as its central point of departure for analyzing and studying the nature and history of spirituality; second, and perhaps more importantly, Christian spirituality studies stands at a critical, though by no means necessarily oppositional, tension with the normative claims of dogmatic, doctrinal, and systematic systems of Western philosophy in general and Christian theology in particular.[13] That

---

11. Gelpi, *Endless Seeker*, 9.

12. Knutson, *American Spaces*, 115, 11, 12–13.

13. See Sheldrake, *Spirituality and History*, 40–65. For a broad overview of the contours of the field of spirituality and its relationship to Christian theology and religious studies more broadly see Holder's excellent edited volume, *The Blackwell Companion to Christian Spirituality*.

is to say that Christian spirituality is intimately related but is not strictly limited to the traditions of practice and systems of belief of official theological and ecclesial structures.[14] As will be argued below, both Edwards and Emerson were deeply involved in these conversations and to a large extent offer novel approaches to the tension between the individual and community.

To that end, I will begin with an analysis of Edwards's view of religious experience and its normative dimension for the category of human experience as a whole. Here, I will ultimately argue that religious experience is for Edwards a phenomenologically observable reality that carries with it significant ontological and aesthetic implications. Secondly, I will argue that Emerson, a leading public intellectual in the United States and central figure in the Transcendentalist movement of the nineteenth century, continued Edwards's work concerning the aesthetic and normative dimensions of religious experience. However, Emerson who was ordained as a Unitarian minister in Boston's Second Church, eventually left the ministry in 1832 to embark on a philosophical, theological, and spiritual journey that would have tremendous influence on religious thought and practice in America right up to this very day. Thus, the manner in which Emerson uses Edwards's aesthetic foundations leads to rather different conclusions, particularly as it relates to the question of the individual and the community. Therefore I will try to bring some clarity to the effect of Emerson's scholarship in relationship to the landscape of contemporary Christian spirituality studies, around the spiritual potential of nature. When placed in conversation with one another, both Edwards and Emerson provide distinct yet complementary models for recovering a more robust and fruitful notion of the human experience of God that helps contextualize the North American tradition of religious experience as inherited through the North American Pragmatist tradition analyzed in the previous chapter. Moreover, the work of these two seminal figures provided the historical, theological, and spiritual roots of the contemporary crisis of conversion discussed in the first chapter.

The Historical Development of Edwards Thought on Religious Experience

Jonathan Edwards (1703–1758) remains a central figure in North American Christian theology. His appeal to scholars of all stripes, from conservative

14. Sandra Schneiders has made important contributions to this particular relationship by arguing persuasively for a methodologically distinct discipline for the study of Christian spirituality in particular as distinct from theology. See specifically, Schneiders, "Theology and Spirituality"; Schneiders, "Spirituality in the Academy"; and Schneiders, "Horizons on Spirituality."

The Crisis of Conversion

Reformed Calvinists to Arminians, liberal Protestants and even Roman Catholic theologians, attests to his particular genius. This eclectic following however, also points to an elusive quality in properly situating his legacy. Is Edwards a pillar of neo-Calvinism,[15] the last Puritan preaching hellfire and brimstone,[16] or a precursor to Modern social ethicists?[17] Moreover, how is Edwards to be properly understood in relationship to his early Enlightenment context? Is Edwards more appropriately seen as a great defender of Christian orthodoxy against the "new philosophy" of Enlightenment deism,[18] a sympathetic Enlightenment philosopher attempting to bring the best thinking of his day to bear on the grand tradition of Christianity,[19] or rather a bridge figure, with points of connection with a variety of contexts and communities?[20] While attempting to definitively settle Edwards's legacy is well beyond the scope of this chapter, these questions help contextualize the work of Jonathan Edwards in relationship to my central point of concern, namely, the issue of spirituality for Evangelical Christianity. Moreover, that these questions, among many others, remain unsettled among recent scholarship suggests that we are in the midst of a resurgence of interest in Edwards.[21] Despite this fact, his cultural-religious influence has become somewhat obscured and remains only implicitly present, if present at all, in the contemporary North American religious ethos.[22] Nevertheless, I find that Edwards develops a phenomenology of religious experience that is informative and constructive for contemporary Evangelical spirituality.

---

15. Caldwell, *Communion in the Spirit*; Crisp, *Jonathan Edwards*.

16. Brand, *Profile of the Last Puritan*.

17. Fiering, *Jonathan Edwards's Moral Thought*.

18. Holmes, *God of Grace and God of Glory*.

19. Miller, "Jonathan Edwards to Emerson," 589–617; Miller, "Jonathan Edwards on the Sense of the Heart," 123–45.

20. McClymond and McDermott, *Theology of Jonathan Edwards*, 22.

21. Schwanda, *Emergence of Evangelical Spirituality*; Hastings, *Jonathan Edwards and the Life of God*; Crisp, *Jonathan Edwards on God and Creation*; McClymond, *Encounters with God*; Withrow, *Becoming Divine*; McDermott, *Understanding Jonathan Edwards*.

22. See one notable exception to this trend is the Neo-Calvinism of the "young, restless, Reformed" movement within contemporary Evangelicalism that continues to popularize and synthesize elements of Jonathan Edwards's thought to lay audiences through the work of pastor/theologian John Piper, and his Desiring God network; http://www.desiringgod.org/topics/jonathan-edwards; Nichols et al., *God Entranced Vision of All Things*; Piper and Edwards, *God's Passion for His Glory*; Piper, *Captive to Glory*; Piper, *Supremacy of God in Preaching*.

Setting the Context: Edwards and Religious Experience

Jonathan Edwards was born in East Windsor, Connecticut in 1703 to the Reverend Timothy Edwards and Esther Stoddard Edwards, the only son of eleven children. His father, Timothy, was the pastor of the church in East Windsor, and his mother, Esther, was the daughter of Solomon Stoddard, the pastor of Northampton, Massachusetts, who Jonathan would later succeed as pastor during the Great Awakening of the 1730s and 1740s. Timothy Edwards played an influential role in a series of early awakenings between 1712 and 1713, which would occasion for the young nine year old Jonathan the first of a series of spiritual experiences that would culminate in his religious conversion in 1721. These early experiences also mark the beginning of his increasing interest in the nature of religious experience, personally and professionally, that would remain throughout the rest of his life. Edwards wrote a spiritual autobiography about his conversion in *Personal Narrative* written in 1740 during the height of the Great Awakening in the Connecticut Valley, though it was not published until after his death in 1765.

While Edwards would come to be associated primarily with his central leadership during the Great Awakening, and the many writings, sermons, and letters he wrote in defense of the revivalistic conversions taking place across New England, he was concerned with and wrote often about various theological, philosophical, and spiritual issues related to religious experience and its relationship to the reality of God throughout his life, before, during, and after the revivals. To help situate Edwards's life in relation to the development of his thought concerning religious experience, I distinguish three phases of his life; namely his Yale period as a child struggling with his own experience of conversion as a student and subsequently a tutor at Yale from 1712–1726; secondly, the Northampton period from 1726–1742 when his pastorate began under the tutelage of his grandfather, Solomon Stoddard, and lasting through the height of the Great Awakening; thirdly, the Awakenings period from 1742–1758 with his revival sermons preached during this time that would eventually become *A Treatise Concerning Religious Affections* published in 1746, to his death in 1758. These three phases represent a loose framework within which we can organize Edwards's work; but these phases should not be seen as mutually exclusive nor should they be seen as representing major shifts in his thinking. Three examples help to show the fluidity of these phases. First, his religious conversion, begun in 1712 and culminating in 1721 in the early Yale period, would serve to ground his later reflections on religious conversion during the Awakenings period, particularly his writing of *Personal Narrative* in 1740. Second, though begun during the Yale period, Edwards's important collection

The Crisis of Conversion

of notes on the philosophy of the mind continued well into the Awakenings phase, and moreover he uses this material in writings published in both the Northampton and Awakenings phases.[23] Lastly, his tenure at the Church in Northampton marks the beginning of his Northampton period, but he would remain in Northampton until 1750, seven years into his Awakenings phase and he would continue to preach on occasion in Northampton as late as October of 1757. In summary, these three phases help to highlight the interplay between the intellectual development of Edwards's philosophical, pastoral, and theological thought as each phase represents a new context and new set of concerns to which Edwards would respond. Although Edwards was an occasional writer rather than a systematic thinker in the traditional sense, there does emerge throughout these phases certain organizing principles that reveal an underlying continuity in Edwards's thought, even as he matured in his thinking along several points related in particular to the articulation and defense of authentic religious affections.[24] Two of these underlying principles that were consistently central in Edwards's writings were a metaphysical theocentric determinism in line with his Calvinist Puritan heritage; and closely connected to this, a theological aesthetics that informed his understanding of our knowledge of God and the dynamics of religious conversion.

Throughout his intellectual development, Edwards identifies a close relationship between the aesthetic nature of God (and by virtue of his deterministic framework, of the nature of reality itself) and the role of human experience in interpreting the world in which we inhabit. In this section, I will flesh out the development of his thought concerning theological aesthetics and human experience by showing how his thought matured yet remained on the whole consistent from his Yale period, through the Northampton and Awakenings period. In particular, his early notebooks "On the Mind" and "The Miscellanies," begun during his Yale period, provide a foundation from which he would work out his mature thought concerning the ethical normativity of human experience in *The End for which God Created the World*, and *The Nature of True Virtue* (c. 1755, published posthumously in 1765 together as *Two Dissertations*),[25] as well as Edwards's arguably most famous and important work, *Religious Affections* (1746). In these works, representing his mature thought, Edwards works out a phenomenological defense of the validity of

---

23. Anderson, "Editor's Introduction," in *WJE*, 6:1–37.

24. McClymond and McDermott, *Theology of Jonathan Edwards*, 113.

25. These works have at times been published as individual volumes, but as Paul Ramsey has persuasively argued in his "Editor's introduction" to *WJE*, 8, these two essays were intended to be published together as a single volume with two parts as several key arguments in *True Virtue* expand and depend on points developed in *The End*. Ramsey, "Editor's Introduction" *WJE*, 8:5–9.

religious experience as a means of highlighting the normative claim of religious conversion on a person's life (primarily in *Religious Affections*), as well as his thinking on the relationship between ontology and experience (primarily in *The End for Which God Created the World*), and the ontological implications of normative religious experience on human society in general (primarily in *The Nature of True Virtue*). I will begin with Edwards's own conversion experience as a spring board to analyze his understanding of the relationship between experience and ontology which, in turn, provides the normative dimension of his theological aesthetics. From there, I will then proceed to consider the aesthetics of religious experience, and finally conclude with a treatment of the normative dimension of aesthetic experience which emerges in Edwards's mature writings on the human experience of God.

Edward's Conversion and the "Sense of the Heart"

As mentioned above, Edwards's first earnest experiences related to his conversion began around 1712–1713, during a time of "remarkable awakening" at his father's church in East Windsor. Edwards, it seems, was caught up in the enthusiasm of the revivals and recounts in his *Personal Narrative* that he would "pray five times a day in secret, and . . . spend much time in religious talk with other boys."[26] Edwards and his friends had constructed a secret prayer booth in the woods, and Edwards had for himself an additional secret place where he alone would go off to pray, a common enough practice for religiously concerned Puritans in the seventeenth and eighteenth centuries, as Tom Schwanda notes.[27] In these early stirrings, Edwards recounts that his religious fervor and the perception of religious affections was very great within him. "My affections seemed to be lively and easily moved, and I seemed to be in my element, when engaged in religious duties."[28] However, Edwards would soon find himself losing interest in these affections, which he had at the time mistaken as the true gracious presence of God. After these early affections wore off, there were several intervening years where Edwards "returned like a dog to his vomit, and went on in ways of sin."[29] These early affections and intervening years conform to the standard Puritan *ordo salutis*, of a spiritually immature person attempting to manufacture their own conversion by means of mere human effort that didn't last, but nevertheless serve as preparatory

---

26. Edwards, *WJE*, 16:790.
27. Tom Schwanda, "Spiritual Practices: Introduction," 153.
28. Edwards, *WJE*, 16:791.
29. Edwards, *WJE*, 16:791.

The Crisis of Conversion

signs that one is on the path toward regeneration.[30] However, it is important to keep in mind that at these stages the outcome of one's conversion was very much unsettled; as we saw in Knutson, this provided the tension between the uncertainty of one's experiences on the one hand, and the certainty of the nature of the covenant between God and human persons on the other that would fuel Edwards's social imaginary of religious conversion.[31] The eminent historian of early American colonial religion, Edmund Morgan, summarizes the Puritan *ordo salutis* into three broad movements:

> First comes a feeble and false awakening to God's commands and a pride in keeping them, but also much backsliding . . . . Sooner or later a true legal fear or conviction enables the individual to see his hopeless and helpless condition and to know that his own righteousness cannot save him, and that Christ is the only hope. Thereafter comes the infusion of saving grace, sometimes but not always so precisely felt that the believer can state exactly when and where it came to him. A struggle between faith and doubt ensues, with the candidate careful to indicate that his assurance has never been complete and that his sanctification has been much hampered by his own sinful heart.[32]

The intervening years between Edwards's initial affections and his experience in 1721 that signaled his conversion were a period of "great and violent inward struggles," whereby he "made seeking my salvation the main business of my life."[33] This period of striving came to a head in the summer of 1721 in three closely connected stages while Edwards was back home in East Windsor from his graduate studies at Yale. Of chief concern for Edwards during this period of struggle and striving was the doctrine of God's sovereignty, a consistent element in Puritan preparations for conversion. He would first come to be intellectually "convinced, and fully satisfied, as to this sovereignty of God, and his justice in thus eternally disposing of men, according to his sovereign pleasure."[34] This conviction however was at the time purely a rational assent to the doctrine. Secondly, while reflecting on 1 Timothy 1:17,[35] Edwards recounts: "there came into my soul, and was as it were diffused through it, a sense of the glory of the divine being; a new sense, quite different from anything I

---

30. Marsden, *Jonathan Edwards*, 25–26; Goen, "Editor's Introduction," 25–26.
31. Knutson, *American Spaces*, 58–59.
32. Morgan, *Visible Saints*, 91.
33. Edwards, *WJE*, 16:791.
34. Edwards, *WJE*, 16:792.
35. "To the King of the ages, immortal, invisible, the only God, be honor and glory forever and ever. Amen" (1 Tim 1:17 NRSV).

ever experienced before . . . . how excellent a Being that was . . . and prayed in a manner quite different from what I used to do; with a new sort of affection."[36] Yet even here, where Edwards's rational consent to God's sovereignty became attached to the idea of the enjoyment of God, it remained merely a possibility for Edwards as he was still experientially disconnected from that enjoyment. He longingly contemplated, "how happy I should be, if I might enjoy that God, and be wrapt up to God in heaven, and be as it were swallowed up in him."[37] Finally, Edwards experiences for himself this enjoyment of God's sovereignty during a walk through his father's pasture, in perhaps the most famous passage of his *Personal Narrative*:

> And as I was walking there, and looked up on the sky and clouds; there came into my mind, a sweet sense of the glorious majesty and grace of God, that I know not how to express. I seemed to see them both in a sweet conjunction: majesty and meekness joined together: it was a sweet and gentle, and holy majesty; and also a majestic meekness; an awful sweetness; a high, and great, and holy gentleness.
>
> After this my sense of divine things gradually increased, and became more and more lively, and had more of that inward sweetness. The appearance of everything was altered: there seemed to be, as it were, a calm, sweet cast, or appearance of divine glory, in almost everything.
>
> God's excellency, his wisdom, his purity and love, seemed to appear in everything; in the sun, moon and stars; in the clouds, and blue sky; in the grass, flowers, trees; in the water, and all nature; which used greatly to fix my mind. I often used to sit and view the moon, for a long time; and so in the daytime, spent much time in viewing the clouds and sky, to behold the sweet glory of God in these things: in the meantime, singing forth with a low voice, my contemplations of the Creator and Redeemer. And scarce anything, among all the works of nature, was so sweet to me as thunder and lightning. Formerly, nothing had been so terrible to me. I used to be a person uncommonly terrified with thunder: and it used to strike me with terror, when I saw a thunderstorm rising. But now, on the contrary, it rejoiced me. I felt God at the first appearance of a thunderstorm. And used to take the opportunity at such times, to fix myself to view the clouds, and see the lightnings play, and hear the majestic and awful voice of God's thunder:

36. Edwards, *WJE*, 16:792–93.
37. Edwards, *WJE*, 16:792.

The Crisis of Conversion

> which often times was exceeding entertaining, leading me to sweet contemplations of my great and glorious God.[38]

Here we see the culmination of nearly two decades of Edwards's spiritual striving towards his conversion. From the experience itself, both in the gradual progression over nearly two decades, as well as this climactic episode, there is a general conformity with the Puritan morphology of conversion as articulated above by Morgan. Moreover, as C. C. Goen argues in his introduction to the *Great Awakenings* volume of the *WJE* series, under Edwards's leadership and theological defense of the awakenings, this morphology of conversion would "become normative in the evangelical churches; and as the revivalism then aborning brought those churches to dominance in American Christianity, this pattern of conversion came to be widely accepted as the normal mode of entry into the Christian life."[39] Goen's argument confirms John Markey's insight from chapter one, that this evangelical expression of conversion continues to be the default understanding across Protestant and Catholic Christianity in North America.[40]

At the same time, however, Edwards's conversion is not simply a recapitulation to earlier seventeenth-century Puritan understandings of conversion. Rather Edwards's reflections in the *Personal Narrative*, written nearly twenty years after the fact, reveal a subtle shift in emphasis, persuasively identified in Knutson's "conductive imaginary." This shift, as noted above, moved the locus of interpretation from an external appeal to a pre-determined covenant to the inner integration of the experiencing subject. In the final episode of Edwards's conversion process, we find the integration of first, the intellectual consent to the sovereignty of God followed by the consent of the will desiring to experience the delight of God's sovereignty, and lastly, an affective consent whereby he experiences the "sweet sense of the glorious majesty and grace of God."[41] Thus the rationalism of the earlier Puritan *ordo salutis* organized as it was covenantally between the elect in general and God, becomes for Edwards an *ordo salutis* organized experientially through the integration of the intellect, will, and affection of elect individuals and God; a process that Edwards would further clarify in his mature thought through the concept the "sense of the heart." While the exact phrase "sense of the heart" does not show up in the *Personal Narrative*, its composite aesthetic structure is embedded in his conversion experience and is used to interpret not only the experience itself,

---

38. Edwards, *WJE*, 16:793–94.
39. Goen, "Editor's Introduction," 26–27.
40. See Markey, *Moses In Pharaoh's House*, 10–11; and pp. 18–19 above.
41. Edwards, *WJE*, 16:793.

but also the nature and quality of God's self revelation in the experience of gracious affections. Edwards mentions a "new sense" or a "sense" related to the change in his experience of the glory, majesty, loveliness, etc., of God as either evidence for, or the manifestation of a result of his conversion, eighteen times in the *Personal Narrative,* and connected with that, the descriptor "sweet" in reference to the enjoyment or pleasureable quality of this new sense of God is mentioned fifty-two times.[42] Compare those statistics with his "Diary" that was begun in the immediate context of his conversion between December of 1722 and May of 1724, where "sense" is used only seven times, and only once in relationship to an experience of God, on December 22, 1722, where he was "Affected with the sense of the excellency of holiness."[43] More striking, is that "sweet" only shows up seven times as well in his "Diary," with only three of those used in a similar manner of describing an experience of God. Interestingly in the "Diary," even those three occurrences are used in a petition to God on May 1, 1723 that he might experience "sweet, calm, delightful love."[44]

If we widen our view and examine Edwards's entire corpus, we find a similar chronological development in terms of Edwards articulating the experience of the sovereignty of God using sense of the heart language. The earliest record of Edwards's use of the phrase is from an untitled and unpublished sermon, dated by Thomas A. Schafer in the Spring of 1728 on the text, II Cor. 3:18(a). There, Edwards teaches that "This sight of the Glory of [Christ] dont [sic] so much consist in the Imagination that it should seem to them as if they saw a visible shape or as if they saw a light with their bodily eyes tho [sic] When the heart is very much affected it often works upon the Imagination but it consists in the inward sense of the heart. He has an [sic] deep sense and impression Given him of the divine excellency of [Christ] he feels it with Power upon his heart."[45] Two other notable examples of early usage of sense of the heart are the popular sermon "A Divine and Supernatural Light" where the phrase is used four times (preached in August of 1733, and published in 1734), and once more in a sermon "False and True Light" (July 1734). In 1739-1740, Edwards uses sense of the heart six times in his notebook "The Miscellanies" twice in entry No. 732, and four times in the centrally important No. 782 (c.

---

42. "Sweet" is mentioned 57 times in total in the *Personal Narrative*, but five of them are in reference to fond reflections of certain congregants in New York, whom he had recently left, and so while they may indeed be referring to this same new sense, being kindled in Christian love, I wanted to focus more exclusively on Edwards's aesthetic language as it relates to experiences of the divine.

43. Edwards, *WJE,* 16:759.

44. Edwards, *WJE,* 16:768.

45. Edwards, *WJEO,* 43:72.

1739),[46] and a sermon "Seeking After Christ" (Dec. 1740). Edwards used the phrase three more times in the *Religious Affections* (1746), and twice more in the index for his "Notes on the Mind" (c. 1747). The latest usage provides an interesting parallel between Edwards's early "Diary" and the later reflections in *Personal Narrative*. Edwards's "Notes on the Mind" were written early during his Yale days as a student and tutor between 1717– 1723, and comprise a series of notes in semi-outline form of a book project that he left unfinished at the time of his death. Noticeably, there are no uses of "sense of the heart" in these original notes. However, Edwards returned to this project in 1747, and wrote out an alphabetical index of his earlier notes, and "sense of the heart" is included as one of the "Subjects to be Handled in The Treatise On The Mind" with a cross-reference to note 14 produced below:

> [14]. Excellence, to put it in other words, is that which is beautiful and lovely. That which is beautiful considered by itself separately, and deformed considered as a part of something else more extended; or beautiful only with respect to itself and a few other things, and not as a part of that which contains all things—the universe—is false beauty, and a confined beauty. That which is beautiful with respect to the university of things has a generally extended excellence and a true beauty; and the more extended or limited its system is, the more confined or extended is its beauty.[47]

The "sense of the heart" language is absent here in the original drafting of Note 14 in the early 1720's, the same as it is absent in the "Diary" and "Resolutions" of the mid 1720's; However, it does show up in Edwards's subsequent reflections on the Mind's appendix dated c. 1747, and the *Personal Narrative* of 1740. This corroborates the work of Ava Chamberlain and Perry Miller who situate the central Miscellany No. 738, and its substantive commentary on the sense of the heart, to have been written between 1739 and 1745[48], and further suggests that Edwards's own understanding of religious experience was undergoing a significant development as the Great Awakening progressed through the 1730s and 1740s.

---

46. Perry Miller's groundbreaking publication of Misc. 782 in his article "Jonathan Edwards on the Sense of the Heart," brought much needed attention to the central philosophical, and theological role that the sense of the heart had for Edwards as his thought matured through his involvement with the Great Awakenings.

47. Edwards, *WJE*, 6:389.

48. Perry Miller suggested a later date of 1745 for this entry, putting it roughly in the same time period that Edwards was completing the *Religious Affections*. However, Ava Chamberlain, in her introduction to *WJE*, 18, has argued persuasively I think, for an earlier date around 1739. Chamberlain, "Editor's Introduction," in Edwards, *WJE*, 18:23.

This development, at least in part, points to the increasing importance of philosophical and theological aesthetics in Edwards's thought. For both Edwards's conversion experience, and the "Notes on the Mind" there is a near synonymous identification with his later reflections on the sense of the heart with the earlier material utilizing aesthetic categories; whether that is the "sweetness" of his experience of conversion, or the "Excellence/Beauty" of his Notes 14. Moreover, Edwards's interest in aesthetics was not limited to his thoughts related to religious experience, but as Roland Delattre has persuasively argued, aesthetics was central to Edwards's philosophical, theological, and ethical development as well, what Delattre calls Edwards's "first principle of being."[49]

Edwards on Aesthetics, the Nature of God, and Human Experience

In 1723, after receiving his master's degree in theology from Yale, Edwards began a series of notes on the philosophy of the mind that laid the foundation for much of his later and more matured thought. Alongside these "Notes on the Mind," as they are called, during this same time Edwards began a separate and significantly more substantial collection of notes entitled "The Miscellanies." While the Miscellanies cover the entire spectrum of Edwards intellectual life related to biblical exegesis, and sermon preparation, as well as theological and philosophical musings which often served as outlines for later manuscripts, the "Notes on the Mind" are a more sustained though still informal discussion on metaphysics and ontology.

"One alone," Edwards writes in note 1 on the mind, "without any reference to any more, cannot be excellent; for in such case there can be no manner of relation no way, and therefore, no such thing as consent."[50] Excellence and consent are two of Edwards's most important concepts and serve as the key in many ways for interpreting Edwards's work as a whole. Excellence and consent are rooted in Edwards's ontology as well as his aesthetics, which in turn will become central in the development of his thought regarding the nature of human experience. For Edwards, beauty, often used interchangeably with the term excellency, is the highest category and first principle of being and thus all being is understood and experienced primarily through the structures of beauty.[51] Beauty for Edwards consists in "similarness, or identity of relation"[52]

49. Delattre, *Beauty and Sensibility*, 1–2.
50. Edwards, *WJE*, 6:337.
51. Delattre, "Aesthetics and Ethics," 277–97.
52. Edwards, *WJE*, 6:334.

and excellency "consists in the similarness of one being to another,"[53] which is ultimately understood as "The consent of being to being, or being's consent to entity."[54] Unsurprisingly, Edwards places God at the top of the chain of being stating, "God is proper entity itself, and these two [that is, excellency and consent] therefore in him become the same; for so far as a thing consents to being in general, so far it consents to him."[55] It is important to note that God is not above or prior to being as such, which here is comprised of both consent and excellency, but rather *is* precisely infinite excellency and infinite consent. Miscellany no. 117 makes this point rather explicitly: "Therefore, if God be excellent, there must be a plurality in God; otherwise there can be no consent in him."[56] The implications of Edwards's dynamic ontology as outlined here would not be fully developed theologically until after he began his pastorate in Northampton.

Instead, during this time, his work concerning the doctrine of God and pneumatology followed predictable Western, Augustinian, and Reformed trajectories. One of his more common analogies during this period is that the three distinctions within God are God, which is the Father, his idea of himself, which is the Son, and his love or delight, which is the Spirit.[57] With respect to the Spirit more specifically, Edwards in this early phase attaches beauty and its composites consent and excellency to the particularity of the Holy Spirit. Miscellany no. 293 written in 1726 reads as follows: "It was more especially the Holy Spirit's work to bring the world to its beauty and perfection out of the chaos, for the beauty of the world is a communication of God's beauty."[58] For Edwards, at this early stage, the Holy Spirit was most properly the beauty, and therefore the excellency and consent of the divine essence, as it pertained to the Trinitarian distinctions within the Divine essence. What is at issue here is that the properties of beauty for Edwards are particular to the Person of the Spirit and come logically after the divine essence itself rather than as the previous note from "The Mind" suggested as constitutive of God in God's essential unity. We see clearly that Edwards is continuing the long tradition of the Western Church positing that the Spirit properly serves, as Augustine suggested, as the bond of love between the Son and Father which forms the "primary" relation of the Godhead, as

---

53. Edwards, *WJE*, 6:336.
54. Edwards, *WJE*, 6:336.
55. Edwards, *WJE*, 6:337.
56. Edwards, *WJE*, 13:284.
57. Edwards, *WJE*, 13:392–93.
58. Edwards, *WJE*, 13:384.

it were.[59] Edwards was concerned from the very beginning in reinforcing the relevance of the doctrine of the Trinity, and in particular the role of the Holy Spirit, as a central component not only of Christian orthodoxy, but as an integral part of the economy of salvation, a believer's personal conversion experience, and the continued spiritual life of the saints.

We may now move on to the second phase of Edward's thinking concerning the Holy Spirit between the start of his Northampton pastorate and the height of the Great Awakening and the beginning of his preaching a series of sermons that would eventually become the *Religious Affections* (1729–1742). It was during this period that Edwards began his "Discourse on the Trinity" which he apparently intended to publish as a complete manuscript, but was however never completed and only published posthumously.[60] Nevertheless, in the "Discourse" we see Edwards integrating his relational ontology begun in "The Mind" with his Trinitarian understanding of the Holy Spirit that reveals a more dynamically social model of the immanent Trinity analogous to but not derived from the models of Eastern Christianity. The "Discourse" is an extended reflection on 1 John 4:7–21, that God is love which according to Edwards, "shows that there are more persons than one in the Deity: for it shows love to be essential and necessary to the Deity, so that his nature consists in it."[61] Here we find Edwards not only continuing to stress the plurality of the persons of the Godhead but we see a shift in emphasis that places the dynamic reality that is love as that which the divine nature consists in. It is in this crucial development that Edwards begins to reorganize his Trinitarian thinking, starting from a notion of reality that is fundamentally plural in nature.

The Trinitarian distinctions do not result in a tri-theistic view of God, but rather reinforce what is the essence of the Divine nature, a dynamic and relational love. This dynamic essence then is inclined to communicate itself, as Edwards argues in Miscellany 107. By combining his original insight of a fundamentally relational ontology, with his identification of beauty as the first category of Being, along with our second exploration of the notion of divine

---

59. See Robert Caldwell's analysis of Edwards's Trinitarian theology that confirms this Western, and Augustinian interpretation of Edwards's theology; Caldwell, *Communion in the Spirit*, 21–29. However, Caldwell ultimately fails to see the continued development of Edwards's trinitarian thought that enlarges the Western traditions exclusive focus on psychological analogies also include social analogies of the Trinity as well. See the dialogue between Amy Plantinga Pauw and Steve Studebaker on this point; Pauw, *Supreme Harmony of All*; Studebaker, "Jonathan Edwards' Trinitarian Theology," 281–301; Studebaker, "Jonathan Edwards's Social Augustinian Trinitarianism," 268–85; Studebaker, "Supreme Harmony or Supreme Disharmony?," 479–85; Pauw, "Response," 486–89.

60. Lee, "Discourse on the Trinity" in Edwards, *WJE*, 21:109.

61. Edwards, *WJE*, 21:114.

beauty, that is excellency and consent, we can now move to the third phase in Edwards thought concerning religious experience more explicitly.

In this final phase (1742–1758), we find an integration of the Immanent and Economic Trinity through the category of human experience. Motivated by the strange and surprising movement of the Holy Spirit that began to sweep through the New England colonies, Edwards sought to defend the often-dramatic conversion experiences that accompanied these awakenings from more conservative detractors keen on preserving the doctrinal purity of Puritan public piety as well as to critique more radical individuals who viewed affective responses themselves as guarantees of a person's conversion.

A Treatise Concerning Religious Affections is impressive in its own right as an exposition into the psychology and phenomenology of religious experience; we are however here most interested in Edwards's rather unique contribution concerning the experience of God through the Holy Spirit. "True religion," Edwards claims, "must consist very much in the affections."[62] And the affections are for Edwards the spring and foundation of all human action. Or to put it another way, "Nothing is more manifest in fact, than that the things of religion take hold of men's [and women's] souls, no further than they affect them."[63] For Edwards, the fundamental distinction between true religious affections and all other affections is the communication of the divine essence itself via the real indwelling of the Holy Spirit in the soul of a given person. Ultimately, it was God, communicating his own proper (immanent) nature that is the essential and necessary foundation for authentic religious affection and true Christian conversion.

Here Edwards combines his aesthetic ontology with God's *ad extra* communication of himself through the indwelling of the Holy Spirit through the sense of the heart, bringing together the mind, will, and affective faculties of the human person into one holistic reality where a person experiences "the supreme beauty and sweetness of the holiness or moral perfection of divine things, together with all that discerning and knowledge of things of religion, that depends on, and flows from such sense."[64] Connected with this sense of the heart is another corollary term, a new spiritual principle, which is the indwelling of the Spirit within the person thereby creating a new source of influence and foundational nature for the individual. This supernatural principle of nature interacts with the sense of the heart in an entirely distinct manner than the natural operations of mind, will, and affections of human persons. And while this spiritual principle of nature and sense of the heart are not new

---

62. Edwards, *WJE*, 2:100.
63. Edwards, *WJE*, 2:100.
64. Edwards, *WJE*, 2:272.

faculties, they nevertheless operate in a categorically different manner from what is properly natural to human persons. The difference is precisely the reality of the Holy Spirit present in the life of the individual. Edwards writes; "The Spirit of God so dwells in the hearts of the saints, that he there, as a seed or spring of life, exerts and communicates himself, in this his sweet and divine nature, making the soul a partaker of God's beauty and Christ's joy."[65]

Thus like we saw from the early Edwards, Beauty here is intimately connected to Being. God is ultimately Beauty itself. The difference that in the end really matters concerning one's religious experience is the real presence, quality, and degree of God's beauty in the experience. In this way, throughout the *Religious Affections,* Edwards is able to make vital distinctions between affections that are not necessarily true religious affections, and those principles that are essential to authentic religious affection. Aesthetics, then, becomes not some tertiary matter of individualistic taste or bourgeois cultural expression, but rather serves as the ground for which human persons come into the knowledge of and a relationship with God. Because of this, through Edwards's notion of beauty as "Being's consent to Being,"[66] and his rather sophisticated work concerning the structures of beauty, he has made the aesthetic dimension of religious experience itself a foundational element of the social expression of the Christian life and thus integrated into the life of Christian community's faith and practice through the indwelling of the Holy Spirit. The Holy Spirit is the communicated beauty of God's loving reality, and furthermore serves as the seal of consent between humanity and God.

We must now move to take up the question of the relationship between Edwards's understanding of human experience in general and religious experience in particular with the question of normativity raised above. That is, how does Edwards's mature thought concerning the relationship between the human experiences of the beauty of God through the Holy Spirit interact with the normative dimension of one's conversion experience?

The Norming Aesthetics of Religious Experience

As has already been stated above, Edwards closely identified aesthetics with ontology in what Roland Delattre calls Edwards's "first principle of being."[67] Moreover, aesthetics is very much in the center of Edwards's understanding of human experience, particularly religious experience. However, what remains

65. Edwards, *WJE,* 2:201.
66. Edwards, *WJE,* 6:336.
67. Delattre, *Beauty and Sensibility,* 1–2.

to be seen is how Edwards relates aesthetics and ontology in the lived-reality of human existence.

For all of the relations between primary and secondary beauty, natural and religious affections, and rational versus affective knowing, Edwards maintains a consistent and firm distinction between their natural or secondary realities on the one hand, and their transcendent or primary realities on the other. We will proceed "from below" as it were, and work from the natural/secondary relations up to the transcendent/primary relations, which is of course the exact opposite order in which they interact according to Edwards, in order to establish more clearly the issue of normativity which will form the conclusion of this analysis.

The subordinate position of these secondary categories should not be thought of as them being less real or somehow ontologically contingent on their primary corollaries for existence. Rather, both the primary and secondary relations are equally and immediately contingent upon God for their existence. The difference is the mode or manner in which the primary and secondary relations are contingent rather than the degree or the ontological prioritization of one over the other. Where the primary relations relate to God through concepts such as the sense of the heart, true virtue, and excellency; the secondary relations relate to God through concepts such as harmony, consent, virtue, and fittingness. Moreover, the primary relations are "over" the secondary ones in that those realities that operate according to the primary relations more perfectly embody or participate in the reality of God than do the secondary relations.[68] Additionally, all beings that have primary relations also have secondary relations, however, the reverse is not necessarily true.

These primary and secondary categories operate in several spheres of Edwards's thought. In aesthetics, Edwards distinguishes sharply between primary beauty (of which only intelligent and spiritual beings have access to) and secondary beauty (that beauty which relates to world of things and nature). For both primary beauty and secondary beauty, Edwards uses the notion of consent to elaborate on the dynamics of their relationships. Consent for primary beauty "consists in concord and union of mind and heart,"[69] whereas consent for secondary beauty which consists "only in uniformity and consent of nature, form, quantity, etc."[70] Additionally, Edwards makes a distinction between general and particular beauty. General beauty is that beauty "by which a thing appears beautiful when viewed most perfectly, comprehensively and universally, with regard to all its tendencies, and its connections with every

68. McClymond and McDermott, *Theology of Jonathan Edwards*, 112–15.
69. Edwards, *WJE*, 8:565.
70. Edwards, *WJE*, 8:565.

thing to which it stands related."[71] And particular beauty is that beauty "by which a thing appears beautiful when considered only with regard to its connection with, and tendency to, some particular things within a limited, and as it were a private sphere."[72] Consent according to primary and secondary beauty are both operative for general and particular beauty for Edwards, as the later distinction is in reference to the scope of beauty whereas the former distinction is in terms of the mode of beauty.[73]

As we saw in the previous section concerning the development of Edwards's thought with regard to the nature of human experience, consent is the key for understanding Edwards's dynamic ontology. Interestingly, Edwards uses the structure of consent to bring together aesthetics and ontology on the one hand and ethics on the other. Virtue, or more precisely true virtue, is for Edwards the highest and ideal expression of ethics. Ultimately, for Edwards, true virtue is the "communication of God's holiness; so that hereby the creature partakes of God's own moral excellency, which is properly the beauty of the divine nature."[74] According to Edwards, this communication of God's own virtue, holiness, moral excellency, and beauty is properly seen as an enlargement of Godself in order to allow for human persons to "partake of him, and [rejoice] in himself expressed in them, and communicated to them."[75] The communication of Godself to the world is expressed via true virtue which is for Edwards "that consent, propensity and union of heart to being in general, which is immediately exercised in a general good will."[76] This communication of God's own nature forms the objective ground of the reciprocal and subjective response of consent from the human person towards true virtue.[77] It is objective precisely because the communication of virtue, as we have already seen with aesthetics in general is rooted in the ontology of God's reality; for "what is communicated is divine, or something of God: and each communication is of that nature, that the creature to whom it is made, is thereby conformed to God, and united to him."[78]

On the other side stands the subject of this divine communication. The subject, according to the nature and dynamics of consent, is not a passive participant in this exchange but rather is actively engaged through his

71. Edwards, *WJE*, 8:540.
72. Edwards, *WJE*, 8:540.
73. Spohn, "Union and Consent with the Great Whole," 21–22.
74. Edwards, *WJE*, 8:442.
75. Edwards, *WJE*, 8:461.
76. Edwards, *WJE*, 8:540.
77. Delattre, *Beauty and Sensibility*, 156.
78. Edwards, *WJE*, 8:442.

or her own consent towards a second major term for Edwards, benevolence. Nearly echoing what we have seen over and again in Edwards's writings, "pure benevolence in its first exercise is nothing else but being's uniting, consent, or propensity to Being."[79] Benevolence, however, is not synonymous with consent, but rather, is expressed through the interior reception of either the secondary delight of beauty (what Edwards terms complacence) or more properly, the primary love of Being (which is true benevolence). Thus there is an added dimension of "value" here, where the subject's consent occurs not only at the level of external ontological or natural relations but also at the level of inner apprehension, appreciation, and appropriation of the beauty of Being. Or in other words, there is in some sense an affinity towards the object of benevolence/complacence as something desirable in itself which in turn is experienced as beautiful or lovely by the subject.[80]

The close correlation between the dynamics of consent and benevolence on the one hand and Edwards's ontological basis for aesthetics and ethics on the other highlight the importance of the category of human experience for Edwards. Experience, or what Edwards refers to as "participation" is an essential component to his thought, even though he does not give much attention to the concept directly in his writings. Nevertheless, in "Notes on the Mind," a running journal that Edwards kept Edwards makes it clear that a "being's consent to being must needs be agreeable to perceiving being . . . because itself is a participation of being in general." That is, the notion of consent necessarily implies a participation in (or experience of) the reality being consented to. This holds true as well for Edwards's aesthetics and ethics. Thus it is not accidental that Edwards places aesthetics and ethics, as well as religious experience as we will see below, strictly under ontology, which is ultimately none other than the Being of God himself. In this way then, the category of human experience underlies the whole of Edwards's thought, for without the subject's participation in the object through consent his entire metaphysical and theological structure would collapse.

In the immediately preceding discussion, I argued that human experience in general is for Edwards ultimately aesthetic and ontological in nature. This holds true in a particular way as well for his view of religious experience. However, whereas Edwards made a general distinction between primary and secondary relations within his aesthetics and to some degree within his ethics as well, the same does not hold true for religious experience. Rather, Edwards takes the general distinction he maintained between the limited nature of virtue and the comprehensive nature of true virtue, from which he ultimately

---

79. Edwards, *WJE*, 8:546.
80. Delattre, *Beauty and Sensibility*, 94–99.

argued that all virtue in the final analysis is either true virtue or not virtue at all, and expands it for the nature of religious experience.[81] Thus Edwards argues that religious experience is distinguished from human experience in general as virtue is distinguished from true virtue. That in the end, and strictly from his onto-aesthetic perspective, for Edwards, the only ultimately real experience is in some sense religious experience.[82]

With that being said however, Edwards makes a very clear distinction between explicitly religious experiences of God, famously called true religious affections, and all other experiences of reality (even of God) that are not explicitly or legitimately religious in nature. These religious affections are indeed at the very center of the Christian faith itself for as Edwards contends, "[nothing] is more manifest in fact, than that the things of religion take hold of men's souls, no further than they affect them."[83] The distinction then between religious affections and all other experiences of God is, as would be expected, aesthetic in nature.

Very early on in his ministry during 1723 Edwards wrote a sermon "A Spiritual Understanding of Divine Things Denied to the Unregenerate (1 Corinthians 2:14)" that introduced several important insights that Edwards would continue to develop throughout his life. In this sermon he identified a fundamental difference between a "notional" knowledge of God and a "spiritual" knowledge of God.[84] The difference lies in the lack of a sensible perception of the beauty, amiableness and excellency in the notional knowledge of God that the spiritual knowledge of God contains. Secondly, Edwards introduces an experiential dimension to this difference between the notional and spiritual knowledge of God, by comparing the two ways of knowing with the analogy of the difference between knowing that honey is sweet and actually tasting the sweetness of honey which is experienced aesthetically as either enjoyment or disgust of the taste of it.[85] And lastly, in this sermon Edwards introduces the different effects that spiritual knowledge produces within a believer that mere notional knowledge does not produce for a "natural" person. These

---

81. Edwards, *WJE*, 8:540.

82. This of course is not to say that individual people do not experience through the course of their lives genuinely natural or non-religious realities, but that from the onto-aesthetic dimension of Edwards metaphysics, even those things are related in some way to Being in General, or God, and thus of a religious quality in one manner or another. In this way, Edwards is also able to take up the problem of evil and sin and reconcile it within his theocentric metaphysics. See his two seminal works on this issue *Original Sin* and *The Freedom of The Will*.

83. Edwards, *WJE*, 2:101.

84. Edwards, *WJE*, 14:74.

85. Edwards, *WJE*, 14:76.

different effects are: (1) spiritual knowledge transforms the heart; (2) spiritual knowledge purifies the believer's life towards obedience to Christ; (3) spiritual knowledge includes a holy joy regarding the things of God; (4) spiritual knowledge cultivates humility.[86] Taken together, these early remarks from Edwards lay the foundation for the aesthetic and ontological arguments that he would continue to develop throughout his life regarding religious experience.

More than twenty years after penning "A Spiritual Understanding," Edwards expands these early insights in *Religious Affections* with two central and interrelating concepts for properly understanding the onto-aesthetic nature of religious experience for Edwards; the indwelling of the Holy Spirit as a new spiritual principle of nature (signs one and seven), and the "sense of the heart." These two central concepts establish the objective and aesthetic dimensions, respectively, of Edwards's view of religious experience. The implications of this onto-aesthetic root of religious experience will be explored in more detail in the following section where we take up directly the question of normativity and the experience of God for Edwards.

The connection between the sense of the heart and the new principle of nature places religious experience in a relationship to human experience in general that is parallel and analogous to the relationship that Edwards establishes between true virtue and virtue in general. That is, religious experience establishes the onto-aesthetic ground for experience in general and at the same time serves as the perfection of all other experiences. Therefore, religious experience, like true virtue, in a certain sense defines and establishes the nature of experience and virtue respectively in general. It is this dynamic that leads us to consider the question of normativity for religious experience.

Sandra Schneiders's spiritual hermeneutic, that we explored in the previous chapter, posits the nature of Scripture as revelatory, or more precisely Scripture as self-disclosive revelation of God.[87] Moreover, for Schneiders divine revelation "as possibility" is "coextensive with human experience."[88] What is of interest here, is the revelatory potential of human experience, that has significant parallels with Edwards's own understanding of religious experience. Schneiders is quick to qualify that in actuality, human experience falls short of being co-extensive with divine revelation, but nevertheless in potentia, there is a correspondence between the mode of revelation as divine self-disclosure and the mode of human experience as encounter that for Schneiders remains in dynamic tension throughout the lived-reality of human existence. By construing the nature of divine revelation as primarily self-disclosure, Schneiders

---

86. Edwards, *WJE*, 14:81–82.
87. Schneiders, *Revelatory Text*, 34–35.
88. Schneiders, *Revelatory Text*, 45.

introduces the role of faith which echoes Edwards's onto-aesthetic notion of religious experience as "an objectively grounded but nonnecessary response" to divine self-disclosure.[89] Thus for Schneiders, the mode of God's self-disclosure to the world, precisely as communication, establishes both an objective/ontological and an subjective/transformative dimension to the human experience of God that highlights the normative dimension of the revelatory act as well as the appropriation of that revelation via the human experience of faith.[90]

For Schneiders normativity is not primarily to be understood dogmatically or epistemologically as that which one must do or believe, but rather, as criterion. That is, the problem or question of normativity is concerned with the relationship between the content/object, in this case the self-disclosive revelation of God, and the reader/recipient of that content.[91] While Schneiders does not develop this relational dimension of normativity in explicitly aesthetic categories as Edwards does, there is nevertheless an inherent aesthetic quality to the mode of this relationship when she affirms that: "For those who realize that the only God worth knowing is a personal God, and that all personal relationships are dialogical and relative, the 'uncontrollability' of God's self-revelation is a source of joyful astonishment and an invitation to the unwavering confidence that only a God of endlessly original love can justify."[92]

While this might allow for an implicit onto-aesthetic connection between Schneiders's understanding of the normativity of Revelation with Edwards's notion of religious experience, the question remains as to whether Edwards's notion of religious experience includes the transformative capacity inherent in Schneiders's normativity. In other words, does Edwards in fact view religious experience as normative for human experience in general? The twelfth sign of the *Affections* provides the answer, yes. The twelfth, final, and by far the longest distinguishing sign of true religious affections has long been noted as the most important in terms of the authentic signs of true religious affections. In short, the twelfth sign is that true religious affections "have their exercise and fruit in Christian practice."[93] The importance of this sign here is not simply that Edwards is dealing with the issue of practice, with all of its attending experiential elements, but rather how Edwards establishes this sign as the chief sign of true religious affections.

Edwards lists three implications of this sign that serve as the main points of commentary for the sign: that practices are directed by Christian rules; that

89. Schneiders, *Revelatory Text*, 51.
90. Schneiders, *Revelatory Text*, 51–53.
91. Schneiders, *Revelatory Text*, 44.
92. Schneiders, *Revelatory Text*, 59.
93. Edwards, *WJE*, 2:383.

The Crisis of Conversion

Christian practices become the most important aspect of an individual's life; and lastly, that these practices continue throughout the entirety of an individual's life until the very end. Clearly from the outset then, there is an immediate parallel between Schneiders's notion of normativity as the criterion from which one organizes and lives their life and Edward's twelfth sign. Moreover, these three implications help to highlight the totality of authentic religious affections in terms of the claim that they make on the individual that is implicit in Schneiders's normativity as criterion.

Moving beyond these organizing principles of Edwards's twelfth sign however, we see that the onto-aesthetic structure that underlies Edwards's metaphysics of experience is at play here as well. The key here is how Edwards understands Christian practice as the tendency and effect of religious affections. First, this suggests that Edwards maintains a distinction between the affections themselves and Christian practice as the fruit or effect of the affections. This reinforces his contention in part two of the *Affections* that the experience and expression of affections in themselves are not signs of true and gracious affections.[94]

Secondly, and more importantly, Christian practice, as the natural tendency and effect of gracious affections points to the ontological and aesthetic dimension of the religious affections and the dynamism of consent. According to Edwards, true religious affections have the effect of Christian practice precisely because it is the Holy Spirit indwelling in the heart of the individual "as an internal vital principle"[95] as we saw above from signs one and seven thus reinforcing the ontological relationship between God and his self-communication via gracious affections. Additionally, that gracious affections ultimately tend toward Christian practice suggests that the dynamics of consent are operating in these affections. Edwards argues that in addition to indwelling the heart, the Spirit also "gives the soul a natural relish of the sweetness of that which is holy."[96]

And finally, the tendency and effect of gracious affections toward Christian practice suggests for Edwards a change of nature. This change is in many ways the natural results of the operation of the sense of the heart through the new spiritual principle of nature that is the indwelling Spirit. However, this change also points to the transformative power of gracious affections as a sign of salvation and conversion through the power of the resurrection of Christ.[97]

---

94. See specifically signs one and two of Part Two on this point, also sign eleven of Part Three. *WJE*, 2:127–35, 376–83.

95. Edwards, *WJE*, 2:392.

96. Edwards, *WJE*, 2:394.

97. Edwards, *WJE*, 2:392–93.

For Edwards, in line with his reformed Calvinism, without the spiritual agency of the sense of the heart and new principle of nature, the natural person is simply unable to recognize and see the beauty and goodness of God's holiness and the pursuit of that holiness through Christian practice without the efficacious grace of God. Morally and socially, there may indeed be many motivations for individuals to behave in certain patterned ways that may mirror or attempt to simulate Christian practice, or what is true virtue; but as we saw above, there is an unbridgeable divide between virtue and true virtue, between the appearance of affections and true gracious affections, and between knowing that God is beautiful and participating in the beauty of Being itself.

Conclusion

Edwards, as I have argued here, provides a solid onto-aesthetic foundation that, in light of the development of the Pragmatist's tradition concerning human experience more broadly, will remain a central pillar throughout the development of American philosophy and theology. Specifically, I find as Edwards shifted the locus of interpretation from the earlier Puritan *ordo salutis*, to one rooted in the aesthetic interpretation of personal experience, he set the stage, as it were, for the emergence of a distinctly American approach to philosophical and theological inquiry. Moreover, by placing personal experience in the center of spiritual and theological discernment, Edwards also represents the North American source of the tension between individual experience and traditional modes of interpreting the presence of God. This tension for Edwards was mediated through a Reformed Calvinist lens and a strong theocentric determinism, that allowed him to navigate between the two extremes of the sheer individualism of the revival enthusiasts on the one hand, and the older Puritan detractors of Great Awakening revivalism on the other. As Puritanism gave way to Arminian Unitarianism at the turn of the nineteenth century, however, this tension would become exacerbated through what Donald Gelpi calls Ralph Waldo Emerson's "expressive individualism,"[98] to which we will now turn.

The Aesthetic Foundations of Ralph Waldo Emerson's Religious Experience

The link between Edwards and Emerson, is not a direct one, but rather as McClymond and McDermott have argued, one that happened through stages

---

98. Gelpi, *Endless Seeker*, 4.

The Crisis of Conversion

"From Edwards to the New Divinity, from the New Divinity to Unitarianism, and from Unitarianism to Transcendentalism."[99] The New Divinity was a pejorative term for the second generation of Edwardseans that tried to carry on the legacy Edwards's middle path between the emerging radical evangelicals to the left, who carried revivalism to perceived excesses, and the Puritans to the right, that maintained a strict rationalism and dismissed affections as a means of grace. A distinctive piece of New Divinity thought that emerged at the end of the eighteenth century had to do with the nature of human sin and the experience of God as a benevolent being. Taking Edwards's thought concerning the basic possibility of the unregenerate natural person as being able to recognize and experience God in some limited fashion (the secondary categories of natural benevolence, and affections above), New Divinity followers held that the strict Calvinist doctrine of imputed sin, a central element in their understanding of original sin, ran counter to Edwards's theological anthropology. Sin was rather willful action, as was holiness, both were available to the natural person. New Divinity still maintained that salvation was a product of Divine grace and not human merit, and so would still hold to a basic Calvinist doctrine of predestination, but in the realm of lived-experience, they held that divine grace was a matter of integrating the heart and the will towards God's own benevolence.[100] As the agency of human experience took on a more proactive role in the economy of salvation for the New Divinity than Edwards himself seemed to have been comfortable with, experience and doctrine became more tenuously connected. Meanwhile, there was a growing rationalist revolt against the more speculative strains of Orthodox theology, particularly Trinitarian theology in New England in this period as well. These rationalists similarly rejected the utterly supernatural metaphysic implied by Calvinist doctrines of imputed righteousness and sin, but in line with traditional Puritanism, rejected the high emotionalism of revivalism, and began to subtly supplant Calvinist soteriology with what Goen refers to as a "crypto-Arminianism that would resurface after the Revolution as Unitarianism.[101] The old Puritan tradition was being threatened from both sides, and when the Harvard Puritan theologian David Tappan died in 1803, a battle ensued over his replacement with the Arminian-leaning faction eventually securing leadership, and according to Bruce Kuklick's narration of the history, by the "end of the second decade of the new century, these Harvard Arminians took the label of 'Unitarians.'"[102] The final link in the chain from Edwards to Emerson

---

99. McClymond and McDermott, *Theology of Jonathan Edwards*, 653.

100. McClymond and McDermott, *Theology of Jonathan Edwards*, 601–06.

101. Goen, "Editor's Introduction," 84.

102. Kuklick, *History of Philosophy in America*, 50.

would happen once Emerson resigned his Unitarian pulpit and would help start the Transcendentalist movement.

Ralph Waldo Emerson (1803–1882) was a leading public intellectual in the United States and central figure in the Transcendentalist movement of the nineteenth century. From the trajectory established by Edwards, Emerson represents the "liberal" stream of American religious identity, though his presence is still present among the "conservative" streams as well, even if that presence is ignored or unrecognized. Part of the reason for Emerson's continued influence is the sort of national synthesis that his thought achieved through his many public lecture tours across the country in the mid-nineteenth century. Additionally, Emerson's thought help to crystallize a particularly American spiritual ethos that transcended strictly theological divides by blending in creative ways the young nation's civic, moral, and religious ideals. Specifically, I will contextualize Emerson's seminal work *Nature* and his overall Transcendental vision, which together function as a sort of call to conversion, within the social upheavals of ante-bellum North America and the crisis of slavery. Nineteenth-century American culture was in the midst of another significant transition, although in content quite different from Edwards's Awakenings a century earlier at the dawn of the American Revolution. Another wave of religious revivals, known as the Second Great Awakening (c. 1790–1840), were reaching their apex during Emerson's career, as were the rallying cries for emancipation and the building tensions between the Northern and Southern states over the issue of slavery. And while a full exposition of the complex and painful reality that was slavery is beyond the scope of this book, it helps to frame Emerson's career and provide a position from which to analyze his work. Specifically, Emerson's insights relate to his transcendental moral vision and call to personal conversion that has significant relevance for contemporary spirituality studies.

The field of Christian spirituality is beneficial for us concerning Emerson's contemporary legacy for at least a couple of reasons; first, as we have seen, spirituality studies takes the category of lived human experience of the divine as its central point of departure for analyzing and studying the nature and history of lived religion; second, and perhaps more importantly, Christian spirituality studies stands at a critical, though by no means necessarily oppositional, tension with the normative claims of dogmatic, doctrinal, and systematic systems of Christian theology. That is to say that Christian spirituality is intimately related but not strictly limited to the traditions of practice and systems of belief of official theological systems and ecclesial structures. However, this critical spiritual stance to theology allows for the possibility for new methods of exploration that can be mutually beneficial for both disciplines, and it is in this hope that I bring Emerson into the conversation. Emerson, as

The Crisis of Conversion

I will argue, stands in a similarly ambiguous relationship to structures of traditional theology as that of spirituality in the sense that Emerson's Christian theological heritage permeates his writings and at the same time he severed himself from the boundaries of Unitarian and perhaps even Christian Orthodoxy broadly conceived as his Transcendentalism developed. Moreover, a similar tension has developed between normative and universalizing schemes and Western thinking more broadly with the rise of Postmodern Deconstructionism that was explored in the first chapter precipitating the contemporary evangelical crisis of conversion. This present analysis will focus primarily on *Nature* as a key text for understanding Emerson's spirituality, with some other contextual references to some of his other work as necessary.

Emerson's Context

Emerson was born on May 25, 1803 in Boston to William and Ruth Haskins Emerson. William, who was the pastor of the First Church in Boston, died while Ralph Waldo was a young child in 1811. Ruth moved the Emerson family of eight children to her hometown, Concord, Massachusetts. In Concord, Ralph became close to his aunt, Mary Moody Emerson, who would have a major influence on Ralph into his early adulthood. Emerson graduated from Harvard University in 1821 and spent four years as a school teacher before returning to Harvard Divinity School. After his graduation from Harvard Divinity in 1825, he suffered a serious illness and nearly went blind. After a convalescence in Florida, he would return to Boston and become ordained in 1829 as the pastor of Second Church, from which he would resign three and half years later in 1832.

Emerson's adulthood includes three key events in his life help us to organize his thought. The first, briefly mentioned above, was his resignation of his pastorate at Boston's Second Church in 1832 due primarily to his growing disdain for the residual Puritan traditionalism of Unitarian church practice that he viewed as stifling the social and moral progress of the church. The second event, was his subsequent trip to Europe during the winter and spring of 1832–1833 where he had a series of ecstatic experiences in the Vatican art museums and the *Jardin des Plantes* in Paris. This trip, and particularly these ecstatic experiences began a period of time which later Emerson would refer to as his "saturnalia of faith," lasting from 1832 up until the death of his son Waldo in 1842.[103] Moreover, it was during the return voyage from Europe that he began one of his most famous essays, *Nature* that became a central work in

---

103. Gelpi, *Varieties of Transcendental Experience*, 100–101.

Retrieving the Foundations of North American Evangelical Spirituality

the emerging movement known as Transcendentalism. The third major event for our purposes here was the passage of the so-called Compromise of 1850 and the Fugitive Slave Act, that forced Emerson's hand in becoming a more public voice against slavery in the US. I will return to these events in more detail in what follows.

During this same time-period, the 1830s through the 1850s, a large and diverse series of cultural reform movements, often referred to as the "American Renaissance,"[104] was developing in the United States alongside the growing national political crisis over slavery. Within this larger cultural context, Emerson stood at the epicenter of a group known as the Transcendentalists. The Transcendentalists, with much in common to the European Romantic movements a few decades before, launched a critique against the perceived excesses of Enlightenment rationalism and scientific empiricism. Similarly, the early stages of the movement came out of Christian liberal circles (Unitarian Calvinism more specifically for Emerson), and by its later stages had extended beyond traditional religious affiliations; evidenced in Emerson's own life by his resignation from his Unitarian pastorate in 1832. Of central concern for the Transcendentalists was what they saw as the failures of Modernist rationalism in fostering personal morality. And finally, the Transcendentalists, like their Romantic forbearers, attempted to retrieve Classical and Medieval emphases on aesthetics and the liberal arts as a corrective to the cold rationalism of the day, which they believed aided, or at least maintained the status quo related to the moral crisis of slavery in the US.

African Slavery came to North America with the European colonists in the seventeenth century and continued up until its abolition at the culmination of the Civil War and the ratification of the 13th amendment to the US Constitution in 1865. While slavery was practiced throughout the American colonies and then newly formed states after the Revolutionary War, it became increasingly associated with the Southern states and territories as evidenced by the passage of the so-called Missouri Compromise of 1820 that created a political border-line along the 36th Parallel line of latitude. States and territories north of that line were to remain free states (with the exception of Missouri which was allowed to enter the Union as a slave holding state), and the states and territories below the line were allowed to continue slavery.

Emerson, while personally and morally opposed to slavery, was hesitant to provide much public support to the abolitionist cause. He turned down several invitations to speak or rally support by various abolitionist leaders around Massachusetts during the 30s and 40s, at the prime of his public influence. Though he drafted several letters and did deliver three public

---

104. Matthiessen, *American Rennaisance*; Reynolds, *Beneath the American Renaissance*.

The Crisis of Conversion

addresses concerning slavery policies in the mid to late 40's, he spent much of his time during this period working out his Transcendental vision of true moral reform of the individual, with little attention given to wider social or public concerns. While it has been common in Emersonian scholarship to interpret Emerson as uninterested or personally unaffected by the social issues surrounding slavery in the US, Len Gougeon, in his editor's introduction to the important publication, *Emerson's Anti-slavery Writings*, argued that it was the development of his Transcendentalism that kept him from taking a more central social stand on the particular issue of slavery.[105] This is to say that Emerson's Transcendentalism itself developed in such a way that the focus of Emerson's moral vision did not extend to arguably the most important moral and social issue of his day. William Westfall, on the other hand, concluded that it was precisely because of the elevation of the private individual inherent in Emerson's Transcendentalism, that abolitionists were able to challenge the prevailing political and social majorities that supported the institution of slavery.[106] In any event, it was not until much later in Emerson's career, with the passage of the Fugitive Slave Act, that he would assume a more public role in anti-slavery and abolitionist causes.

The Fugitive Slave Act compelled all US citizens to actively seek out and return runaway slaves.[107] Prior to this act, many northern cities including Emerson's Boston, were safe havens for escaped slaves, who were able to maintain their public freedom without fear of being arrested and returned to their former masters. Emerson, and many other Northerners, perhaps grew complacent in these policies and deemed themselves personally freed from the guilt of Southern slavery as a result of these Northern policies of simple goodwill toward escaped slaves. This new law now forced Northerners sympathetic with emancipation to either willfully break the law and risk the consequences on the one hand, or to directly enter into pro-slavery activities by turning in suspected escaped slaves on the other.[108] For reasons that will be explored in more detail in what follows, this situation became unbearable for Emerson. For our present purposes, I am interested in the role that Emerson's mystical vision of the world, developed in the saturnalia of his faith during the 1830's and 40's, served as a catalyst for public transformation from the 1850's onward. In particular, I will analyze Emerson's Transcendental theory of Nature as both a method of preparation leading to personal conversion, and the foundation for his public platform in relation to the social crisis of slavery.

105. Gougeon, "Historical Background," xxxv–xliii, liii–lvi.
106. Westfall, "Tocqueville, Emerson, and the Abolitionists," 62–63.
107. Gougeon, "Historical Background," xxxv–xliii.
108. Gura, *American Transcendentalism*, 240–47.

Retrieving the Foundations of North American Evangelical Spirituality

Transcendentalism and Emerson's Aesthetic Moral Vision

Emerson and the transcendentalists were closely committed to a Platonic realism rooted in the immediacy of intuition as the means of accessing Truth and Goodness, through the revelatory capacities of Beauty. Unlike other groups within the American Renaissance, Emerson and several other leading Transcendentalists utilized explicitly religious language and vocabulary in their writings. For them, Beauty, particularly as experienced through the natural world, served a very important spiritual role; it established and revealed an essential unity between the divine and the human soul. Moreover, the experience of the divine through the Beauty of Nature provided Emerson with an inspired language with which he expressed his moral vision.

In one of Emerson's essays "The Poet," published in his *Second Series* in 1844, Emerson provides us with a sense of the centrality of aesthetics in his thought by placing two important elements within the category of Beauty. The first element in Emerson's aesthetics is a linguistic semiotics where he notes that nature is a "picture language," "A symbol, in the whole, and in every part."[109] This nature-semiotics is not simply a theory concerning the processes of the communication of nature, but is instead that which mediates Goodness, Truth, and Beauty, or in other words, reality itself. This semiotic mediation is viewed by Emerson as a "holy place . . . where Being passes into Appearance, and Unity into Variety."[110] Ultimately Emerson's metaphysical construction of this transcendent semiotics rests upon Beauty; "All form is an effect of character . . . and for this reason, a perception of beauty should be sympathetic, or proper only to the good."[111]

Emerson's aesthetic semiotics is composed of three elements; Nature, Spirit, subject, that in relation with one another have a tendency to move towards unification through difference. Secondly, the aesthetic element in Emerson's thought serves as the mediating and experiential entry point into an experience of the divine through Nature, primarily seen in his essay of the same name. *Nature*, published in 1836 is not only Emerson's most popular work, but indeed is arguably one of his most important works that established him as central figure in the emerging American intellectual tradition that would come to be known as Transcendentalism. This work, as noted by Emersonian commentator Donald Gelpi, sought to establish "a religious formula which would somehow unite mind and heart, reason and intuition, in a

---

109. Emerson, *Essays and Lectures*, 452.
110. Emerson, *Essays and Lectures*, 453.
111. Emerson, *Essays and Lectures*, 452.

felt, creative response to divine Beauty."[112] Gelpi's insight here underscores an important synthesis often overlooked by Emersonian scholarship that moves toward integrating rather than a distinguishing between a Christian theological/religious reading and a spiritual/philosophical reading of *Nature*. For Emerson, the aesthetic is both the essence of transcendent unity of Nature as well as the particular mode of mediation between Nature and human persons. Moreover, it appears that just beneath the surface of Emerson's Unitarian/Platonic structure, there lies a close affinity with the Trinitarian tradition of the Church, as received primarily through the writings of Jonathan Edwards. I will follow Gelpi's insight and suggest that the study of spirituality offers a new way of reading Emerson's *Nature* in a way that develops both a spirituality of nature born out of his recovery of aesthetics as a normative category of human reality and that this aesthetic turn offers some interesting implications concerning religious conversion.

The second key piece in Emerson's metaphysics is temporality perceived as history. As we saw above with his linguistic semiotics as the mode of perceiving reality, for Emerson history "is the universal nature which gives worth to particular men and things."[113] For Emerson there is a direct correlation between the reality of the past and the reality of the present. This correlation however must be mediated via history. And while it is apparent that History is very much a genuine element of all that is reality, there is a fundamental difference between history and the nature-semiotics discussed above. The difference is something that is inherent in history itself, which exists as a construct of the human mind. Emerson claims at the outset of his essay "there is one mind common to all individual men. Every man is an inlet to the same and to all of the same."[114] He continues by asserting that history in itself is nothing other than the record of the works of this singular and universal mind. These comments appear to suggest that history is in some since merely a derivative constituent of reality rather than a fundamental principle of reality itself, however it is important to remember that like his semiotics above, for Emerson history in itself is fundamentally one universal reality that is mediated via the particularities of a given place, person, event, etc. yet through this mediation history itself does not lose its essential unity. "Epoch after epoch," Emerson writes, "camp, kingdom, empire, republic, democracy, are merely the application of his [i.e. history's] manifold spirit to the manifold world."[115]

---

112. Gelpi, *Varieties of Transcendental Experience*, 102.
113. Emerson, *Essays and Lectures*, 238.
114. Emerson, *Essays and Lectures*, 237.
115. Emerson, *Essays and Lectures*, 237.

When viewed in this light, the structure and nature of history functions in parallel with what we saw of Emerson's semiotics; namely, the essential unity of reality perceived via the mediation of particularity. This system is of course consistent with platonic substance metaphysics, where all apparently diverse reality is merely a mediated form of the One. What is of interest however, are the implications of Emerson's notion of history for his aesthetics. The key for this connection is the idea of history as the mediation of worth, or value. History, perhaps unlike his semiotics, is not simply a mediating reality, but rather history also mediates the perception of value inherent within reality; or to use Emerson's language, history is the recorded perception of worth. Emerson places a constructive element in the perception of history, that is less clear in his semiotics. This constructive element allows for Emerson to on the one hand affirm a certain immediacy between Reality and individual persons by virtue of the mediated value of temporality; yet on the other hand, allows him to dismiss the reified traditions of previous eras, particularly in Nature, the dogmatism of Christian Orthodoxy.

By placing history itself within the subjective category of value Emerson accomplishes two things; first, he challenges the Enlightenment presupposition from Descartes through Hegel that human persons have recourse to history objectively through rationality and the overcoming of the personal biases of the contemporary reader. Instead, Emerson claims that history in its creation is necessarily a mediated reality, from its source and thus the reality perceived in the present, in all of its biases and incompleteness, is on equal footing with the reality transmitted to us historically. It is by virtue of this critique that he writes "I have no expectation that any man will read history aright, who thinks that what was done in a remote age . . . has any deeper sense than what he is doing to-day."[116]

Secondly, this critique elevates the category of the aesthetic, the Beautiful, as the arbiter of history so that rather than placing aesthetics in opposition to reason, as with Kantian metaphysics, Emerson elevates the aesthetic as the ground for the mediation of reality in the present as well as the mediation of the past. In this way, Emerson is similar to Edwards, who both are attempting to establish human experience as a legitimate locus for interpreting the nature of reality. Aesthetics, then, forms the ground for which all of the rest of Emerson's work is established in that humanity perceives reality through the aesthetic meaning of signs/nature/language and the aesthetic value of history. In short the True (meaning) and the Good (value) are mediated through

---

116. Emerson, *Essays and Lectures*, 239.

The Crisis of Conversion

the Beautiful (aesthetic). We may turn to consider the aesthetic of nature and Emerson's development of a spirituality of Nature.[117]

"Build, therefore, your own world":[118] Emerson's Spirituality of Nature

As we begin our discussion of Emerson's spiritual aesthetics in *Nature*, it is perhaps helpful to situate the overall argument with our above analysis of Emerson's metaphysical structure. From the outset, it must be pointed out that Emerson did not write a systematic treatise, nor does his collection of essays naturally lend themselves to be organized systematically. However, as Gelpi and others have suggested, Emerson's own thought went through several internal shifts that do warrant a systematic analysis and which form a sort of lens by which Emerson viewed the world.

Consistent with his critique of Enlightenment rationality briefly outlined above, Emerson's *Nature* seems to be an extended response to this question found in the introduction to the work: "Why should not we have a poetry and philosophy of insight and not of tradition, and a religion by revelation to us, and not the history of theirs?"[119] This question appears to prefigure the two metaphysical elements of Emerson's matured Transcendentalist thought; the semiotic, or experiential mode of reality, and the leveling of the playing field between the present and the past via the constructive mediation of history. It is also of note that being published in 1832, the same year that Emerson left Boston's Second Church, we see the beginning of his break with religious tradition itself that would culminate in his 1838 address to Harvard Divinity School. What remains to be seen, however, is to determine in what manner this metaphysical stance informs Emerson's idea of Nature[120] as a spiritual practice.

117. For a thorough analysis of Emerson's metaphysical development see Gelpi's careful treatment in, *Endless Seeker*. In particular Gelpi argues for a three-stage development of Emerson's metaphysic; the pre-Transcendentalist stage included his years as a student, and Unitarian minister coming to a close when he left the pulpit of Second Church in 1832; Emerson's second Transcendental phase occurred between 1832–1841; and the final post-Transcendental phase from 1841–1875 which is marked by a revision and dampening of the lofty character that marked the Transcendental phase. Nature, as well as our previous metaphysical analysis occupy the middle two phases of Gelpi's scheme, with *Nature* falling in the early stages of his Transcendental phase and the metaphysical material characterizing the matured Transcendental phase and early post-Transcendental thought.

118. Emerson, *Essays and Lectures*, 48.

119. Emerson, *Essays and Lectures*, 7. This is also a striking parallel to Emerson's younger contemporary William James and his notion of the essence of religious experience, *Varieties*, 31.

120. A note for clarification, when I use Nature in a capital and non-italicized style it is referring to what Emerson is referring to as the Transcendental reality of Nature itself.

The work itself is comprised of eight chapters that attempt to tease out various aspects, purposes, and uses of Nature as they relate to humanity. Central to this Nature-human relationship is its near if not actual identification with the divine-human relationship. In fact, Emerson's apparent pantheism throughout *Nature* as well of the rest of his work during his Transcendental period is a distinguishing mark that helps to define the shift from his 'pre-Transcendental' period. This theme is repeated throughout his work during this time, as evidenced by the poem at the start of this essay; "There is nothing else but God."[121] While there can be little doubt that Emerson's writing concerning the divine-human relationship may very well be labeled pantheist, in this specific instance it appears that his Edwardsean background is most responsible for this theocentric phrase. It should also be remembered that Edwards's work would remain a strong influence through to the end of his life and thus calls into question giving Emerson the unequivocal label of a pure pantheist.[122]

Nature, like Emerson's semiotic mysticism (i.e. the mediation of divine through language) serves as a mediator of reality, that is conceived here ultimately as Spirit. Emerson's conception of Spirit should not be confused with the Continental *Geist* of Hegel, as a synthesis of subjective becoming.[123] Rather, in a more organically Neoplatonic conception, Spirit is strictly speaking the only being whatsoever, the One, that is experienced in the diversity of Nature. It is mediated emanation of being, rather than the mediated becoming of subject. Here, Emerson is continuing an emerging theme within the North American religious tradition where Spirit, perceived reality, and ultimate reality, are mediated through human experience. An early example of this is Edwards, explored above. Emerson argues; "that spirit, that is the Supreme Being, does not build up nature around us, but puts it forth through us, as the life of the tree puts forth new branches and leaves through the pores of the old."[124] It is in fact the reality of the Spirit that establishes the foundation upon which any reality may be perceived at all.

This transcendent Spirit, perceptible in human experience, and mediated through Nature, establishes the experience of Spirit through Nature in its

---

Italicized *Nature* refers to Emerson's text, and nature lower case refers to common usages of nature (including the natural world human nature, specific internal properties inherent to a given thing, etc.).

121. Emerson, *Collected Poems and Essays*, 337.

122. In particular, Gelpi notes Jonathan Edwards's strict divine determinism heavily influenced Emerson throughout is life, and that coupled with a strong Neoplatonic idealism leads me to ascribe a radical form of panentheism to Emerson's theological philosophy. See Gelpi's full argument in *Varieties of Transcendental Experience*, 87–133.

123. Schlitt, *Experience and Spirit*, 77–80.

124. Emerson, *Essays and Lectures*, 40.

The Crisis of Conversion

temporally perpetual present-at-handedness as the most fundamentally valid means of entering into a spiritual journey, and by extension into the virtuous life. For Emerson, it is not merely *the idea* of Nature that is spiritually transformative, though he would not deny that; it is rather Nature in its widest totality *as experienced* that is transformative and transcendent. "Nature," he writes, "in its ministry to man, is not only the material, but is also the process and the result. All the parts incessantly work into each other's hands for the profit of man."[125] Moreover, this natural material ministry towards humanity is not something that is true only after the fact or as a result of the efforts of human agency, but rather, "there seems to be a necessity in spirit to manifest itself in material forms . . . [that] preexist in necessary forms in the mind of God, and are what they are by virtue of preceding affections, in the world of spirit." Thus Emerson can claim that Spirit is immediately perceptible in Nature, precisely because that is the nature of Spirit. There is a co-naturality about the manner in which Nature is perceived and the reality of transcendent Spirit. Moreover, by virtue of the fact that "Nature is the symbol of spirit" according to Emerson, he is able to assert that the present-ness of Nature as reality is able to semiotically mediate Spirit in a way that other modes of revelation are not.[126]

In chapter three of *Nature* entitled 'Beauty,' Emerson provides us with a fairly clear portrait of how his notion of aesthetics serves as the ground for much of his thinking, especially as it relates to Nature. Beauty, at least in its metaphysical relationship to Nature, is conceptually divisible into three aspects; simple perception; the presence of a higher and spiritual element in that perception; and that this simple-yet-spiritual perception becomes "an object of the intellect."[127] This parallels Edwards's structure of Beauty through consent, though lacks the multi-layered sophistication of Edwards's primary and secondary modes. Moreover, the three elements of Beauty begin to reveal how Emerson incorporates spirituality, which is the human participation with Nature through the category of experience just as we saw above with Edwards's consent to Being in general.

Emerson's aesthetics, in concert with his general philosophical/theological framework is a combination of Neoplatonic and Edwardsean influences. There are several significant parallels between the aesthetics of Edwards and Emerson, as we have begun to see. First, both thinkers start from a relational epistemology, that is, that knowledge comes from perception of relations

---

125. Emerson, *Essays and Lectures*, 12.

126. See specifically, the connection between Language and spiritual mediation from chapters 4 and 7, "Language" and "Spirit" respectively. Emerson, *Essays and Lectures*, 20–25, 40–42.

127. Emerson, *Essays and Lectures*, 18.

between objects, concepts, subjects, etc. Emerson writes in this chapter; "nothing is quite beautiful alone . . . A single object is only so far beautiful as it suggests this universal grace."[128] From the above discussion of Edwards's relational metaphysics this passage from *True Virtue* is particularly enlightening as to the similarity between these two thinkers.

> "There is a general and a particular beauty. By particular beauty I mean that by which a thing appears beautiful when considered only with regard to its connection with, and tendency to, some particular things within a limited, and as it were a private sphere. And a general beauty is that by which a thing appears beautiful when viewed most perfectly, comprehensively and universally, with regard to all its tendencies, and its connections with every thing to which it stands related."[129]

Granted that Edwards's entire aesthetics is far more complex than what Emerson has developed here in *Nature*, but nevertheless, both thinkers place relationality at the very center of what is the Beautiful. This relational aesthetics carries with it some significant implications as far as Emerson is concerned, for it very fittingly agrees with his metaphysical semiotics, conceived of as systems of relations.[130] We can therefore see a structural similarity between the relationality of Emerson's and Edwards's aesthetics and ontology.

When we move to consider Emerson's threefold structure of Beauty in light of this semiotic aesthetics, we finally arrive at the heart of this argument, the emergence of Emerson's spirituality of Nature. Recalling briefly this structure of simple perception, the presence of a spiritual element, and it becoming an object of the intellect, we now can see a clear example of a primary semiotic relationship: Spirit as the perceived sign by a human subject(s). Nature, like Emerson's semiotic metaphysics (i.e. the mediation of history through language) serves as a mediator of reality, which is conceived here ultimately as Spirit. It is in fact the reality of the Spirit, with the notable absence of the distinctly Trinitarian formulation that we saw in Edwards, that establishes the foundation upon which reality may be perceived at all. Therefore, as mentioned above, whatever pantheistic overtones are present in Emerson, it is a Pantheism that is in some sense Theocentric/transcendent rather than anthropocentric/immanent.

---

128. Emerson, *Essays and Lectures*, 18.
129. Edwards, *WJE*, 8:540.
130. Emerson, *Essays and Lectures*, 20.

Conclusion

To return to Emerson and the pre-war abolitionists, we find that Emerson's mystical aesthetics served as the basis for his personal moral stand against slavery, a situation that is inherently un-natural; while at the same time resulted in his aversion to championing the socio-political cause of the abolitionists. Emerson's Transcendentalism is ultimately a supreme moral vision of universal proportions, or to use Emersonian language, "a sally of the soul into the unfolding infinite"[131] through the mystical unity of Natural Beauty. Emerson's sense of duty, his moral compass, and the motivation for all right action, is rooted in and sustained by the mystical awareness of the unity of the whole of reality glimpsed through the partiality of finite existence. Thus for Emerson, any single social platform, no matter how noble it may appear to be—abolitionism, temperance, poverty, illiteracy, world peace, etc.—are inherently limited and thus fail to grasp the truth of Transcendental virtue. This transcendental vision rests solely on the individual soul standing in an immediate mystical relationship with the divine. While slavery is a grotesque distortion of the natural dignity of human persons, so too social institutions are a distortion of the divine dignity of the individual. A loose connection may be made here between the idealism of Emerson's metaphysics creating such distinction between limited and transcendental value, with Edwards's similarly structured primary and secondary categories of consent, and benevolence that we saw above. One important difference between the two however, is the specifically moral/theological character of Edwards's sense of divine determinism, that becomes a more nebulous and benign determinism in Emerson's system.

Public institutions and communal sentiment are nothing more than distractions from the individual soul's true potential. Emerson's mysticism is simultaneously universal in transcendent scope and utterly individualistic in its application, leaving little room for either social agendas or a motivation to legislate or attempt to direct a public morality. Consistent with his critique of Enlightenment rationality briefly outlined above, Emerson's *Nature* seems to be an extended response to this question found in the Introduction to the work: "Why should we not have a poetry and philosophy of insight and not of tradition, and a religion by revelation to us, and not the history of theirs?"[132] His response is that the history of tradition is one of compromise,

---

131. Emerson, *Essays and Lectures*, 47.

132. Emerson, *Essays and Lectures*, 7. This is also a striking parallel to Emerson's younger contemporary William James and his notion of the essence of religious experience in *Varieties*, 31.

inefficiencies, corruption, and oppression. These, in turn, enslave individual human potential in the name of social norms, convention, and the so called common good. It is with these sentiments in mind that Emerson can make the quite surprising remark: "I ask primary evidence that you are a man, and refuse this appeal from the man to his actions."[133] Emerson is giving voice to a peculiarity of American mysticism; the paradoxical relationship between a vision of universal divine harmony and unity through the national ideals of liberty and freedom on the one hand, and a bitterly divisive individualism that focuses exclusively on the sphere of the self as the only place where this divine vision is perceptible on the other. Thus the Anglo North American mystical tradition, particularly from Emerson through William James, lacks a proper socio-communal foundation from which their mystical insights may serve as a catalyst for social change.

As a response to this form of critique, Emerson suggests that humanity, in humanity's material quest for ecological and economic mastery buttressed by social institutions, has been reduced to a half-life comprised of "pen-wisdom," utilitarianism, and a Spirit-less world. To restore the proper life again to Nature is nothing short than the "the redemption of souls."[134] Thus, Emerson suggests that the transcendental expanse of Spirit in nature, as articulated through his aesthetic semiotics, provides an occasion for conversion. Returning to Knutson's "conductive imaginary," Emerson's *Nature* is offered as an experience of preparation, and an invitation to experience religious conversion. Ultimately it then appears that the problem is not so much that society has surpassed the crude naturalism of antiquity, but rather that by the very act of progressing beyond Nature, humanity has become disunited with itself. Emerson can challenge us all to "build, therefore, your own world,"[135] precisely because Nature in its essential unity of spirit exists to be perceived, to be encountered, to participate in the reality of life. The practice of Nature is nothing other than "a sally of the soul into the unfolding infinite."[136] It is, to put it simply, the agreeable perception of the unity of Beauty and the "consent of being to Being."[137]

However, despite the latent optimism in Emerson's *Nature*, and the admittedly powerful ideals that it contains, a question arises in terms of the application of this transcendental vision. In other words, how might Emerson's call to embrace his aesthetic call result in one's own personal transformation? With Edwards, given his thoroughly theocentric vision and pastoral concern

133. Emerson, *Essays and Lectures*, 263.
134. Emerson, *Essays and Lectures*, 46–47.
135. Emerson, *Essays and Lectures*, 48.
136. Emerson, *Essays and Lectures*, 47.
137. Edwards, *WJE*, 8:546.

The Crisis of Conversion

through his career, the implications of his work related to conversion were naturally more well-defined. With Emerson, the end for which *Nature* is calling appears vague. In his own life, Emerson realized this, and during what Gelpi refers to as his post-transcendental phase, the sheer optimism of *Nature* becomes much more muted in the face of the finitude of human life. Knutson, similarly, highlights the ambiguous application and difficulty in adequately living out Emerson's transcendentalism, though she situates this problem philosophically and intellectually, rather than religiously or spiritually. Ultimately I find that this question reveals a significant flaw in Emerson's work, namely an aggressive individualism that contradicts Emerson's own objectives in cultivating a sense of personal conversion towards a better and more free life. This critique is most clearly seen in Emerson's response to the greatest cultural crisis of his day, slavery.

Conclusion: Edwards, Emerson, and the Quest for Conversion

Jonathan Edwards's exposition of the Christian life in terms of the dynamic relationship between God and human persons highlights the centrality of conversion through faith and the experience of God as the source and foundation of salvation that is normative for Christianity in general and Evangelical Christianity in particular. Moreover, by connecting this normative encounter of God with his aesthetic ontology, Edwards opens up the category of human experience and provides an opportunity for a more central role within an evangelical experience of faith. At the same time, Edwards does not give experience itself a blank check as it were to define for itself what is authentic Christian practice or not. Rather, Edwards's onto-aesthetic notion of experience places the self-disclosive revelation of God as the criterion for religious experience. Thus, religious experience itself is bound up and rooted in Scripture as the word of God, which as Schneiders argued is itself a revelatory encounter of divine self-communication.

Emerson's Transcendental vision provides an aesthetic approach to personal conversion through self-discovery and by removing the shackles imposed upon human individuality through custom and tradition, particularly the heavy-handed dogmatism of his Puritan-Unitarian heritage. There are significant resonances here with Schneiders's work on the method and nature of spirituality as lived experience, particularly her two dynamics of life-integration and self-transcendence, which lead towards her horizon of infinite value. Within this system, Emerson's work finds a good fit in terms of the overall method and structure of the process of transformation via experience that both Schneiders and Emerson present.

Moreover, both Edwards and Emerson help to articulate just how deep-seated the tension between individual experience and the authority of religious tradition lies at the heart of the crisis of conversion. On the one hand there is Edwards, who through a relational metaphysics attempts to integrate the triune revelation of Godself to the world and the human experience of that revelation as aesthetic in nature and ethically normative in relation to one's engagement with the world. On the other hand, Emerson embodies a more radical individualism that places the inner and immediate relationship between the soul and God as the source for one's own spiritual and ethical identity. However, following Edwards, Emerson's aesthetic of Nature parallels Edwards's normative structure, but leaves the Trinitarian implications implicit if present at all. For both men, there is an undeniable relationship between the structure of aesthetics and the structure of reality in its transcendent and immanent dimensions that provide the foundation of the human experience of God. This tension was mirrored in the previous discussion between James and Royce and the development of a Pragmatist semiotics of religious experience at the turn of the twentieth century.

In summary, Edwards and Emerson together lay the foundation of an aesthetically rooted notion of the process of religious transformation, or conversion, through the category of human experience that would help the later Pragmatist tradition articulate the contours of the nature of human experience more broadly. Moreover, Edwards and Emerson individually, represent two divergent streams of the North American religion-spiritual ethos, with Edwards representing the central role of organized religion that continues to exert tremendous influence in shaping, or attempting to shape the civic values of society; and with Emerson representing the spirit of American individualism that similarly exerts tremendous influence in shaping our shared values. This tension on the larger social level finds particular theological expression in the evangelical crisis of conversion, which in its own way has been deeply formed by both the forces of tradition and individual expression. However, that both Edwards and Emerson place the categories of experience and aesthetics in the center of their thought presents an opportunity for evangelicalism to recover a more robust and nuanced appreciation for the constructive and normative role that human experience in general plays in our understanding and interpretation of reality, particularly the reality of God. These constructive and normative insights, as articulated in the North American tradition from Edwards, Emerson, James, Royce, to Schneiders, find a contemporary evangelical theological expression in the creative work of Amos Yong.

4

Conclusion

Toward a Postmodern Evangelical Spirituality

Retracing Our Steps

IN THE PRECEDING CHAPTERS I have traced the main contours of what I have called the crisis of conversion as it relates to the problematic situation of religious experience in relationship to the authority of the Bible within evangelical Christianity. Before moving to the constructive development of my conclusion, I would like to take stock of what has been said up to this point.

The work Jonathan Edwards related to the revivals of the First Great Awakening during the 1730s and 1740s gave shape to a particularly American expression of the larger emerging evangelical spirituality that was developing throughout Western Christianity in the middle of the eighteenth century. Edwards would both help to cultivate this new and surprising work of God through his role as a preacher and pastor of the church in Northampton and the surrounding Connecticut River Valley of New England, as well as articulate a theological and spiritual defense of the centrality of the experience of conversion which reoriented the soul of individual persons to perceive in a new way the glory of God, as a legitimate—and perhaps even necessary—element of true Christianity. This experience of conversion, or "gracious affections" for Edwards, placed the individual in a more or less direct encounter with God, whereby a person began to work out their own salvation through the indwelling of the Holy Spirit as an "internal vital principle," that integrated and reoriented the intellect and will towards God through the affective perception of the "sweet and divine nature, making the soul a partaker of God's beauty and Christ's joy," the first sign of gracious affections according to Edwards.[1] The indwelling of the Spirit, in turn, opens up a new avenue for spiritual insight through the "sense of the heart," Edwards's fourth sign, whereby the "beauty and sweetness of the holiness or moral perfection of divine things" becomes connected to the "knowledge of things of religion."[2] And together, the presence of the indwelling Spirit and sense of the heart are publicly confirmed through the cultivation of habits in the "exercise and fruit" of Christian practice observed in an individual's life, the twelfth and final of sign of religious affection.[3] As I argued in the previous chapter, through these cumulative and progressive signs of true gracious affections, Edwards blends a theocentric aesthetics with his Reformed Calvinist doctrine of election in the experience of religious conversion, in a way that becomes normative for the individual and is confirmed through the visible discernment of habits of Christian piety throughout that person's life. In this way, Edwards's reorienting the process of conversion to the individual's experience of God from the older Puritan Covenantal model established what would become the standard expression of American evangelical Christianity.

A century later, Ralph Waldo Emerson would both continue and modify the experiential and aesthetic foundations of Edwards's articulation of evangelical conversion, through his public leadership during the Transcendental renaissance at the tail end of the Second Great Awakening in the 1830s through the1850s. Whereas Edwards was keen to defend the authenticity of people's conversion experiences during the revivals of his time from the rigid formalism of Puritan Covenantal theology, Emerson's growing frustration with the lifeless Enlightenment rationalism of New England Unitarianism led him beyond the pulpit out into the world where he would find the "advancing spirit" of the Transcendent in the experience of inner conversion mediated through Nature, "the symbol of spirit."[4] Conversion for Emerson, like Edwards, was found in the integration of the will and the intellect through the affective dimension of the experience of the transcendent. For Emerson, this integration begins in the "love of beauty," which is first experienced in the "simple perception of natural forms" as "delight."[5] Second, this delight reveals a "spiritual element" through the integration of the perception of delight and

1. Edwards, *WJE*, 2:201.
2. Edwards, *WJE*, 2:272.
3. Edwards, *WJE*, 2:383.
4. Emerson, *Essays and Lectures*, 49, 20.
5. Emerson, *Essays and Lectures*, 14.

The Crisis of Conversion

the human will so that the experience of beauty becomes the "mark God sets upon virtue."[6] And Lastly, the cultivation of virtue through the perception of the soul's delight in beauty transforms the intellect which "searches out the absolute order of things as they stand in the mind of God," and in concert the intellect, virtuous will, and affective perception of delight "succeed each other" so that the "exclusive activity of the one, generates the exclusive activity of the other."[7] This experience of conversion through the aesthetic dimension of spirit, similarly results in the cultivation of new habits of life for Emerson. However, one's conversion is not directed towards an obedience to the will and glory of God, but rather the "self-recovery" of the individual who has become "dis-united with himself," which in turn leads to the restoration of the original and eternal beauty of the world through the building of one's own world.[8] However, as I argued above, Emerson's idealistic "self-reliant" individualism, resulted in a fractured moral vision that couldn't properly address even the most morally egregious evil of his day, slavery.

When taken together, then, the experiential and aesthetic dimensions of conversion in Edwards and Emerson, expose the historical foundations of the contemporary crisis of conversion; namely the ambiguous relationship between an individual's experience and the normative/ethical demands of our larger social reality. Edwards attempted to mediate the tension through his Reformed, theocentric, and transcendent determinism, and Emerson attempted to mediate it via a Neo-platonic and immanent determinism; however, this determinism seems to undercut the otherwise robust role that experience itself has in the total reality of conversion that both Edwards and Emerson want to preserve. Furthermore, this ambiguity concerning religious experience would next be taken up by the American Pragmatist philosophical tradition at the turn of the twentieth century, particularly by William James and Josiah Royce.

The turn to the Pragmatist tradition signals two major shifts in context, first away from the pulpit and ecclesial concerns of Edwards and Emerson to the lecture halls of the university and professional academics; and second, away from the emotional pastoral/theological concerns of religious revivalism and personal salvation, to the reflective depths of sustained systematic inquiry. This is not to suggest that James and Royce were not concerned with the things of religion, nor, on the other hand, that Edwards and Emerson were uncritical thinkers, but rather the respective professional roles and methods of inquiry were quite different for James and Royce than from those of Edwards

---

6. Emerson, *Essays and Lectures*, 16.
7. Emerson, *Essays and Lectures*, 18.
8. Emerson, *Essays and Lectures*, 47, 48.

and James. This change in context allowed the Pragmatists to engage with the questions of human experience and religious experience in a unique way, namely through the fields of logic and semiotics. Despite these shifts, however, the work of James and Royce provide key insights for the question of human experience that help illuminate the tension between experience and tradition found in Edwards and Emerson.

James's work on religious experience, principally in his *Varieties*, continues the trajectory from Edwards and Emerson in locating the root of religious belief in the "feelings, acts, and experiences"[9] directed towards the divine that "goes direct from heart to heart, from soul to soul, between man and his maker."[10] Similarly, James articulates the integrative nature of religious experience has for the individual, where the "attainment of belief" result in "rules for action" and that religious experience as a whole is "one step in the production of habits."[11] The aesthetics of religious experience that was central for both Edwards and Emerson, however is absent in James. In fact, James's account of the phenomenology of mysticism, the keystone for his analysis of religious experience as a whole, is noticeably devoid of an affective dimension; rather it is organized according to four psychological elements, ineffability, noetic insight, transiency, and passivity.

Here James is reporting as an outside observer, attempting to articulate *what* a religious experience is and to articulate what religious experience means for the formation of religious belief. Edwards and Emerson, on the other hand, were articulating *how* religious experience happens, in the hopes of guiding others into the experience themselves as an expression of a previously attained religious belief, or at least interested curiosity. James's most significant contribution for our present purposes is his latter question concerning the nature of the relationship between experience and belief. As I argued above, James links the noetic insight of religious experience, as that element of human experience that gives an "absolute addition to the subject's range of life,"[12] with the normative dimension of belief which results in the production of habits. That is, the persuasive power of religious belief is rooted in and even dependent on, an individual's experience, thus confirming the basic trajectory from Edwards through Emerson as to the centrality of experience itself for authentic religious belief. At the same time however, by ignoring the external traditions and institutions that preserve and interpret religious belief from generation to generation, James's account of religious experience

9. James, *Varieties*, 32.
10. James, *Varieties*, 31.
11. James, *Varieties*, 338.
12. James, *Varieties*, 44.

The Crisis of Conversion

ultimately suffers from the same individualism as that of Emerson. For both of them, a fundamental problem remains as to how one moves from the confines of personal religious experience to putting the habits of belief cultivated through experience, into lived-practice which would, in turn, form and shape our larger social life, institutions, and traditions of belief.

Royce helps to answer that question by reconceiving James's pragmatic notion of personal religious experience into social and triadic categories. With Royce all experience is the interpretation of signs, which is comprised of three interrelated elements; the interpreter, the interpretant, and the interpretation, the latter of which is mediated via larger social and cultural realities that Royce calls "communities of interpretation." For Christian religious experience specifically, an individual's awareness of the presence of God is mediated through the church as the community of interpretation, and is experienced by the individual as the Holy Spirit. The Holy Spirit, then, serves as both the self-interpreter of God to the individual via the Church, but also the interpretant, or that which is interpreted by the individual and the church as community.[13] This double role of the Spirit suggests that religious experience is not only a matter of the individual and God, though it definitely includes that, but is also a matter of the community and the individual, both of which are mediated through the presence of the Spirit.

Here then, we have a semiotics of experience that helps to illuminate Edwards's notion of the sense of the heart and the indwelling spirit as a vital principle. Additionally, the concept of loyalty provides a normative or ethical/moral quality to the notion of religious experience that requires an integration of will and belief through the "the willing and thoroughgoing devotion of a self to a cause."[14] Thus Royce allows us to conceive of both individual and communal experience as processes of interpretation that do not require a deterministic metaphysics like we saw with both Edwards and Emerson. Rather, the concept of loyalty provides an underlying structure that supports both the continual unfolding of the presence of God as interpreted by and mediated to individuals and the church, precisely because a constituent part of the mediating and mediated nature of the community is Godself in the Spirit. Thus, even when individuals and the Church fail or fall short of its true ideal, we can trust that the presence of God can still be experienced precisely because of God's fidelity to Godself via the mediating and mediated nature of the Spirit.

The work of James and Royce help to illuminate certain elements of Edwards's and Emerson's earlier thought related to the experience of conversion. First, through James, there is a clarification of the relationship between the

---

13. Royce, *Problem*, 95, 233–34.
14. Royce, *Problem*, 83.

experience of conversion and the source of authentic belief that supports Edwards's basic defense of the revivals as being on the whole a legitimate activity of the work of God. James also clarifies the individualist strain from Emerson, by relativizing the formative role that larger social and cultural realities have on the individual, and reducing religious experience to a merely internal and personal phenomenon. This is, however, ultimately untenable in light of the teleological element in the nature of religious experience in both Emerson and James, which states that authentic human experience—including religious experience—leads to the production of habits of life, which signals a move out beyond the self, toward larger social realities in the realms of ethics, morals, and culture. Royce helps to recover religious experience at this point, by regrounding the category of experience within these wider social realities and the normative dimension of the process of interpretation, which for religious experience includes the active self-mediation of God via the Spirit, who in turn interprets the nature and reality of God to the individual and the community. In this way, Royce illuminates the morphology of conversion as articulated in Edwards, while critiquing Emerson's and James's individualistic reductionism. At the same time, Royce critiques both Edwards and Emerson on their capitulation back to a deterministic metaphysics in favor of a semiotics of experience that includes its own normative structure through his concept of loyalty.

This critique concerning the normative dimension of human experience serves as an important conceptual link to the contemporary study of Christian spirituality, particularly as it emerges in the late twentieth century in the work of Sandra Schneiders. Schneiders's helped create space within the various fields of religious studies for a new approach to studying religious identity, by placing the category of experience as the formal and material object of study for spirituality.[15] Additionally, her definition of spirituality places our understanding of religion and religious belief more specifically within the category of human religious experience as we have seen with Edwards, Emerson, James, and Royce. Her definition of spirituality as "the experience of conscious involvement in the project of life-integration through self-transcendence toward the horizon of ultimate value one perceives,"[16] and specifically her self-integrating dynamic within religious experience, connects to the integrative dimension of affect, intellect, and will that was central to Edwards's and Emerson's understanding of religious experience. As the key definition of the "hermeneutical" type, I argued that the interplay between the self-transcendence and the horizon of ultimate value raise immediate questions related to the normative

15. Schneiders, "Approaches," 5.
16. Schneiders, "Approaches," 16.

dimension of experience, or the "self-implicating" nature of religious experience on the one hand, and Schneiders's methodological bracketing of normative claims from the realms of philosophy and theology. Once again, as we saw with Edwards, Emerson, and James, the problem of the subjectivity of individual experience in light of wider social concerns and patterns of thought and behavior becomes apparent. Royce's semiotics of the process of interpretation, and particularly with the dual mediating and mediated Spirit, provide an important clarification that helps to resolve the dualistic nature of the tension between the individual and the community. Therefore, I propose that by reading Schneiders's work on the nature of Christian spirituality, specifically as she articulates the horizon of ultimate value as experienced through an experience of the self-disclosive revelation of God through the interpretation of the Scriptures as the "word of God" through the lens of Royce's semiotics of experience as interpretation, the stage is set to recover both the centrality of personal experiences of conversion on the hand, and the role of communities of interpretation and the process of traditioning on the other as irreducible and co-constitutive elements for evangelical Christianity. To that end, I will return to the work of Amos Yong, who helpfully articulates a more explicitly theological interpretation of Royce's semiotics, and bring him into constructive dialogue with Schneiders, and by way of conclusion offer a recommendation of their work as a model for exploring and articulating a Postmodern evangelical spirituality.

The Pneumatological Imagination as Christian Spirituality: Yong and Schneiders in Constructive Dialogue

One central factor in the contemporary crisis of conversion within evangelical Christianity, is the general trend towards reductionism, as symptomatic and correlative to evangelicalism's increasing individualistic spirit. In both cases, I have articulated these trends through the parallel movement of the articulation of the centrality of religious experiences of conversion as an essential component of one's religious identity, alongside of an increasing separation between the individual's experience and larger social concerns related to theological or ecclesial institutions through the work of Edwards and Emerson as representative voices for American religiosity in general. These trends, however have been identified across the evangelical spectrum in both European and North American contexts through the scholarship of historians and theologians such as Bebbington, Hindmarsh, Larson, Grenz, and others.

Conclusion

This reductionism, has, in turn, severely truncated the notion of religious experience for evangelicals on the one hand, and has distorted their understanding of the nature of human experience itself, particularly in its interpretive/constructive dimensions on the other. In this regard, the recovery of a semiotics of religious experience through the work of James, Royce, and Schneiders help to reverse this trend by providing for a more expansive, and therefore adequate articulation of the nature of human experience in general, and religious experience in particular as it is actually lived.

When combined, evangelicalism's reductionist/individualist spirit and its truncated/distorted approach to religious experience has therefore become situated within a false dichotomy; putting personal religious experience on the one hand in oppositional tension with the interpretation of God on the other. It is here that the methodological work of Schneiders's articulation of Christian spirituality and the creative pneumatology of Yong provide an alternative way forward for evangelical Christianity.

Revisiting the Pneumatological Imagination

At the end of chapter one, I laid out in summary fashion the main contours of Yong's pneumatological imagination which serves as a guiding methodological insight that informs his large and continually expanding body of work. This early insight has been expanded and clarified throughout his career in such texts as, *Spirit-Word-Community: Theological Hermeneutics in Trinitarian Perspective*, and *The Dialogical Spirit: Christian Reason and Theological Method in the Third Millennium*.

The main objective of chapter one's analysis of the pneumatological imagination was twofold; first to place it within the larger context of the demise of early modern foundationalism in light of the post-foundationalist and anti-foundationalist critiques of postmodern thinkers that has exacerbated the evangelical crisis of conversion. Second, to articulate the trialectical shape of the hermeneutical structure of the pneumatological imagination expressed as "Spirit-Word-Community" as an initial corrective strategy to Grenz's anthropological and dialectical proposal of the "ecclesial self," which, as I argued there, ultimately failed to provide an adequate alternative to Enlightenment foundationalism. We are now in a position to flesh out, in a more constructive way, Yong's pneumatological imagination in light of the aesthetic and experiential foundations of evangelical religious experience as explored in Edwards and Emerson, as well as the methodological and semiotic articulation of religious experience more broadly with Schneiders's notion of spirituality, as read through the lens of the Pragmatist tradition. Here I will argue that Yong's

The Crisis of Conversion

"pneumatological engine" provides a methodologically sound platform from which to interpret and engage the presence of God in the world, through the experience of the Holy Spirit.

Yong's proposal of a pneumatological starting point is born out of a series of contextual considerations. First, from his own Pentecostal/charismatic spiritual context, the "encounter with the Holy Spirit which . . . shapes their engagement with world," positions Yong to "provide a pneumatological account for the transformative character of human experience in general and the experience of ultimate salvation in particular."[17] Secondly, and from this foundational spiritual context, Yong's pneumatological starting point helps to illuminate and mediate four overarching contexts that characterize the "exceedingly pluralistic world" that we find ourselves in the twenty-first century, of which three are of particular importance for the present discussion; namely "an epistemological environment after the demise of early modern foundationalism," a "cultural period after the passing of Christianity as a politically dominant reality," and "a late if not postmodern era within which the meeting of the religions portends either to a clash of civilizations or a debilitating subjectivism and relativism."[18] These contextual considerations help to show what is at stake for the future of Christianity on the one hand, and serves as the crucible within which the evangelical crisis of conversion exists.

Taking into account the trialectical shape of his hermeneutics, Yong's pneumatological starting point mitigates both the reductionist spirit of evangelical individualism and its deficient semiotics of religious experience in two important ways. First, Yong roots the interpretive dimension of human experience in the Spirit who is—theologically and experientially—"both universal and particular, both the Spirit of God and the Spirit of Jesus the Christ."[19] That is, for Yong, the Spirit and her attending pneumatological characteristics mediate individual's experience of the presence of the Spirit of God specifically as the revelation of Jesus Christ via the scriptures and the historical unfolding of the Church as the Body of Christ; while simultaneously mediating

---

17. Yong, *Discerning the Spirit(s)*, 311.

18. Yong, *Dialogical Spirit*, 283. Yong also includes a fourth overarching context, "an information age beyond the sacred-secular divide that brings science and the religions together in the public square in new ways," which is an important element in his development of a theology of religions. However, our interests here are more narrowly confined within an ecumenical context relating to a more or less internal discussion within the Christian tradition of the west, and as such we will not explore in any substantive way Yong's theory of religions specifically, nor the important implications that Yong's thought has for a theological engagement with the sciences.

19. Yong, *Beyond the Impasse*, 21.

the experience of the activity of the Spirit of God in the world in general.[20] This pneumatologically-rooted hermeneutical strategy then radically expands the potential for the category of human experience to serve as the locus for the particular religious experiences of conversion to the presence of God in Christ, and for more general, though no less religious experiences of the work of God in the world. Here, Yong points to a religious dimension of human experience "in which there is a heightened sense of truth, beauty, excellence, goodness and reality." Here Yong helps to bring together insights from the aesthetic dimension at the heart of Edwards's and Emerson's notions of religious experience, the phenomenological quality of James's notion of religious experience involving an "absolute addition to the Subject's range of life,"[21] and Royce's insight concerning the mediated and mediating nature of the holy Spirit in the process of the interpretation in community.

Secondly, Yong's pneumatological hermeneutic helps to clarify the normative—Schneiders's self implicating—dimension of human experience by highlighting three biblical root metaphors inherent in the experience of the Holy Spirit; namely, the experience of the Spirit's "*dynamos* or power of creation and life,"[22] the experience of the "relationality" of the Spirit that integrates the "affective, volitional, and the spiritual dimensions of human experience,"[23] and the experience of the Spirit as both axiological yet ambiguous, taken from the biblical imagery of the Spirit as "wind" or "breath," which highlights that the experience of the Spirit is not value-free, thereby stressing the need for spiritual discernment.[24] Taken together, these three characteristics of the experience of the Spirit connect the insight from Edwards and Emerson of the internally integrative nature of religious experience, driving the affect, intellect, and will towards the cultivation of habits of action. Additionally, these characteristics inform the ineffable, noetic, transient, and passive qualities of James's articulation of mystical experience. And lastly, these characteristics provide a point of connection between the self-implicating nature of Schneiders's notion of religious experience, and her "horizon of ultimate value."

This first root metaphor, of the experience of the Spirit's power, orients us in two directions simultaneously. On the one hand, it orients us toward the soteriological power of the presence of the Spirit in the economy of salvation. This is the redemptive power that is attributed to the Spirit in the Old and New Testaments, and is made manifest through conversion into new life in

20. Yong, *Discerning the Spirit(s)*, 123–25.
21. James, *Varieties*, 44.
22. Yong, *Spirit-Word-Community*, 134.
23. Yong, *Spirit-Word-Community*, 136.
24. Yong, *Spirit-Word-Community*, 139–40.

The Crisis of Conversion

the resurrection of Christ. This experience of the Spirit's power highlights the transcendent frame of divine agency, in contradistinction to human finitude and passivity evoking our need for reconciliation and salvation. For Yong, in particular, this experience of the Spirit is a distinguishing mark of the Pentecostal experience of the anointing of the Spirit and the displays of the Spirit's power through the receiving of charismatic gifts. Secondly, the experience of the Spirit's power orients us towards the foundational activity of the Spirit in the world. This is the productive, creative, and dynamic energy of the Spirit's activity in the world. Here, the immanent frame of divine agency is highlighted, which animates, convicts, prompts, and equips us to cooperative action with the Spirit who is always-already active in the world. Yong makes a helpful distinction here theologically, between ecclesial pneumatology on the one hand, corresponding to the soteriological power of the Spirit, and foundational pneumatology, corresponding to the power of the Spirit in the world. The experience of the Spirit's power informs the self-implicating dimension of Schneiders's work primarily in the "experience of conscious involvement" and "self-transcending" components of her definition, in that the experience of the Spirit's soteriological power actualizes our self-transcendence toward the horizon of ultimate value in Jesus, while also empowering us towards conscious involvement with the presence and activity of the Spirit in the world. Moreover, the intentionality inherent in human experience for Schneiders, similarly orients teleologically towards the object of our experience, which is ultimately the horizon of ultimate value, or Yong's soteriological power.[25]

Yong's Second root metaphor, the experience of the Spirit's relationality, similarly orients us ecclesially and foundationally, and is the central experience related to the interpretive dimension of Yong's pneumatologically-rooted hermeneutics as we saw above. Here we experience the Spirit relating interpersonally as both the "Spirit of God" and the "Spirit of Christ" as we saw above, and also intra-personally, through the integration of the affective, intellectual, and spiritual dimensions within ourselves. Moreover, Yong suggests that this relational aspect of the Spirit has an othering effect, meaning that "the Spirit never calls attention to herself, but is always rather the relational pointer to the other."[26] This captures an important insight related to evangelicalism's individualism, that while one's own experience of God is foundational for their evangelical identity, nevertheless, as Yong comments in *Discerning the Spirit(s)* our experience of God "relates us to a dimension of being that includes us but is not exhausted by normal experience."[27] In this way, one's

---

25. Yong, *Spirit-Word-Community*, 134–36.
26. Yong, *Spirit-Word-Community*, 136.
27. Yong, *Discerning the Spirit(s)*, 122.

appeal to experience alone becomes inappropriate, while at the same time, it forces each of us to take seriously the experiences of others, as no one experience "exhausts" the reality of God. Royce, once again, is instructive here, as his dynamic interpretive process within communities of interpretation both expand the context of experience beyond the control of any one person or group, and also appropriately relativizes particular experiences within the overarching interpretive process of the community itself.[28]

In terms of the normative dimension of the experience of the relationality of the Spirit, Schneiders's bracketing becomes informative, though perhaps counterintuitively. As I argued in chapter two, Schneiders's argument for the methodological bracketing of normative claims introduced an apparent tension in her work vis a vis the self-implicating nature of human experience. However, this tension, methodologically speaking, has more to do with Schneiders's early struggle to create the disciplinary space for spirituality studies from which to establish the category of human experience as the formal and material object of study.[29] Moreover, when we consider the method of bracketing in the work of Husserl from chapter one, we see that he similarly utilized bracketing as a hermeneutical strategy to clear away the space for phenomenological investigation. This suggests that bracketing serves an originating rather than teleological function in the overarching process of phenomenological investigation. This is a crucial piece in the larger postfoundationalist and postmodern critique of Enlightenment rationality. What is bracketed, for Husserl and Schneiders, is the *a priori* appeal to normative claims, so that a proper phenomenological inquiry is made possible. For Schneiders in particular, this allows for experience, as the formal object, or the "how" spirituality is studied—as experience of—to be properly analyzed as such.[30] Experience though, when read through the pragmatic lens of James, Dewey, and especially Royce, mediates interpretation as a constitutive element of the dynamic process of experience; and moreover, interpretation should not be, and indeed cannot be, abstracted from the very experience itself. Schneiders's appeal to bracketing, therefore, provides the methodological link between the intentionality of lived experience as the primary mode of investigation on the one hand, and the dynamic processes of life-integration and self-transcendence on the other. This initial bracketing allows for the interpretation one's experience to be teleologically oriented towards the "horizon of ultimate value, that one perceives" rather an *a priorily* asserted, as would be the case in foundationalist approach. This horizon of ultimate value is again

---

28. Royce, *Problem*, 85.
29. Schneiders, "Study of Christian Spirituality," 39.
30. Schneiders, "Study of Christian Spirituality," 40–41.

supplied by and emerges from the interpretive dimension of lived experience.³¹ This precludes the legitimacy of appeals abstracted from the realm of experience as authentic or authoritative interpreters of the experience itself. In a similar fashion, the othering effect of Yong's experience of the Spirit's radical relationality has a similar effect in that it both elevates human experience as the mode of perceiving the Spirit, and also orients us teleologically towards the ever-unfolding self-revelation of the Spirit by continually pointing us further into the process of interpretive inquiry, towards the "already-but-not-yet" kingdom of God.³²

This brings us to consider Yong's third root metaphor, the experience of the Spirit as axiological yet ambiguous. This experience of the Spirit calls to attention both the mysterious movement of the Spirit's agency in the world "the wind blows where it chooses . . . but you do not know where it comes from or where it goes" (Jn 3:8a), and also to the presence of a "variety of spirits operative in the world."³³ In both cases, this points to the need to cultivate an attitude of spiritual discernment. For Edwards, this connects with the process of authenticating one's experience of the divine through the manifestation of the "exercise and fruit [of] Christian practice."³⁴ Similarly, in the Pragmatist tradition, there is a correlation to James's "production of active habits,"³⁵ and Royce's community of interpretation made manifest through the cohesion of the individuals together through a shared loyalty, rooted in the experience of Jesus mediated through the individual and cumulative interpretation of and with the Spirit.³⁶

Additionally, Yong indicates that this experience of the Spirit points to the pneumatological component in all things, thus mitigating any attempt to dualistically construe the world into metaphysically distinct realms of spirit and mater, or in like manner, of good and evil. This suggests an essentially incarnational view of the world, and furthermore reinforces the pneumatological orientation toward the "other" that we saw previously. At this point there is considerable agreement with Schneiders's notion of the potentially revelatory nature of all things, a central piece of the spiritual stance in her biblical hermeneutics analyzed above. Here again, the issue of normativity requires nuance. The spirit, as axial, or value-laden indicates that there is a normative dimension to the experience of the Spirit, yet this normativity is

---

31. Schneiders, "Theology and Spirituality," 268, 271–73.
32. Yong, *Spirit-Word-Community*, 137
33. Yong, *Spirit-Word-Community*, 139.
34. Edwards, *WJE*, 2:383.
35. James, *Varieties*, 338.
36. Royce, *Problem*, 176–79.

realized through the interpretive function of discernment of the experience. This would seem to suggest that discernment would be an essential component for each discreet experience of the Spirit. It would also follow that through the sustained "exercise and fruit [of] Christian practice"[37] that the relative aptitude of spiritual discernment would result in cumulatively more accurate and expansive interpretations of experiences of the Spirit throughout the life of an individual and community. This "traditioning" of the experience of the Spirit, an element that is central to the ongoing life of Royce's community of interpretation through the actualization of loyalty to the Spirit, might in some way illuminate the Roman Catholic notion of the *sensus fidelium* as the collective listening back-and-forth between the laity and the magisterium under the guidance of the Spirit.[38] Moreover, this might also help to connect Schneiders's notion of the self-implicating nature of human experience with the teleological orientation of religious experience towards the horizon of ultimate value, by making more explicit the socio-communal nature of human experience as articulated through the Pragmatist tradition. At the same time, Schneiders's feminist hermeneutic of "suspicion and retrieval" related to the misogynistic history of the Church and its interpretation of the revelation of God in the world, introduces a critical activism at the level of an individual's interpretation and discernment of the experience of the Spirit that might further accentuate the ambiguous dimension of Yong's analysis at this point; blurring the lines of the mysterious movement of the Spirit and the relative success and, more importantly, failure of human persons and communities adequately interpreting that movement.[39]

Thus far, I have engaged Yong's pneumatological "engine" as a hermeneutical strategy at the level of the experience of the Spirit, in constructive dialogue with Schneiders's hermeneutical approach and the preceding historical analyses of religious experience in a North American context. This has to a certain extent highlighted more explicitly the dynamic interplay between the Spirit-Community relation of Yong's trialectic in an effort to articulate some of the methodological implications of spirituality as experience. The phenomenon of religious experience, as articulated in the previous chapters, is not strictly a purely individual phenomenon, although the individual is an irreducible component. Rather, it is on the whole a fundamentally hermeneutical phenomenon that necessarily includes at least; individual and social, affective

---

37. Edwards, *WJE*, 2:383.

38. Markey, *Creating Communion*; Markey, "Clarifying the Relationship between the Universal and the Particular Churches," 299–320; Markey, "Communion as Salvation," 119–37.

39. Schneiders, *Revelatory Text*, 182–83.

The Crisis of Conversion

and intellectual, material and spiritual, objective and subjective, noetic and ineffable, active and passive, transcendent and immanent, discreet and cumulative, conscious and unconscious, and normative and volitional components. It is finite and perspectival in its mode, fallible in its expression, expansive in its trajectory, and is the point of contact with all reality, including ourselves. This however, does not mean that one's experience is literally all there is. Through this discussion, an alternative way forward has begun to emerge as it relates to the evangelical crisis of conversion, particularly in the reductionistic and individualistic tendencies within the larger evangelical tradition on the one hand, and by resituating the category of human experience on the other. Specifically, I have endeavored to show that the experiential insight within the spiritual tradition of North American evangelicalism stemming from Edwards and Emerson, and becoming more clarified through the Pragmatist tradition and through the contemporary concerns of Schneiders and Yong, needs to cultivated, particularly in light of the epistemological challenges posed by postmodernity. Moreover, I have suggested that this cultivation of a spirituality of experience need not be placed in opposition with the theological pursuit of religious truth. To draw out our that suggestion more explicitly, I will now engage Yong's pneumatological "imagination" as a hermeneutical strategy at the level of theological reflection that will more explicitly incorporate the dimension of the Word within the trialectical hermeneutics of Spirit-Word-Community, without losing the other two dimensions of Spirit and Community.

As I showed in chapter one, reason and experience became problematically situated in opposition together through the larger intellectual disputes during the Enlightenment and later Romanticist movements, particularly for evangelicals with Schleiermacher's reconceiving of the Pietist emphasis on feeling and the rise of classical Liberal Protestantism. Moreover, with the advent of postmodern thought, the battle lines and presuppositions of the modernist debates began to be called into question the adequacy of foundationalist epistemologies, both liberal and conservative. Postmodern anti-/non-/post-foundationalist approaches have not solved all of our epistemological questions, nor provided consistent or compatible pathways forward; for example the rapid increase of our technological lives has tended to single out materialistic interpretations of the world and reality that suggests a tragic loss of imaginative capacities on the one hand, while on the other hand technological advances have produced an "explosion of images" signaling for Yong, "perhaps the third coming of imagination following the ancients and the early modern romanticists and transcendentalists."[40] In both of these cases post-

---

40. Yong, *Spirit-Word-Community*, 142

modern values of "local knowledge and concrete experiences" are privileged over "universal reason or abstractions of the mind."[41] In the latter case, Yong suggests that imagination may be reemployed as an ally in theological reflection, particularly in its natural aspirations toward the transcendent by virtue of its "inherently religious activity of worldmaking."[42] Through the worldmaking activity inherent in the nature of human imagination, Yong sees a potential epistemological benefit by engaging the imagination as a part of theological reflection, specifically in the imagination's basic transcendental orientation to see more than is simply there. Following the work of Robert Cummings Neville, Yong comments on the basic function of the imagination which "constitutes the lived-world in its totality, including its farthest horizons, sometimes expanding these horizons and transforming them from possibility (fancy) into actuality, and other times going beyond them speculatively."[43] However, imagination by itself is not helpful, given that its creative energy exceeds the nature of reality in the realm of sheer possibility. Here, interpretation comes in to "specify the vague possibilities suggested by imagination."[44]

When placed together in an explicitly theological context, ideally the interpretive dimension of theological reflection "ensures that revelation is being adequately engaged, even if not altogether understood . . . " whereas the imaginative dimension serves as "the necessary mediator that enables theologizing—considered as orthodoxy and orthopraxy—to take place."[45] For Yong, his basic epistemological assumptions, rooted in the Pragmatist tradition of Peirce, James, and Royce, are not what he is arguing for. What Yong is arguing for here is the explicit engagement with the synthetic, transcendent, and creative processes of the imagination as a constitutive element in the mediated process of theological reflection as adequate engagement with revelation. In this way, Yong perhaps is trying to position himself in a middle path, analogous with Edwards, between the polar alternatives of cold rationalism on the one hand, and unfettered enthusiasm on the other. But rather than articulating a space for the affective dimension of religious experience as an element in adequate engagements with revelation, Yong is here articulating a space for the creative dimension of religious imagination as an element in adequate engagements with revelation.

---

41. Yong, *Spirit-Word-Community*, 142.
42. Yong, *Spirit-Word-Community*, 141
43. Yong, *Spirit-Word-Community*, 144.
44. Yong, *Spirit-Word-Community*, 144.
45. Yong, *Spirit-Word-Community*, 146.

The Pneumatological Imagination and the Revelatory Text

Yong connects the worldmaking possibility of human imagination with theological reflection through the pneumatological imagination at three basic levels. First the pneumatological imagination "recognizes that whatever there is to be encountered is multi-dimensional, in that it is a result of being acted upon as well as being a creative . . . actor in its own right";[46] second it "engages the process of worldmaking holistically; combining valuational, affective, and spiritual sensitivities";[47] and third, it "engages the task of worldmaking axiologically and normatively."[48] Here Yong's the trialectical structure of the pneumatological imagination as theological reflection parallels the trialectical structure of the pneumatological imagination as experience of the Spirit above in its dynamic, integrative, and axiological dimensions. The difference between the two is their respective and relative temporal position within the overarching trialectical shape of Yong's pneumatological imagination as a hermeneutical strategy. The function of these two interconnected levels is analogous to the three-fold nature of experience that I outlined in the work of John Dewey, and, as Yong notes, is heavily dependent on the foundational work of C. S. Peirce's articulation of a triadic semiotics of experience.[49] The key insight here is that for Yong, theological reflection is rooted in and arises from the basic triadic process of religious experience.

Yong's analysis of the three levels of worldmaking that is engaged through the pneumatological imagination proceed in a similar fashion to his analysis of the trialectical experience of the Spirit in that it orients us transcendently and immanently; situates us relationally within ourselves, in the world, to the other, and toward the divine; while also providing an "epistemic corrective to the ideological tendencies that otherwise plague human knowledge"[50] by virtue of the Spirit's axiological and spontaneous reality. That is, the pneumatological imagination is both "Christomorphic" in that its theological

---

46. Yong, *Spirit-Word-Community*, 147.

47. Yong, *Spirit-Word-Community*, 147.

48. Yong, *Spirit-Word-Community*, 148.

49. As mentioned in several places throughout my analysis of the Pragmatist traditions work related to religious experience, James, Dewey, and Royce are developing insights first articulated through Peirce's original thought. Throughout his work, Yong interacts with Peirce more directly than I have here, primarily because Peirce's thought is more explicitly rooted in formal logic and semiotics, whereas James and Royce apply Peirce's categories to question of religious experience more directly. For Yong's more sustained interaction with Peirce in *Spirit-Word-Community*, see chapters 3 "Toward a Foundational Pneumatology: Metaphysics and Ontology," 83–118 (esp. 91–118), and chapter 5 "The Pneumatological Imagination and Truthful Discernment," 151–84 (esp. 151–65).

50. Yong, *Spirit-Word-Community*, 148.

orientation is incarnational by virtue of the Spirit being the "Spirit of Christ," while also "Pentecostal"—used as a descriptor of the presence and activity of the Spirit in the world, rather than ecclesially here—thus exhibiting the "providential extension and constitution of otherness itself." And so it is "only in the form of Christ and the power of the Spirit that true integrity, authenticity and autonomy is achieved."[51] This "Pente-Christic" integrity of the pneumatological imagination in the process of the theological reflection helps to not only give shape and guidance as to the adequate subject of theological reflection, which is God; but also helps clarify the hermeneutical embeddedness of the self-world-other-God in the task of theological reflection, through Yong's trialectic, Spirit-Word-Community.[52]

This integral dimension of Yong's pneumatological imagination brings us, finally, to consider the question of normativity for both religious experience and theological reflection born out of experience. This normative question will, in turn, help to integrate key insights from Schneiders's spiritual hermeneutics of scripture as the "word of God" discussed in chapter two, and will allow me to offer by way of a tentative conclusion, a potential solution to the contemporary crisis of evangelical spirituality.

As we have seen, the trialectic shape of Yong's pneumatological imagination informs his understanding of the experience of God in the Spirit. The same holds true for his understanding of theological reflection which, "consists of an ongoing spiral of Spirit and Word in community."[53] For Yong, the pneumatological imagination is central for adequate theological reflection, particularly as it is informed through the interpretation of scripture. In this process of interpretation, the pneumatological imagination "seeks not only the habitual application and transformation of the text in our lives, but also our transformation according to the christomorphic character of the living Christ,"[54] thereby insisting that "interpretation is a normative act,"[55] ultimately

---

51. Yong, *Spirit-Word-Community*, 148.

52. Here, Yong may be responding to some critiques of his earlier *Discerning the Spirit(s)*, and *Beyond the Impasse* in which he stressed the distinct and independent mission and presence of the Spirit from those of Christ, in an effort to get past the "christological impasse" for the development of his theology of religions. While he never absolutized this distinction, he nevertheless still wants to maintain the Spirit's alterity and autonomy as this protects the "freedom" of the Spirit from being subordinated under christological categories. For more on this critique see: Yong, *Beyond the Impasse*; Yong et al., "Christ and Spirit," 15–83; Merrick, "Spirit of Truth as Agent in False Religions?," 107–25; Richie, "Spirit of Truth as Guide into All Truth."

53. Yong, *Spirit-Word-Community*, 151.

54. Yong, *Spirit-Word-Community*, 162.

55. Yong, *Spirit-Word-Community*, 163.

meaning that "truth necessarily emerges through the coherence of the entire set of interpretants."[56] In this process, the "truth" related to the nature of God or the scriptures is not ultimately propositional, but rather interpreted. Truth, in this way, is connected to ontology, or the nature of reality for Yong. This does not mean that any and all interpretations of a given reality are true, but that the truth of a given reality is only understood through the process of interpretation. This process of interpretation, is, as we saw above, rooted in the trialectical hermeneutics of Spirit-Word-Community, which is actualized through the pneumatological imagination. The dynamic relationship that Yong has traced here between truth, interpretation, and transformation illuminates our previous discussion of Yong in chapter one and his understanding of conversion, following the foundational theology of Lonergan and Gelpi.[57] Conversion, then, is both the result of the transformative interpretation of the truth of God, and also the process by which the transformative truth of God is interpreted, precisely through the pneumatological imagination's hermeneutical function at the levels of experience and theological reflection simultaneously.

In a similar way, Schneiders argues that personal transformation is the proper primary objective in the interpretation of scriptures, at least from her spiritual/existential stance that is concerned with dealing with the "truth-claims" contained within the text.[58] Moreover, Schneiders makes this claim by appealing to the experience of the reader as they read the text. In her analysis of the Gospel of John, Schneiders argues that the purpose of John as a text "is to bring the reader, as much as possible, into the truth, not just to abstract knowledge in the factual sense of the word but to that existential involvement with the truth to which the Jesus of John's gospel invites his hearers."[59] And it is this experience of transformative encounter, as the main objective of the text, that is fundamental to her understanding of scripture as the "word of God." As outlined above in chapter two, Schneiders's designation of scripture as the word of God, refers primarily to its "privileged position" by "witnessing to the foundational revelation [of God in Jesus Incarnate] constitutes a privileged possibility of revelation in the present."[60] Schneiders nicely summarizes this relationship between revelation and the text of scripture by stating that "[revelation] is *rooted* in the life of Jesus in Palestine in the first century. But

---

56. Yong, *Spirit-Word-Community*, 171.

57. Yong, *Spirit-Word-Community*, 222–23.

58. Schneiders, *Revelatory Text*, 13–14; Schneiders, *Written That You May Believe*, 18–22.

59. Schneiders, *Revelatory Text*, 14.

60. Schneiders, *Revelatory Text*, 46.

Conclusion

it *occurs* in the faith life of believers in the community shaped by the text of scripture."[61] That is, scripture as potentially revelatory becomes actually revelatory through the act of interpreting the truth claims of the text, unfolding into the process of transformation, through the experience of Jesus occasioned by the reading of the text.

On the other hand, the scriptures are not the only things that can be the occasion for revelation. For Schneiders, rather, "as possibility, divine revelation must be seen as coextensive with human experience." Where it is only in Jesus of Nazareth that divine revelation was actually coextensive with human experience, but because for Schneiders, God desires to reveal Godself to us, "all of human experience is meant to be revelatory." Human sinfulness and the finite nature of reality preclude the full actualization of the revelatory potential of human experience, but it is fundamentally important for Schneiders that human experience really is potentially revelatory.[62]

Schneiders's definition of spirituality: "the experience of conscious involvement in the project of life-integration and self-transcendence toward the horizon of ultimate value that one perceives,"[63] serves then as the hermeneutical method whereby the actualization of the potentially revelatory nature of human experience occurs, including the experience of transformative interpretation of scripture; the specific dynamics of which I explored above in chapter two. Here, however, the relationship between human experience and the normative implications of the process of transformation needs further clarification in light of Schneiders's understanding of the hermeneutics of interpretation.

Following closely the work of Paul Ricœur, the hermeneutical method that Schneiders develops seeks to show "how text and reader interact in the experience of biblical revelation."[64] This method is summarily outlined as the means by which a reader "enters into and appropriates the world of meaning that the text projects and is thereby changed."[65] Interpretation, for Schneiders, refers to both an object "the meaning" and to a dialectic process "between explanation and understanding, between the use of methods to clarify the sense-reference content of the text and the holistic assimilation of that content as expansion of one's being."[66] This dialectical process unfolds through a series of steps beginning with one's pre-understanding that they bring with

---

61. Schneiders, *Written That You May Believe*, 10.
62. Schneiders, *Revelatory Text*, 45.
63. Schneiders, "Approaches," 5.
64. Schneiders, *Revelatory Text*, 157.
65. Schneiders, *Revelatory Text*, 157.
66. Schneiders, *Revelatory Text*, 157

The Crisis of Conversion

them to the text in their initial engagement and informs their basic and initial understanding of "what the text is about and what it says."[67] As the reader engages the text with their preunderstanding, they move into the process of explanation, which is the "more or less methodical interrogation of the text through techniques of investigation."[68] For biblical studies these techniques would include such things as exegesis and historical and literary methods which then present before the reader a variety of possible understandings of the text, which are then in turn investigated further. This dialectical back-and-forth between explanations and understandings of the text eventually "comes to rest in an experience of meaning that is satisfactory and that we will finally call, following Ricœur, appropriation or, as I prefer, transformative understanding."[69] And it is the capacity of the dialectic between explanation and understanding to transform the reader that "grounds the possibility of the biblical text functioning as revelatory medium."[70]

Closely related to this, is the relationship between meaning and understanding. Again, following Ricœur, Schneiders understands meaning to be the goal of interpretation, whereas understanding is the grasping of meaning. Here another dialectic emerges between "sense (what is said) and reference (what it is said about)."[71] Here, meaning is achieved when the reader comes to understand both the sense and reference of the text. Grasping the sense of a text, is our basic ability to read the text (and also the text's basic ability to communicate) according to grammatical and syntactical norms. I cannot make sense of something that either is in a foreign language that I cannot read, or that is improperly or poorly communicated, such that there is no basic understanding of what the text is about. At the level of sense, questions about the text's truth or falsity are left aside. At the level of understanding the reference of the text, however, refers to the "proposition's claim to attain reality."[72] Here, to achieve understanding one must be able to come to some degree of recognition of what the text is referencing and subsequently adjudicate the adequacy of the text's proposition to its intended reference. Basic meaning is achieved when the reader is able to identify what the text is trying to communicate, and then come to some conclusion about the relative success or failure of the text's ability to say something about it. Once meaning has been achieved, the final step in Schneiders's hermeneutical method is "appropriation" or the process

---

67. Schneiders, *Revelatory Text*, 158.
68. Schneiders, *Revelatory Text*, 158.
69. Schneiders, *Revelatory Text*, 158.
70. Schneiders, *Revelatory Text*, 158.
71. Schneiders, *Revelatory Text*, 161.
72. Schneiders, *Revelatory Text*, 146.

of transformation, by which the reader moves from an unreflective reception towards a transformational understanding through critical investigation. This is in short form, Ricœur's move from first to second *naiveté*.[73]

This transformational reading of the text is, as was stated above, the primary objective of the scriptures as texts for Schneiders, and it is at this level of transformation that her hermeneutics becomes integrated with her notion of spirituality as experience and brings us to consider the normative dimension of both Schneiders's understanding of spirituality as lived experience, as well the scriptures as revelatory texts. In both cases, Schneiders refers to Gadamer's seminal notion of the "fusion of horizons" to help articulate the nature of the transformational meaning of the text that involves a "radical personal engagement with . . . the truth claims of the text. [Which are] not merely dogmatic propositions . . . but the presentation of reality that offers itself to us as a way of being."[74] In the process of transformation the world that the text projects becomes fused into our own horizon of being in a way that transforms our own sense of reality in a way that necessarily changes who we are and the world about us.

Here I find both great compatibility between Schneiders and Yong and also a significant point of departure between them. In terms of their compatibility, both Schneiders and Yong are interested in exploring and more clearly articulating the transformative capacity of human experience in reference to our understanding of God. Both of them are careful to point out that experience in itself is not necessarily transformative, nor that even when it is transformative it is not absolutely so. Moreover, they both place human experience in a central role in their understanding of scriptural interpretation (Schneiders) and theological reflection (Yong), in a way that is compatible with their understanding of human experience in general. And finally, there seems to me to be a great deal of substantive compatibility between Schneiders's notion of "transformational interpretation" and Yong's "pneumatological imagination," particularly as they both function respectively to decenter, expand, and deepen an individual's engagement with and understanding of themselves, the world, and God.

However, I find that there are certain advantages in the trialectical shape of Yong's hermeneutical structure than the dialectical shape of Schneiders's in more adequately addressing the question of the normativity of religious experience vis a vis the normativity of scripture, or the church, etc. The problem or deficiency I find in Schneiders's hermeneutics, is more properly aimed at an underlying problem with dialectical structures more generally and their

---

73. Schneiders, *Revelatory Text*, 169–72.
74. Schneiders, *Revelatory Text*, 174.

under-developed sense of mediation, often resulting in either the collapsing of one pole of the dialectic into the other, e.g., fundamentalism/relativism; or requiring an abstracted or transcendental point from which to synthesize the difference, e.g., Descartes, Kant, and Hegel; or by rejecting the dialectic itself—either immediately through some form of authoritarian objectivism, dogmatic assertion, or nihilistic skepticism, or more gradually through an infinite regression of deferral e.g., deconstructionism. That is to say, with only two elements, the object and the subject, a dialectical hermeneutics seems destined to be trapped in the problems inherent in foundationalist epistemologies, post-, anti-, or otherwise. This does not suggest that these epistemological problems reach successful conclusions in triadic systems, but, rather, by locating the process of interpretation within a triadic structure that includes mediating realities as irreducible components, these problems can be wrestled with in a way that corresponds more adequately to the self-implicating nature of the human experience of reality, which is full of mediating realities such as language, communities, societies, traditions, habits, norms, beliefs, and cultures.

When considering Schneiders's specific contributions; with her notions of transformational interpretation, the revelatory potential of text and experience, and in particular her definition of spirituality, I find them to sit uncomfortably alongside of her dialectical hermeneutics. The dynamic energy and expansive potentiality inherent in these contributions seemed to surpass the simple back-and-forth between text and reader, and in fact within Schneiders's notion of the transformational understanding, the dialectic breaks down precisely through the presence of a third. Transformation occurs for Schneiders not simply between the text and the reader but between God and the reader, mediated or occasioned in the experience of reading the text. This is the case in her articulation of the nature of revelation as well, the revelatory capacity is not rooted in the phenomena of the text or the category of human experience, nor in the reader or experiencing subject, but rather through the presence of God similarly occasioned by and mediated through the experience as lived or the text as read. And finally, when reconsidering Schneiders's notion of spirituality, a similar triadic shape emerges in the interaction between "the conscious experience of"—"the project of life-integration and self-transcendence"—toward the "horizon of ultimate value." In all three of these instances, Schneiders's original insights seem to betray the dialectical shape of her hermeneutics.[75]

---

75. In a similar way, James's eventual conclusions concerning the nature of religious experience sat uncomfortably alongside of his previous articulation of Peirce's triadic semiotics of religious experience. I also critiqued him at this point, precisely because his

Conclusion

The uncomfortable situation of Schneiders's conclusions vis a vis her hermeneutics become much more comfortable when similarly situated within Yong's triadic pneumatological imagination as articulated and developed through the Pragmatist tradition of Peirce and Royce. First, in addressing the question of the normativity of religious experience, Yong's pneumatological imagination is not solely reliant on the relative ability of the individual to perceive, interpret, and actualize his or her experience, but rather finds hermeneutical recourse through the pre-existing communities of interpretation that they find themselves in. These communities, in turn, exist for this individual in relative degrees of importance, relevance, and competence, and which, correlative to these degrees, help mediate the individual's experience both consciously and subconsciously. This larger and multi-dimensional context—Schneiders's "coextensive with human experience"—from which the individual lives and engages reality and is itself a part of the individual's reality and thus is capable of being—Yong's "acted upon as well as being a creative and more-or-less powerful actor in its own right."[76]

Additional parallels are found when comparing Schneiders's dynamics of life-integration and self-transcendence and Yong's pneumatological imagination in its "combining valuational, affective, and spiritual sensitivities," and "Pente-Christic" nature; and perhaps most importantly between Schneiders's horizon of infinite value and Axiological/Normative worldmaking of the pneumatological imagination. As previously argued, Schneiders's understanding of human experience helps get more clarity when read through the lens of a Pragmatist semiotics of religious experience, and so here I will simply conclude this section by suggesting that Schneiders's biblical spirituality, and by extension the discipline of spirituality as a whole, might benefit from engaging some of the methodological, hermeneutical, and experiential categories as developed in the North American Pragmatist tradition.

The Pneumatological Imagination and the Crisis of Conversion: A Modest Proposal Toward a Postmodern Evangelical Spirituality

In this book, I have attempted to identify and articulate a fundamental tension within the North American Evangelical tradition that I have called the crisis of conversion concerning the ambiguous status of the category of human

---

conclusions as deduced from abstractions failed to adequately conform to the semiotics of religious experience he had been developing up to that point.

76. Yong, *Spirit-Word-Community*, 147.

The Crisis of Conversion

experience as it relates to evangelical life and practice on the one hand, and theological reflection on the other. In the former case, as evidenced through the grand tradition of religious revivalism and the importance of one's conversion experience as a marker for one's Christian identity, the writings of Jonathan Edwards and Ralph Waldo Emerson have clearly demonstrated the central role that "experience" has played in history of North American religious expression. This trajectory furthermore confirms the more recent scholarly analyses of evangelicalism by David Bebbington, D. Bruce Hindmarsh, Timothy Larson, and others that conversionism and activism, or experiential piety, are core distinguishing marks of evangelical identity.

In the latter case, I showed that with the rise of Liberal Protestantism and the theology of Friedrich Schleiermacher, evangelical theology became more suspect of human experience as viable category for receiving and interpreting divine revelation. This coincided with an intensification of the role of the Bible as the sole medium from which evangelicals might come to know and understand God. Here again Bebbington's definition of evangelicalism is instructive in highlighting its biblicist and crucicentric markers. Moreover, as the epistemological foundationalism of Enlightenment Rationalism came under increasing criticism and suspicion, the problem of the objective and the subjective in terms of the attainment of knowledge, this also threatened evangelicalism's basic approach to the interpretation of scripture. By the time of the advent of postmodern criticism, evangelicalism found itself in a precarious position both theologically and spiritually as both their experiential and biblical foundations became more and more tenuous and precarious.

As an effort to propose a solution to this apparent crisis, I attempted three primary things. First, I attempted to reconsider the nature of religious experience through the methodological insights of Sandra Schneiders and the disciple of Christian spirituality as way of clarifying the nature of experience both phenomenologically and normatively in relation to the evangelical tension between experience and revelation. Second, I attempted to contextualize the nature of religious experience in a North American context in an effort highlight the central role that human experience and religious experience played in the history of the United States' religious and cultural life. For human experience more broadly, the Pragmatist philosophical tradition at the turn of the 20th century who played a central in developing and articulating a philosophical semiotics of religious experience through the work of C. S. Peirce, William James, and Josiah Royce, among others. In terms of the influence that religious experience has had on the shaping of North America, I analyzed the work of Jonathan Edwards and his role during the Great Awakenings of the eighteenth century, and Ralph Waldo Emerson's Transcendentalism during the mid-nineteenth century as representative figures that provided original insights and helped to place religious experience into the center of the North American religious and spiritual ethos in a way that is still operative today.

Third, I attempted to provide a tentative solution to this crisis of conversion in light of the methodological and historical retrieval of the central role that religious experience has had for North American evangelical spirituality. And to that end, I returned to the work of Amos Yong and his pneumatological imagination in an attempt to recover a more vibrant notion of religious experience on the one hand, and mediate the tension between individual experience and scriptural authority on the other that has precipitated the crisis of conversion. In conclusion, I propose that Yong, as informed by the Pragmatist tradition, and placed in constructive dialogue with some the historical insights from Edwards and Emerson, as well as some insights from Schneiders as I have articulated above, does indeed provide a viable pathway forward for the recovery of a solid epistemological method that retains both the centrality of religious experience for evangelical spirituality, and the centrality of the Bible for evangelical theology.

Bibliography

Agnew, Una, et al., eds. *With Wisdom Seeking God: The Academic Study of Spirituality.* Studies in Spirituality 15. Leuven: Peeters, 2008.
Balmer, Randall. *Mine Eyes Have Seen the Glory: A Journey into the Evangelical Subculture in America.* 4th ed. Oxford: Oxford University Press, 2006.
Bebbington, David. "The Evangelical Quadrilateral: A Response." *Fides et Historia* 47 (2015) 87–96.
———. *Evangelicalism in Modern Britain: A History from the 1730s to the 1980s.* London: Routledge, 1989.
Bellah, Robert N., et al. *The Good Society.* New York: Knopf, 1991.
Bloesch, Donald G. *The Crisis of Piety: Essays towards a Theology of the Christian Life.* 2nd ed. Colorado Springs: Helmers & Howard, 1988.
———. *The Evangelical Renaissance.* Grand Rapids: Eerdmans, 1973.
———. *The Future of Evangelical Christianity: A Call for Unity amid Diversity.* 1st ed. Garden City, NY: Doubleday, 1983.
Borgmann, Albert. *Crossing the Postmodern Divide.* Chicago: University of Chicago Press, 1992.
Brand, David C. *Profile of the Last Puritan: Jonathan Edwards, Self-Love, and the Dawn of the Beatific.* American Academy of Religion Academy Series 73. Atlanta: Scholars, 1991.
Brantley, Richard E. *Coordinates of Anglo-American Romanticism: Wesley, Edwards, Carlyle and Emerson.* Gainesville: University Press of Florida Press, 1993.
Bremer, Francis J. *The Puritan Experiment: New England Society from Bradford to Edwards.* London: St. James, 1977.
Brueggemann, Walter. *Old Testament Theology: An Introduction.* The Library of Biblical Theology. Nashville: Abingdon, 2008.
Buckham, John Wright. "The Contribution of Professor Royce to Christian Thought." *Harvard Theological Review* 8 (1915) 219–37.
Buttrick, George Arthur, ed. *The Interpreter's Bible.* 12 vols. New York: Abingdon, 1952.
Caldwell, Robert W. *Communion in the Spirit: The Holy Spirit as the Bond of Union in the Theology of Jonathan Edwards.* Studies in Evangelical History and Thought. Eugene, OR: Wipf & Stock, 2007.

Bibliography

Cenkner, William. "Theme and Counter-Theme in Contemporary Spirituality." *Horizons* 9 (1982) 87–95.
Cochran, Pamela. *Evangelical Feminism: A History*. New York: New York University Press, 2005.
Cohen, Charles Lloyd. *God's Caress: The Psychology of Puritan Religious Experience*. Oxford University Press, 1986.
Cone, James H. *A Black Theology of Liberation*. New York: Orbis, 1990.
Crisp, Oliver D. *Jonathan Edwards on God and Creation*. Oxford: Oxford University Press, 2012.
Dayton, Donald W., and Robert Johnston. *The Variety of American Evangelicalism*. Eugene, OR: Wipf & Stock, 1997.
Delattre, Roland A. "Aesthetics and Ethics: Jonathan Edwards and the Recovery of Aesthetics for Religious Ethics." *Journal of Religious Ethics* 31 (2003) 277–97.
Delattre, Roland André. *Beauty and Sensibility in the Thought of Jonathan Edwards: An Essay in Aesthetics and Theological Ethics*. Eugene, OR: Wipf & Stock, 2006.
Derrida, Jacques, and Gayatri Chakravorty Spivak. *Of Grammatology*. Fortieth-Anniversary Edition. Baltimore: Johns Hopkins, 2016.
Dewey, John. *Experience and Nature*. 2nd. ed. Paul Carus Foundation Lectures Series l. La Salle, IL: Open Court, 1958.
———. *The Quest For Certainty*. London: Allen & Unwin, 1930.
Dochuk, Darren. "Revisiting Bebbington's Classic Rendering of Modern Evangelicalism at Points of New Departure." *Fides et Historia* 47 (2015) 63–72.
Dreyer, Elizabeth, and Mark S. Burrows, eds. *Minding the Spirit: The Study of Christian Spirituality*. Baltimore: Johns Hopkins, 2005.
Dupré, Louis. *Passage to Modernity: An Essay in the Hermeneutics of Nature and Culture*. New Haven, CT: Yale University Press, 1993.
Edwards, Jonathan. *The Works of Jonathan Edwards, Volume 2, Religious Affections*. Edited by John E. Smith. New Haven, CT: Yale University Press, 2009.
———. *The Works of Jonathan Edwards, Volume 4, The Great Awakening*. Edited by C. C. Goen. The Great Awakening. New Haven, CT: Yale University Press, 2009.
———. *The Works of Jonathan Edwards, Volume 6, Scientific and Philosophical Writings*. Edited by Wallace Earl Anderson. New Haven, CT: Yale University Press, 1980.
———. *The Works of Jonathan Edwards, Volume 8, Ethical Writings*. Edited by Paul Ramsey. New Haven, CT: Yale University Press, 1989.
———. *The Works of Jonathan Edwards, Volume 13, The Miscellanies: A–500*. Edited by Thomas A. Schafer. New Haven, CT: Yale University Press, 1994.
———. *The Works of Jonathan Edwards, Volume 16, Letters and Personal Writings*. Edited by George S. Claghorn. New Haven, CT: Yale University Press, 1966.
———. *The Works of Jonathan Edwards, Volume 18, The Miscellanies: Entry Nos. 501–832*. Edited by Ava Chamberlain. New Haven, CT: Yale University Press, 2000.
———. *The Works of Jonathan Edwards, Volume 21, Writings on the Trinity, Grace, and Faith*. Edited by Sang Hyun Lee. New Haven, CT: Yale University Press, 2003.
———. *The Works of Jonathan Edwards Online, Volume 43, Sermons, Series II, 1728–1729*. Jonathan Edwards Center at Yale University, 2008.
Eliade, Mircea. *A History of Religious Ideas*. Chicago: University of Chicago Press, 1978.
———. *The Quest: History and Meaning in Religion*. Chicago: University of Chicago Press, 1969.

———. *The Sacred and the Profane; the Nature of Religion*. New York: Harcourt, Brace, 1959.

Elliott, Kelly R. "The Bebbington Quadrilateral Travels into the Empire." *Fides et Historia* 47 (2015) 46–53.

Emerson, Michael O., and Christian Smith. *Divided by Faith: Evangelical Religion and the Problem of Race in America*. Oxford; New York: Oxford University Press, 2000.

Emerson, Ralph Waldo. *Collected Poems and Translations*. Edited by Harold Bloom and Paul Kane. The Library of America 70. New York: Library of America, 1994.

———. *Emerson's Antislavery Writings*. Edited by Len Gougeon and Joel Myerson. New Haven, CT: Yale University Press, 1995.

———. *Essays and Lectures*. Edited by Joel Porte. The Library of America. New York: Viking, 1983.

Fiering, Norman. *Jonathan Edwards's Moral Thought and Its British Context*. Williamsburg, VA: University of North Carolina Press, 1981.

Fortman, Edmund J. *The Triune God: A Historical Study of the Doctrine of the Trinity*. Eugene, OR: Wipf & Stock, 1999.

Frohlich, Mary. "Spiritual Discipline, Discipline of Spirituality: Revisiting Questions of Definition and Method." *Spiritus: A Journal of Christian Spirituality* 1 (2001) 65–78.

Gadamer, Hans Georg. *Truth and Method*. 2nd rev. ed. New York: Continuum, 2003.

Gelpi, Donald L. *The Conversion Experience: A Reflective Process for RCIA Participants and Others*. New York: Paulist, 1998.

———. "Conversion: The Challenge of Contemporary Charismatic Piety." *Theological Studies* 43 (1982) 606–28.

———. *Encountering Jesus Christ: Rethinking Christological Faith and Commitment*. Marquette Studies in Theology 65. Milwaukee, WS: Marquette, 2009.

———. *Endless Seeker: The Religious Quest of Ralph Waldo Emerson*. Lanham, MD: University Press of America, 1991.

———. *Grace as Transmuted Experience and Social Process: And Other Essays in North American Theology*. Lanham, MD: University Press of America, 1988.

———. *The Gracing of Human Experience: Rethinking the Relationship between Nature and Grace*. Eugene, OR: Wipf & Stock, 2008.

———. *Inculturating North American Theology: An Experiment in Foundational Method*. Studies in Religion / American Academy of Religion 54. Atlanta: Scholars, 1988.

———. *Varieties of Transcendental Experience: A Study in Constructive Postmodernism*. Collegeville, MN: Liturgical, 2000.

Ghose, Aurobindo. *The Life Divine*. New York: E.P. Dutton, 2013.

Gillespie, Michael Allen. *The Theological Origins of Modernity*. University of Chicago Press, 2009.

Gilpin, W. Clark. "The Theology of Solitude: Edwards, Emerson, Dickinson." *Spiritus: A Journal of Christian Spirituality* 1 (2001) 31–42.

Grenz, Stanley J. "Christian Spirituality and the Quest for Identity: Toward a Spiritual-Theological Understanding of Life in Christ." *Baptist History and Heritage* 37 (2002) 87–105.

———. "Concerns of a Pietist with a PhD." *Wesleyan Theological Journal* 37 (2002) 58–76.

———. *The Named God and the Question of Being: A Trinitarian Theo-Ontology*. Louisville, KY: Westminster John Knox, 2005.

———. *Renewing the Center: Evangelical Theology in a Post-Theological Era*. Grand Rapids: Baker, 2000.

Bibliography

———. *Revisioning Evangelical Theology: A Fresh Agenda for the 21st Century.* Downers Grove, IL: InterVarsity, 1993.
———. *The Social God and the Relational Self: A Trinitarian Theology of the Imago Dei.* Louisville, KY: Westminster John Knox, 2001.
———. *Theology for the Community of God.* Nashville, TN: Broadman & Holman, 1994.
Grenz, Stanley J., and John R. Franke. *Beyond Foundationalism: Shaping Theology in a Postmodern Context.* Louisville, KY: Westminster John Knox, 2001.
Grenz, Stanley J., and Roger E. Olson. *20th-Century Theology: God and the World in a Transitional Age.* Downers Grove, IL: IVP Academic, 1993.
Grenz, Stanley J., and Jay T. Smith. *Created for Community: Connecting Christian Belief with Christian Living.* 3rd ed. Grand Rapids: Baker Academic, 2014.
Gura, Philip F. *American Transcendentalism: A History.* New York: Hill and Wang, 2008.
Gutierrez, Gustavo. *A Theology of Liberation: History, Politics, and Salvation.* Rev. ed. Maryknoll, NY: Orbis, 1988.
Habermas, Jürgen. *Jürgen Habermas on Society and Politics: A Reader.* Edited by Steven Seidman. Boston: Beacon, 1989.
Haight, Roger. *Spirituality Seeking Theology.* Maryknoll, New York: Orbis, 2014.
Hall, Richard A. S., ed. *The Contribution of Jonathan Edwards to American Culture and Society: Essays on America's Spiritual Founding Father (the Northampton Tercentenary Celebration, 1703–2003).* Lewiston, NY: Edwin Mellen, 2008.
Hambrick-Stowe, Charles E. *The Practice of Piety: Puritan Devotional Disciplines in Seventeenth-Century New England.* Williamsburg, VA: University of North Carolina Press, 1982.
Harrison, Douglas. "Toward a Theology of Experience: Belief and Incapacity in Edwards, Emerson, and William James." PhD diss., Washington University, 2005.
Hastings, Ross. *Jonathan Edwards and the Life of God: Toward an Evangelical Theology of Participation.* Minneapolis: Fortress, 2015.
Hawkins, J. Russell, and Phillip Luke Sinitiere, eds. *Christians and the Color Line: Race and Religion after Divided by Faith.* New York: Oxford University Press, 2014.
Haykin, Michael, and Kenneth Stewart, eds. *Advent of Evangelicalism: Exploring Historical Continuities*, 2006.
Helminiak, Daniel A. *Spiritual Development: An Interdisciplinary Study.* Chicago: Loyola Press, 1987.
Helminiak, Daniel A. "The Role of Spirituality in Formulating a Theory of the Psychology of Religion." *Zygon: Journal of Religion and Science* 41 (2006) 197–224.
Higgins, J. August. "The Aesthetic Foundations of Religious Experience in the Writings of Jonathan Edwards and Ralph Waldo Emerson." *American Journal of Theology and Philosophy* 38 (2017) 152–66.
———. "Spirit and Truth: Gadamer's Fusion of Horizons and Contemporary Spirituality Studies." *Philosophy and Theology* 28 (2016) 469–90.
Hindmarsh, D. Bruce. *The Evangelical Conversion Narrative: Spiritual Autobiography in Early Modern England.* Oxford: Oxford University Press, 2005.
———. "The Great Awakening Revisited: A Review Essay." *Crux* 44 (2008) 37–42.
———. *The Spirit of Early Evangelicalism: True Religion in a Modern World.* New York: Oxford University Press, 2018.
Hinson, E Glenn. "Baptist Approaches to Spirituality." *Baptist History and Heritage* 37 (2002) 6–31.
Holder, Arthur. *The Blackwell Companion to Christian Spirituality.* Wiley, 2010.

Bibliography

Holmes, Stephen R. *God of Grace and God of Glory: An Account of the Theology of Jonathan Edwards*. Grand Rapids: Bloomsbury, 2001.

Hooper, John. *Later Writings of Bishop Hooper: Together with His Letters and Other Pieces*. Edited by Charles Nevinson. Cambridge: Cambridge University Press, 1852.

Howard, Evan B. *The Brazos Introduction to Christian Spirituality*. Grand Rapids: Brazos, 2008.

Hughes, R. Kent, and John H. Armstrong, eds. *The Coming Evangelical Crisis: Current Challenges to the Authority of Scripture and the Gospel*. Chicago: Moody, 1996.

Husserl, Edmund. *Ideas: General Introduction to Pure Phenomenology*. Routledge Classics. London: Routledge, 2012.

James, William. *The Varieties of Religious Experience: A Study in Human Nature*. Oxford World's Classics. Oxford: Oxford University Press, 2012.

Johnson, Luke Timothy. *Prophetic Jesus, Prophetic Church: The Challenge of Luke-Acts to Contemporary Christians*. Grand Rapids: Eerdmans, 2011.

Desiring God. "Jonathan Edwards." https://www.desiringgod.org/topics/jonathan-edwards.

Kaminsky, Jack. "Dewey's Concept of an Experience." *Philosophy and Phenomenological Research* 17 (1957) 316–30.

Kant, Immanuel, et al. *Religion within the Boundaries of Mere Reason and Other Writings*. Cambridge Texts in the History of Philosophy. Cambridge: Cambridge University Press, 1998.

Kearney, Richard. *The Wake of Imagination: Toward a Postmodern Culture*. Minneapolis: University of Minnesota Press, 1988.

Kidd, Thomas S. "The Bebbington Quadrilateral and the Work of the Holy Spirit." *Fides et Historia* 47 (2015) 54–57.

Knox, Marv. "Editorial: A Rock, a Hard Place, and a Home for All Kinds of Baptists." Baptist Standard. https://www.baptiststandard.com/opinion/editorials/editorial-a-rock-a-hard-place-and-a-home-for-all-kinds-of-baptists/.

Knutson, Andrea. *American Spaces of Conversion: The Conductive Imaginaries of Edwards, Emerson, and James*. New York: Oxford University Press, 2011.

Koopman, Colin. "Pragmatism as a Philosophy of Hope: Emerson, James, Dewey, Rorty." *Journal of Speculative Philosophy* 20 (2006) 106–16.

Kraybill, Donald B. *The Upside-Down Kingdom*. 25th anniversary. Scottdale, PA: Herald, 2003.

Kuklick, Bruce. *A History of Philosophy in America, 1720–2000*. Oxford: Clarendon, 2001.

Kyle, Richard G. *Evangelicalism: An Americanized Christianity*. New Brunswick, NJ: Transaction, 2006.

Lamm, Julia A. "The Early Philosophical Roots of Schleiermacher's Notion of Gefühl, 1788–1794." *Harvard Theological Review* 87 (1994) 67–105.

Larsen, Timothy, and Daniel J. Treier, eds. *The Cambridge Companion to Evangelical Theology*. Cambridge: Cambridge University Press, 2007.

Lash, Nicholas. *Easter in Ordinary: Reflections on Human Experience and the Knowledge of God*. The Richard Lectures for 1986, University of Virginia. Charlottesville, VA: University Press of Virginia, 1988.

Lévi-Strauss, Claude. *The Savage Mind*. Translated by George Weidenfeld. Chicago: University of Chicago Press, 1966.

Lewis, C. S. *Mere Christianity*. Rev. ed. San Francisco: HarperOne, 2015.

Bibliography

———. *Surprised by Joy: The Shape of My Early Life*. New York: Harcourt, Brace, Jovanovich, 1966.
Lips, Roger Cameron. "The Spirit's Holy Errand: A Study of Continuities of Thought from Jonathan Edwards to Ralph Waldo Emerson." PhD diss., The University of Wisconsin, 1976.
Lombard, C. "Biblical Spirituality and Interdisciplinarity: The Discipline at Cross-Methodological Intersection." *Religion and Theology* 18 (2011) 211–12.
Markey, John J. "Clarifying the Relationship between the Universal and the Particular Churches through the Philosophy of Josiah Royce." *Philosophy and Theology* 15 (2003) 299–320.
———. "Communion as Salvation: Josiah Royce and J.-M. R. Tillard, O.P." *Science et Esprit* 60 (2008) 119–37.
———. *Creating Communion: The Theology of the Constitutions of the Church*. Hyde Park, NY: New City, 2003.
———. *Moses in Pharaoh's House: A Liberation Spirituality for North America*. Winona, MN: Anselm Academic, 2014.
Marsden, George M. *Jonathan Edwards: A Life*. New Haven, CT: Yale University Press, 2003.
Martin, Valerie Lynn. "A Beholding and Jubilant Soul: Spiritual Awakening in the Thought of Jonathan Edwards and Ralph Waldo Emerson." PhD diss., University of North Texas, 1980.
Martinez, Gaspar. *Confronting the Mystery of God Political, Liberation, and Public Theologies*. New York: Continuum, 2001.
Marty, Martin E. *The New Shape of American Religion*. New York: Harper, 1959.
Mathews, Mary Beth Swetnam. *Doctrine and Race: African American Evangelicals and Fundamentalism between the Wars*. Religion and American Culture. Tuscaloosa: University of Alabama Press, 2017.
Matthiessen, F. O. *American Renaissance: Art and Expression in the Age of Emerson and Whitman*. New York: Barnes & Noble, 2009.
McClendon, James Wm., and Ryan Andrew Newson. *The Collected Works of James Wm. McClendon, Jr.: Volume 2*. Waco, TX: Baylor University Press, 2014.
McClymond, Michael James. *Encounters with God: An Approach to the Theology of Jonathan Edwards*. Religion in America Series. New York: Oxford University Press, 1998.
McClymond, Michael James, and Gerald R. McDermott. *The Theology of Jonathan Edwards*. New York: Oxford University Press, 2012.
McDermott, Gerald R. *Understanding Jonathan Edwards*. Oxford University Press, 2009.
McGinn, Bernard, ed. *The Essential Writings of Christian Mysticism*. Modern Library Classics. New York: Modern Library, 2006.
———. *The Foundations of Mysticism*. New York: Crossroad, 1991.
———. "Mystical Consciousness: A Modest Proposal." *Spiritus: A Journal of Christian Spirituality* 8 (2008) 44–63.
———. *The Varieties of Vernacular Mysticism, 1350–1550*. New York: Crossroad, 2012.
McGrath, Alister E. *Evangelicalism and the Future of Christianity*. London: Hodder & Stoughton, 1996.
McLoughlin, William G., and Robert N. Bellah, eds. *Religion in America*. Boston: Beacon, 1968.

Merrick, James R A. "The Spirit of Truth as Agent in False Religions?: A Critique of Amos Yong's Pneumatological Theology of Religions with Reference to Current Trends." *Trinity Journal* 29 (2008) 107–25.

Milder, Robert. "From Emerson to Edwards." *The New England Quarterly* 80 (2007) 96–133.

Miller, David L. "Josiah Royce and George H. Mead on the Nature of the Self." *Transactions of the Charles S. Peirce Society* 11 (1975) 67.

Miller, Perry. *Errand into the Wilderness*. New ed. Cambridge, MA: Belknap, 1956.

———. "Jonathan Edwards on the Sense of the Heart." *The Harvard Theological Review* 41, (1948) 123–45.

———. *Jonathan Edwards to Emerson*. Bobbs-Merrill Reprint Series in History H-150. Indianapolis: Bobbs-Merrill, 1940.

———. "Jonathan Edwards to Emerson." *The New England Quarterly* 13 (1940) 589–617.

———. *The New England Mind: From Colony to Province*. Cambridge, MA: Harvard University Press, 1953.

———. *The New England Mind: The Seventeenth Century*. Cambridge, MA: Harvard University Press, 1983.

Morgan, Edmund S. *Visible Saints: The History of a Puritan Idea*. Ithaca, NY: Cornell University Press, 1965.

Morris, T. Asher. "Jonathan Edwards and Pragmatism." PhD diss., West Chester University of Pennsylvania, 1980.

Nichols, Stephen J., et al. *A God Entranced Vision of All Things: The Legacy of Jonathan Edwards*. Edited by John Piper and Justin Taylor. Wheaton, Il: Crossway, 2004.

Noll, Mark A. *America's God: From Jonathan Edwards to Abraham Lincoln*. Oxford: Oxford University Press, 2002.

———. "Noun or Adjective?: The Ravings of a Fanatical Nominalist." *Fides et Historia* 47 (2015) 73–82.

———. *The Rise of Evangelicalism: The Age of Edwards, Whitefield, and the Wesleys*. Downers Grove, IL: InterVarsity, 2009.

———. *The Scandal of the Evangelical Mind*. Grand Rapids: Eerdmans, 2008.

Nuttall, Geoffrey F. *The Holy Spirit in Puritan Faith and Experience*. Chicago: University of Chicago Press, 1946.

Olson, Roger E. *Essentials of Christian Thought: Seeing the World through the Biblical Story*. Grand Rapids: Zondervan, 2016.

———. *The Journey of Modern Theology: From Reconstruction to Deconstruction*. Downers Grove, Il: IVP Academic, 2013.

———. *The Mosaic of Christian Belief: Twenty Centuries of Unity and Diversity*. Downers Grove, Il: IVP Academic, 2002.

Pauw, Amy Plantinga. "A Response from Amy Plantinga Pauw." *Scottish Journal of Theology* 57 (2004) 486–89.

———. "'The Supreme Harmony of All': Jonathan Edwards and the Trinity." PhD diss., Yale University, 1990.

———. *"The Supreme Harmony of All": The Trinitarian Theology of Jonathan Edwards*. Grand Rapids: Eerdmans, 2002.

Peirce, Charles S. *Collected Papers*. Cambridge, MA: Belknap Press of Harvard University Press, 1960.

———. "On a New List of Categories." *Proceedings of the American Academy of Arts and Sciences* 7 (1868) 287–98.

Bibliography

Perkins, Tasi. "Beyond Jacques Derrida and George Lindbeck: Toward a Particularity-Based Approach to Interreligious Communication." *Journal of Ecumenical Studies* 48 (2013) 343–58.

Perrin, David B. *Studying Christian Spirituality*. London: Routledge, 2007.

Phan, Peter C., ed. *The Cambridge Companion to the Trinity*. Cambridge Companions to Religion. Cambridge: Cambridge University Press, 2011.

Phillips, Charlie. "Roundtable: Re-Examining David Bebbington's 'Quadrilateral Thesis.'" *Fides et Historia* 47 (2015) 44–45.

Piper, John. *Captive to Glory: Celebrating the Vision and Influence of Jonathan Edwards*. Edited by Jonathan Parnell. Desiring God, 2013.

———. *The Supremacy of God in Preaching*. Rev. and exp. ed. Grand Rapids: Baker, 2015.

Piper, John, and Jonathan Edwards. *God's Passion for His Glory: Living the Vision of Jonathan Edwards*. Crossway, 2006.

Porterfield, Amanda. "Bebbington's Approach to Evangelical Christianity as a Pioneering Effort in Lived Religion." *Fides et Historia* 47 (2015) 58–62.

———. *Female Piety in Puritan New England: The Emergence of Religious Humanism*. Oxford: Oxford University Press, 1992.

Principe, Walter H. "Theological Trends: Pluralism in Christian Spirituality." *The Way* 32 (1992) 54–61.

———. "Toward Defining Spirituality." *Studies in Religion* 12 (1983) 127–41.

Proudfoot, Wayne. "From Theology to a Science of Religions: Jonathan Edwards and William James on Religious Affections." *The Harvard Theological Review* 82 (1989) 149–68.

———. *Religious Experience*. Berkeley: University of California Press, 1985.

Rah, Rah, and Soong-Chan Rah. *Next Evangelicalism: Freeing the Church from Western Cultural Captivity*. Downers Grove, IL: InterVarsity, 2014.

Rambo, Lewis R. *Understanding Religious Conversion*. New Haven, CT: Yale University Press, 1993.

Ramsey, Bennett. "The Ineluctable Impulse: 'consent' in the Thought of Edwards, James, and Royce." *Union Seminary Quarterly Review* 37 (1983) 303–22.

Reynolds, David S. *Beneath the American Renaissance: The Subversive Imagination in the Age of Emerson and Melville*. New York: Oxford University Press, 2011.

Richie, Tony Lee. "The Spirit of Truth as Guide into All Truth: A Response to R. A. James Merrick, 'The Spirit of Truth as Agent in False Religions? A Critique of Amos Yong's Pneumatological Theology of Religions with Reference to Current Trends.'" *Cyberjournal for Pentecostal-Charismatic Research* 19 (January 2010).

Ricoeur, Paul. *Hermeneutics and the Human Sciences: Essays on Language, Action, and Interpretation*. Translated by John B. Thompson. Cambridge: Cambridge University Press, 1981.

———. *Oneself as Another*. Chicago: University of Chicago Press, 1992.

———. *The Symbolism of Evil*. Boston: Beacon, 1967.

———. *Time and Narrative*. Chicago: University of Chicago Press, 1984.

Robinson, David. "The Road Not Taken: From Edwards, Through Chauncy, to Emerson." *Arizona Quarterly: A Journal of American Literature, Culture, and Theory* 48 (2014) 45–61.

Rosenthal, Sandra B. "John Dewey: From Phenomenology of Knowledge to Experience as Experimental." *Philosophy Today* 22 (1978) 43–49.

Royce, Josiah. *The Basic Writings of Josiah Royce Vol. 1.* Edited by John J. McDermott. 2 vols. The Basic Writings of Josiah Royce. Chicago: University of Chicago Press, 1969.

———. *The Problem of Christianity.* Washington DC: Catholic University of America Press, 2011.

———. *The Sources of Religious Insight.* CreateSpace, 2011.

Ruether, Rosemary Radford. *Sexism and God-Talk : Toward a Feminist Theology.* Boston: Beacon, 1983.

Runn, Courtney. "The Year of Jen Hatmaker—Texas Monthly." https://www.texasmonthly.com/articles/year-jen-hatmaker/.

Schleiermacher, Friedrich. *The Christian Faith.* Edited by H. R Mackintosh and James Stuart Stewart. Berkeley, CA: The Apocryphile, 2011.

———. *Friedrich Schleiermacher: Pioneer of Modern Theology.* Edited by Kieth Clements. The Making of Modern Theology: Nineteenth- and Twentieth-Century Texts. Minneapolis: Fortress, 1991.

Schleiermacher, Friedrich, and Julia A. Lamm. *Schleiermacher: Christmas Dialogue, the Second Speech, and Other Selections.* Classics of Western Spirituality. New York: Paulist, 2014.

Schlitt, Dale M. *Experience and Spirit: A Post-Hegelian Philosophical Theology.* New York: Peter Lang, 2007.

Schneiders, Sandra M. "Approaches to the Study of Christian Spirituality." In *The Blackwell Companion to Christian Spirituality*, edited by Arthur Holder, 15–33. Hoboken, NJ: Wiley, 2010.

———. *The Revelatory Text: Interpreting the New Testament as Sacred Scripture.* 2nd ed. Collegeville, MN: Liturgical, 1999.

———. "Spirituality in the Academy." *Theological Studies* 50 (December 1989) 676–97.

———. "The Study of Christian Spirituality: Contours and Dynamics of a Discipline." *Studies in Spirituality* 8 (1998) 38–57.

———. "Theology and Spirituality: Strangers, Rivals, or Partners?" *Horizons* 13 (1986) 253–74.

———. *Written That You May Believe: Encountering Jesus in the Fourth Gospel.* Rev. and exp. ed. New York: Crossroad, 2003.

Schneiders, Sandra Marie, et al., eds. *Exploring Christian Spirituality: Essays in Honor of Sandra M. Schneiders.* New York: Paulist, 2006.

Schwanda, Tom, ed. *The Emergence of Evangelical Spirituality: The Age of Edwards, Newton, and Whitefield.* The Classics of Western Spirituality. New York: Paulist, 2016.

———. "'Hearts Sweetly Refreshed': Puritan Spiritual Practices Then and Now." *Journal of Spiritual Formation and Soul Care* 3 (2010) 21–41.

Scott, Barbara Jean Pamela. "Faith and Chaos: The Quest for Meaning in The Writings of Jonathan Edwards and William James." PhD diss., Syracuse University, 1979.

Sewell, Keith C. *The Crisis of Evangelical Christianity: Roots, Consequences, and Resolutions.* Eugene, OR: Wipf & Stock, 2016.

Shaw, Nancy Joy. "Speaking for the Spirit: Cotton, Shepard, Edwards, Emerson." PhD diss., Cornell University, 1988.

Sheldrake, Philip. *Explorations in Spirituality: History, Theology, and Social Practice.* New York: Paulist, 2010.

———. *Spirituality: A Brief History.* 2nd ed. Hoboken: John Wiley & Sons, 2013.

———. *Spirituality and History: Questions of Interpretation and Method.* Maryknoll, NY: Orbis, 1998.

Bibliography

Shurden, Walter B. *The Baptist Identity: Four Fragile Freedoms*. Macon, GA: Smyth & Helwys, 1993.
Simon, Marianna. "Sentiment Religieux et Sentiment Esthétique dans la Philosophie Religieuse De Schleiermacher." *Archives de Philosophie* 32 (1969) 69–90.
Smith, Jay Todd. "A Generous Theology: Reinterpreting Convertive Piety as Trinitarian Participation in the Work of Stanley J. Grenz." PhD diss., University of Bristol, Trinity College, 2013.
Spener, Philipp Jakob. *Pia Desideria*. Philadelphia: Fortress, 1964.
Spohn, William C. "Union and Consent with the Great Whole: Jonathan Edwards on True Virtue." *Annual of the Society of Christian Ethics* 5 (1985) 19–32.
Stackhouse, John G., ed. *Evangelical Futures: A Conversation on Theological Method*. Grand Rapids: Baker, 2000.
———. *Evangelical Landscapes: Facing Critical Issues of the Day*. Grand Rapids: Baker Academic, 2002.
Studebaker, Steve. "Jonathan Edwards's Social Augustinian Trinitarianism: An Alternative to a Recent Trend." *Scottish Journal of Theology* 56 (2003) 268–85.
———. "Supreme Harmony or Supreme Disharmony?: An Analysis of Amy Plantinga Pauw's 'The Supreme Harmony of All': The Trinitarian Theology of Jonathan Edwards." *Scottish Journal of Theology* 57 (2004) 479–85.
Tarnas, Richard. *The Passion of the Western Mind: Understanding the Ideas That Have Shaped Our World View*. New York: Ballantine, 1993.
Taylor, Charles. *Sources of the Self: The Making of the Modern Identity*. Cambridge, MA: Harvard University Press, 1989.
Thandeka. "Schleiermacher's Affekt Theology." *International Journal of Practical Theology* 9 (2005) 197–216.
Thomas, Owen, C. "Some Problems in Contemporary Christian Spirituality." *Anglican Theological Review* 82 (2000) 267–81.
Tibbetts, Paul. "John Dewey and Contemporary Phenomenology on Experience and the Subject-Object Relation." *Philosophy Today* 15 (1971) 250–75.
Tocqueville, Alexis de. *Democracy in America*. Translated by Henry Reeves. A Penn State Electronic Classics Series Publication. University Park, PA: Penn State Press, 2002.
Vinson, Richard Bolling. *Luke*. The Smyth & Helwys Bible Commentary. Macon, GA: Smyth & Helwys, 2008.
Wells, David F. *No Place for Truth: Or Whatever Happened to Evangelical Theology?* Grand Rapids: Eerdmans, 1993.
Westfall, William. "Tocqueville, Emerson, and the Abolitionists." *Journal of Thought* 19 (1984) 56–63.
Winthrop, John. "A Model of Christian Charity." 1630. https://history.hanover.edu/texts/winthmod.html.
Withrow, Brandon. *Becoming Divine: Jonathan Edwards's Incarnational Spirituality within the Christian Tradition*. Eugene, OR: Cascade, 2011.
Wolfteich, Claire E. "Animating Questions: Spirituality and Practical Theology." *International Journal of Practical Theology* 13 (2009) 121–43.
Worthen, Molly. "Defining Evangelicalism: Questions That Complement the Quadrilateral." *Fides et Historia* 47 (2015) 83–86.
Yong, Amos. *Beyond the Impasse: Toward a Pneumatological Theology of Religions*. Carlisle, Cumbria, UK: Paternoster, 2003.

———. *The Dialogical Spirit: Christian Reason and Theological Method in the Third Millennium*. Eugene, OR: Cascade, 2014.

———. *Discerning the Spirit(s) A Pentecostal-Charismatic Contribution to Christian Theology of Religions*. Eugene, OR: Wipf & Stock, 2019.

———. *The Hermeneutical Spirit: Theological Interpretation and Scriptural Imagination for the 21st Century*. Eugene, OR: Cascade, 2017.

———. *Hospitality and the Other: Pentecost, Christian Practices, and the Neighbor*. Faith Meets Faith Series. Maryknoll, NY: Orbis, 2008.

———. "In Search of Foundations: The Oeuvre of Donald L. Gelpi, SJ, and Its Significance for Pentecostal Theology and Philosophy." *Journal of Pentecostal Theology* 11 (2002) 3–26.

———. *Spirit, Word, Community: Theological Hermeneutics in Trinitarian Perspective*. Eugene, OR: Wipf & Stock, 2006.

———. "The Word and the Spirit or the Spirit and the Word: Exploring the Boundaries of Evangelicalism in Relationship to Modern Pentecostalism." *Trinity Journal* 23 (2002) 235–52.

Yong, Amos, et al. "Christ and Spirit: Dogma, Discernment, and Dialogical Theology in a Religiously Plural World." *Journal of Pentecostal Theology* 12 (2003) 15–83.

Ziegenhals, Gretchen E. "Women in Ministry: Beyond the Impasse." *Christian Reflection* (2009) 77–87.

Subject Index

aesthetics, 93–105
    theological, 82, 86–87, 93
affection/s, 65, 86–91, 96–97, 105–6, 116
    gracious, 81, 91, 104–5, 122–23
    religious, 86, 96–98, 101–4, 123
anthropology, 28, 42, 70
    theological, 15, 27–28, 37, 106
Arminian, 9–10ff, 81, 105–6
authority, 1, 4, 9, 17–18, 26, 60
Awakening, First Great, 7, 122
Awakening, Second Great, 107, 123

Baptist, 8–9
beauty, 92–101, 105, 111–12, 116–19, 123–24, 131
Bebbington, David, 8–10, 20
Bible, 5, 8–10, 18–21, 23, 29–30, 43, 54, 57, 77, 80, 122, 146, 147

Calvinist, 10ff, 80–81, 86, 105–6, 123
    Christianity, 4, 17, 19, 22, 37–38, 71–72, 75;
    Catholic, 6, 8, 11, 90
    evangelical, see evangelical/ism
    North American, 1, 3, 11–12, 83
    Protestant, 6–7, 9–10, 17, 19, 21, 23, 71, 90
community, 4, 14, 20, 23, 25, 28–29, 37–43, 70, 72–76, 97, 126–29, 131, 133–36, 139–41
consciousness, 31–32, 34, 50, 50ff, 52

consent, 89–90, 93–94, 96–100, 104, 116, 118–19
conversion, 1, 5, 11–17, 39–40
    experience of, 4, 9, 20, 80–81, 85, 93, 122, 124, 126–27
    morphology of, 90, 127
    religious, 3–4, 5ff, 10–11, 22, 40, 80–82, 85, 87, 112

Dasein, 31–32, 34
deconstruction, see Derrida, Jacques
Derrida, Jacques, 33–37
Dewey, John, 67–69
Divinity, New, 106

Edwards, Jonathan, 3, 5, 7, 80–81, 83–105, 120, 122–23
Eidos, 31–32
Emerson, Ralph Waldo, 3, 81–82, 105–20, 123–24
    Enlightenment, 21–22, 25, 84, 109
engine, pneumatological, see Yong, Amos
epistemology
    Enlightenment, 2
    foundationalist, 21, 23–24, 77
    post-Enlightenment, 31–32
    relational, 116
Epoche, 32
Erlebnis, 31, 33
evangelical/ism, 1–2, 4–11, 17–21, 30, 129
    North American, 3, 22–23, 136, 145

Subject Index

excellence, 92–93, 131
experience, 4, 9, 12–14, 17–20, 26, 30–33, 35, 40–41, 43, 47–55, 57, 68, 73, 93, 100, 110–11, 115–16, 132–34, 14
evangelical, 120
conversion, see conversion, experience of
mystical, 63–64, 78, 131
nature of, 2, 33, 49, 62–63, 67, 76, 102, 138, 146
religious, 3–4, 17, 26, 43–44, 53–58, 61–67, 69–78, 81–85, 87, 97, 101–3, 124–31, 135, 137–39, 143, 146–47

Foucault, Michel, 23–24, 27
Fugitive Slave Act, 109–10

Gadamer, Hans Georg, 21, 53, 56ff, 143
Gefühl, see Schleiermacher, Friedrich
Gelpi, Donald, 13–16
Grenz, Stanley, 22–30, 37, 42

Habermas, Jürgen, 21ff, 56ff
habit/s, 12, 37, 62, 66–67, 123–27, 131, 134, 144
heart, sense of the, 80–81, 90–93, 96
hermeneutic/s, 22, 28–30, 36, 46, 54, 56ff, 58, 102, 130–32, 139–41, 143, 145
biblical, 26, 134
dialectical, 39, 144
trialectical, 38–41, 135–36, 140
Hindmarsh, D. Bruce, 8, 10
Holy Spirit, 8, 10, 42, 48, 72, 95–97, 102, 104, 122, 126, 130–31
Husserl, Edmund, 31–34
hypermodernity, 26–27

imaginary, conductive, see Knutson, Andrea
imagination, pneumatological, see Yong, Amos
imago Dei, 27–30, 40, 42
immediacy, 33–34, 61, 63, 68–69, 78, 111, 113
individualism, 3, 8, 24–28, 38, 58, 119–21

interpretation, 28, 33–35, 39, 43, 53, 56ff, 57, 68–71, 80–82, 90, 105, 121, 126, 136, 140
biblical/scriptural, 8, 17, 20, 41, 56ff, 77, 128, 139, 143, 146
community of, 72–78, 126, 128, 131, 133–35, 145
transformative, 141, 143–44

James, William, 60–67, 69–71, 73–78, 119, 124–27, 131
Jesus, 4–5, 8–12, 15–16, 28–29, 42, 48, 55, 71–72, 75–76, 130, 132, 134, 140–41
Christ, 15, 18, 29, 39, 41–42, 48, 88, 139

Kant, Immanuel, 19–21, 68–69
kingdom of God, 16, 52, 76, 78, 134
Knutson, Andrea, 80–82

Larsen, Timothy, 10–11
Lévi-Strauss, Claude, 23–24
Lewis, C.S., 4, 27
loyalty, 71, 75–76, 126–27, 134–35
Lyotard, Jean-François, 27

Markey, John, 11–13,
McGinn, Bernard, 46, 50ff
Mead, George Herbert, 27
mediation, 67, 69, 72, 111–15, 117, 127, 144
metaphysics, 93, 101ff, 104, 112–13, 118
deterministic, 126–27
relational, 117, 121
semiotic, 3, 117
Miller, Perry, 59, 92
mysticism, 46, 63, 115, 118–19, 125

Nietzsche, Friedrich, 23–24, 27
normativity, 34, 49, 63, 86, 102–4, 134, 138, 143, 145

ontology, 37, 87, 93–94, 100, 140
aesthetic, 96–99, 117, 120
phenomenological, 31
relational, 27, 95

162

Subject Index

ordo salutis, 80–81, 88, 90

Pannenberg, Wolfhart, 27
Peirce, Charles Sanders, 62, 66, 67ff, 72ff, 138ff
phenomenology, 12, 29, 31–32, 46, 58, 78, 82, 84, 96, 125
Pietist/s, 6–7, 17–19, 136
piety, 1, 9, 17, 45, 59, 81, 96, 123, 146
Plain, Sermon on the, 15–16
pneuma, 45–46
pneumatology, 4, 94, 129, 132
postmodern/ity, 21–23, 25–26, 26ff, 31–37, 145–47
post-structuralist, 24, 35–36, 56ff
pragmatist, 44, 60, 66, 82, 121, 124
Principe, Walter, 37
Puritan/s, 6–7, 59–60, 80–81, 88, 90

Quadrilateral, Evangelical, see Bebbington, David

Rambo, Lewis, 11ff, 12
reductionist, 8–9, 17, 129–30, 136
regeneration, 7, 80, 82
religion, 7–8, 19–20, 35, 37, 45, 61–67, 70–71, 75, 77, 96, 101, 121, 123–24, 127, 130
revelation, 8–9, 17, 20, 29–30, 135, 140–41
divine, 14, 19, 35, 44, 54, 102, 146
revival/ist, 5–7, 85
Ricoeur, Paul, 21, 50, 56ff, 141–43
Romanticism, 19, 109
Royce, Josiah, 70–78, 126–28, 131, 133–35

Saussure, Ferdinand de, 23, 35–36

Schleiermacher, Friedrich, 17–20
Schneiders, Sandra, 40, 50–58, 64–65, 69–70, 77, 102–3, 133, 140–45
Scripture, 8–10, 18–20, 29–30, 37, 41, 44, 54–55, 56ff, 57, 77, 102, 120, 128, 130, 139–41, 143
self-implication, 54, 63
semiotic/s, 30, 31, 34–37, 57–58, 60, 63, 78, 111–17, 119, 126–30
sensus fidelium, 135
Sheldrake, Philip, 45–46, 48, 50ff
Shurden, Walter, 8–9
spirituality, 3, 44–47, 49–53, 64–65, 107, 116, 141–42
biblical, 54–58
Christian, 2, 47–48, 50, 54, 77, 82, 107, 127
evangelical, 1–4, 11, 17, 38, 41, 82, 84, 122, 139, 147
structuralist, 23, 35–36, 56ff
subjectivity, 21, 24–25, 31–34, 51, 53, 65, 73, 128

Transcendentalist/Transcendentalism, 107–11, 118
Trinity, 95–96

Unitarian/ism, 81, 106

Wesley, Charles, 6
Wesley, John, 4, 6, 10
Whitefield, George, 5–6, 8, 10
Winthrop, John, 59–60
Wittgenstein, Ludwig, 36

Yong, Amos, 3–4, 37–42, 129–40, 143–45

www.ingramcontent.com/pod-product-compliance
Lightning Source LLC
Chambersburg PA
CBHW050819160426
43192CB00010B/1818